CULTURE

IS BAD

FOR

YOU

Manchester University Press

Culture is bad for you

Inequality in the cultural and creative industries

Orian Brook, Dave O'Brien, and Mark Taylor

Manchester University Press

The right of Orian Brook, Dave O'Brien and Mark Taylor to be identified
as the authors of this work has been asserted by them in accordance with the
Copyright, Designs and Patents Act 1988.

Published by Manchester University Press
Altrincham Street, Manchester M1 7JA
www.manchesteruniversitypress.co.uk

British Library Cataloguing-in-Publication Data
A catalogue record for this book is available from the British Library

ISBN 978 1 5261 4416 4   paperback

First published 2020

The publisher has no responsibility for the persistence or accuracy of URLs
for any external or third-party internet websites referred to in this book,
and does not guarantee that any content on such websites is, or will remain,
accurate or appropriate.

Typeset by Newgen Publishing UK
Printed in Great Britain
by Bell & Bain Ltd, Glasgow

Contents

List of figures   vii

List of tables   x

Preface: Inequality, cultural occupations, and COVID-19   xi

Acknowledgements   xv

1   Introduction   1

2   Is culture good for you?   26

3   Who works in culture?   54

4   Who consumes culture?   77

5   When does inequality begin in cultural workers' lives?   109

6   Is it still good work if you're not getting paid?   136

7   Was there a golden age?   165

8   How is inequality experienced?   190

9   Why don't women run culture?   221

10   What about the men?   249

11   Conclusion   273

Contents

Appendix 1: Interviewee profiles   284
Appendix 2: Further reading   292

Notes   294
Bibliography   326
Index   353

Figures

Graphics by Nigel Hawtin, nigelhawtin.com

3.1a   Composition of the creative workforce.
       Source: Labour Force Survey 2019   59
3.1b   Percentage of women in the creative workforce.
       Source: Labour Force Survey 2019   60
3.1c   Percentage White in the creative workforce.
       Source: Labour Force Survey 2019   61
3.2   Class origins in creative occupations.
       Source: Labour Force Survey 2014–2019   64
3.3   Analysis of British Election Study data.
       Source: Fieldhouse *et al.*, British Election Study   69
3.4   How responses cluster around meritocracy or
       social reproduction. Source: *Panic!* survey 2018   71
3.5   Who do our creative workers know?
       Source: *Panic!* survey 2018   74
4.1   Overall attendance at different events
       (percentages). Source: Taking Part
       survey 2017–2018   80
4.2   Overall participation in different
       forms (percentages). Source: Taking Part
       survey 2017–2018   81

Figures

4.3	Overall participation in different free time activities (percentages). Source: Taking Part survey 2017–2018	82
4.4	Attendance at different events, by social class: percentages within each group. Source: Taking Part survey 2017–2018	85
4.5	Attendance at different events, by gender (percentages). Source: Taking Part survey 2017–2018	87
4.6	Attendance at different events, by ethnic group (percentages). Source: Taking Part survey 2017–2018	88
4.7	Attendance at different events, by age group. Source: Taking Part survey 2017–2018	90
4.8a	Multiple correspondence analysis of how people spend their time (cultural activities). Source: Taking Part surveys 2005–2006, 2012–2013	94
4.8b	Multiple correspondence analysis of how people spend their time (occupational groups). Source: Taking Part surveys 2005–2006, 2012–2013	95
4.9	Comparing attendance figures from ticketing and survey data. Source: Audience Finder	103
4.10	Distribution of ticket sales and self-reported attendance by Index of Multiple Deprivation. Source: Taking Part survey 2017–2018 and Audience Finder	105
5.1	Reported participation/attendance in different activities while growing up. Source: Taking Part surveys 2005–2006, 2008–2009, 2010–2011, 2012–2013	118

Figures

6.1	Fractions of interviewees having ever worked for free. Source: *Panic!* survey 2018	147
6.2	Fractions of interviewees having undertaken an unpaid internship. Source: *Panic!* survey 2018	149
6.3	Fractions of interviewees not having been paid for all hours worked in the last month. Source: *Panic!* survey 2018	150
7.1	Percentage of LS members in core cultural vs any job, by parental NS-SEC. Source: ONS Longitudinal Study, authors' analysis	179
7.2	Odds ratios, probability of ever having a core cultural job 1981–2011. Source: ONS Longitudinal Study, authors' analysis	182
7.3	Odd ratios, ever having a core cultural job by education. Source: ONS Longitudinal Study, authors' analysis	186
9.1	People in the same core creative occupation ten years on (percentages)	227
9.2	People not in work ten years on (percentages)	228

Table

7.1   ONS-LS cohort sizes, by occupational group   178

Preface: Inequality, cultural occupations, and COVID-19

Culture is bad for you is published at an uncertain time for cultural and creative industries. At the time of writing this preface, the death toll from the virus, along with the virus' impact on global society and economy, suggest a crisis of unique proportions.

The crisis looks to be especially grave for the cultural and creative industries. It is unclear how cultural activity taking place in venues and shared public spaces will reopen, if the pre-pandemic business models will be sustainable in the future, and how many individuals will lose their jobs. How long the recovery will take, and any possibility of returning to some form of 'business as usual' for artistic and cultural life as seen before the crisis, is still impossible to determine.

The danger signs are ominous, irrespective of whichever cultural industry or cultural occupation we assess. The impact of streaming and the importance of live performances for the music industry mean many musicians face a collapse in their income. The uncertainty of reopening schedules, along with possible social distancing measures, means performance spaces, whether for theatre, dance, or music, may no longer be sustainable. The collapse of visitor numbers has already closed venues, with museums, galleries, and heritage sites especially vulnerable.

Film and television production, with its dependence on studios or on-location work and large numbers of crew, and sometimes cast, faces difficulties. This is to say nothing about the changes in release schedules, the collapse in advertising revenue, and the continued existence of cinemas and even television channels.

Governments, faced with increased financial pressures as a result of the crisis and subsequent, predicted, economic depression, may struggle to offer continued *direct* funding and investment to the cultural sector. Decisions about welfare and support schemes for the economy and for society in general may focus on areas besides the cultural sector.

The industry-level impacts will be felt by workers most directly. Many of our cultural sectors are based on project work and staffed by a mixture of freelancers, self-employed, and part-time workers. Many of these workers will not qualify for furlough or other government support. As we discuss in Chapter 6 of the book, precariousness is endemic to particular cultural occupations and at particular stages in cultural careers.

The uneven distribution of childcare responsibilities, an issue we discuss in Chapter 9, will impact women's creative careers more heavily than their male counterparts. This uneven distribution has become a narrative offered by decision-makers in specific sectors, such as film and television, to explain the lack of progress for women's careers. We are likely to see this narrative continue, masking existing sexist assumptions in hiring and commissioning practices.

The importance of networks to access work will mean greater difficulties for those without social, cultural, and economic resources, a theme we explore in Chapter 8. The closure of key parts of infrastructure, such as festivals that provide early career opportunities, mean some will be denied the chance to 'get in' to cultural careers; any contraction of cultural labour markets will mean fewer opportunities to 'get on' for those already in cultural occupations.

As we show throughout the book, the impact of the basic issue of access to jobs will not hit the workforce evenly. For women, people of colour, and those from working-class origins, we will see earlier exits from cultural labour markets than might otherwise have happened. As competition for the smaller numbers of cultural and creative careers intensifies, we should expect our cultural occupations to become even more elite than they are now.

We're choosing to comment on these examples as they highlight how the impact of the pandemic is not a result of individual actions or choices. Rather, the impact of the pandemic is shaped by the structures of business models, labour markets, and funding settlements, alongside government policy and scientific advice. Our examples from film and television, music, theatres, and museums and galleries, reflect longstanding issues of inequalities. These are the issues our book analyses.

At the same time as we are fearful for the future of cultural workers, businesses, and organisations, culture has been crucial to sustaining individuals, communities, and nations during the pandemic. Culture has been a vital resource during periods of lockdown. We have seen renewed examples of, and a renewed faith in, the way culture is good for you.

Everyday cultural production, including painting, craft, writing, and making music seems to have been an important source of wellbeing for people during the crisis. Digital platforms and technologies have enabled new forms of cultural activity and accelerated sharing of artistic and cultural practices.

Cultural consumption, aided by an expansion in digital modes of delivery, has also been crucial. Books, with films, television, streaming of theatre and musicals, virtual visits to galleries and museums, and radio and podcasts, have all played a role in helping people through the crisis. Some parts of the cultural sector, for example digital content platforms seeing new subscribers and new audiences, may even be thriving.

There is a distinct irony in this uptake of cultural resources. It comes just as the sustainability of the cultural producers in the sector, and the ability of individual cultural workers to sustain themselves from their work, is most under threat. Even the stories of success, such as digital platforms, may hide new uneven power relationships and unequal divisions of revenue and profit.

In this context, with the fear for the future of culture and the hope of new forms of production and consumption, it may seem strange to suggest we foreground an analysis of inequality. Yet this is almost certainly the most important moment for that analysis.

Early signs are that our digital cultural life under lockdown, whether as consumers or producers, as watchers and readers or as makers, will follow many of the existing patterns of inequality we discuss in Chapters 4 and 5. The labour market, as we demonstrate in Chapter 3, was highly unequal *before* the crisis. The analysis throughout the book shows how inequality is likely to be worse, not better, as a result of the structural issues we discuss. In particular, as Chapter 10 indicates, who makes decisions, who has power, and how they understand inequality, is especially important. We know culture matters. As Chapter 2 illustrates, culture can be powerfully good for you. Understanding inequality is a starting point for the task of rebuilding after COVID-19. It means the present moment gives us a chance to create a fairer and more just cultural sector.

Acknowledgements

This book is the result of a great collaboration. It has been a collaborative effort between the three authors, but it has also been a collaboration with others far beyond the writing team. We are deeply grateful for everyone who has worked directly on the research projects and published papers underpinning this book. They include Heather Carey, Rebecca Florisson, Sam Friedman, Laurie Hanquinet, Daniel Laurison, Neil Lee, Siobhan McAndrew, Andrew Miles, and Kate Oakley. In particular we are especially indebted to Jordan Tchilingirian and Sara De Benedictis, along with Nikki Kane and Bozena Wielgoszewska. It is also a collaboration that has been possible as a result of the support of the UK's Arts & Humanities Research Council, as well as support from the ESRC's Impact Accelerator Account at the University of Edinburgh, and the Edinburgh Futures Institute's research development funding. Orian was granted a postdoctoral fellowship from the Institute for the Advanced Studies of the Humanities at University of Edinburgh to support a period of the writing of this book.

For reading the text, as well as commenting on the cover design, we would like to thank Mae Smith and Jo Maudsley. Kate Oakley, Anamik Saha, Sam Friedman, and the anonymous reviewers for Manchester University Press were crucial in developing the book from its first draft, as was Tom Dark's editorial work.

We would also like to thank the people who we have worked alongside while undertaking the research that this book is based on, including everyone at the Sheffield Methods Institute at the University of Sheffield, and other colleagues across the institution, along with University of Edinburgh, Edinburgh College of Art, and Goldsmiths.

We have also had a great deal of feedback that has been essential in developing the arguments in the book. This has been both from people who have asked us difficult questions when we have presented early versions of the research, and from people who have offered their insight on written drafts and technical issues. Those people include – but are in no way limited to – our academic colleagues, people working in different policy spaces, and some crucially important creative workers. We would like to thank everyone who has contributed in this way.

We would like to thank Paul Lambert, Patrick Sturgis, Lindsay Paterson, and anonymous reviewers for their comments on our analysis of social mobility.

The permission of the Office for National Statistics to use the Longitudinal Study is gratefully acknowledged, as is the help provided by staff of the Centre for Longitudinal Study Information & User Support (CeLSIUS). CeLSIUS is supported by the ESRC Census of Population Programme (Award Ref: ES/K000365/1). The authors alone are responsible for the interpretation of the data.

We would of course like to thank all of our families and friends for their support throughout this project.

Acknowledgements

Finally, and most importantly, we would like to acknowledge and recognise the importance of our survey respondents and especially our interviewees. They gave us time and insights, and the book would not have happened without them. We hope we have done justice to the stories they were generous enough to share with us – both those who have experienced exclusion and lack of opportunity, but also those whose stories have been of success and luck. All are important in helping us to explain and illustrate the social exclusions in our creative economy.

1

Introduction

Culture is good for you.

Culture will help keep you fit and healthy. Culture will bring communities together. Culture will improve your education[1] and get you higher wages during your career.[2] Culture will transform your village, town, or city for the better.[3] Culture is what makes countries successful. This is the message from governments,[4] as well as from arts and cultural organisations.[5]

Culture is an essential part of most people's lives.[6] Culture is watching a gripping television show or getting absorbed in the world of a video game. It is reading a book or writing a poem, going to see a band, discussing a film with friends. Culture is singing in a choir, acting on stage, or crafting a gift for the family.

These activities are just a few examples of culture. Culture captures what people make, what they participate in, and what they attend. Culture is a central part of what it means to be human.

This book explains why we need to be cautious about culture. We will demonstrate that culture is closely related to inequality in society.

Who produces culture reflects social inequality. The workforce in cultural occupations and cultural industries is highly unequal.[7] To 'make it' in a cultural job you need the sort of economic, social, and cultural resources that are not fairly shared within society.[8]

Who consumes culture reflects social inequality.[9] The audience attending artforms including theatre, classical music, opera, ballet, jazz, and exhibitions is a minority of the population.[10]

Participation has similar patterns. Painting, playing instruments, singing, dancing, writing, and performing are only done by a minority of the population.

The way we define culture reflects social inequality. What counts as culture, and what is excluded from the definition, is a site of long-standing debate.[11]

We know about attendance and participation from government surveys. These surveys contrast everyday activities, such as shopping, DIY, and listening to music, with formal cultural activity, such as attending a theatre or participating in a choir.[12]

Decisions in survey methods reflect that some cultural forms are given high social status, with considerable state funding and support. Other cultural forms are the preserve of commercial and community organisations. What counts as 'high' and 'everyday' culture reflects historical struggles over legitimacy.[13] What counts also reflects social inequalities associated with class, race, and gender.

These are just a few introductory examples of the relationship between culture and inequality. If producing, consuming, and even defining, culture is closely related to inequality, perhaps we should be asking whether culture is bad for you.

Henna's story

To start to understand the relationship between inequality and culture we can hear from Henna. Henna was one of 237 creative and cultural workers we interviewed for the research and analysis presented in this book. Like the rest of our participants we've given her a pseudonym, so she could be honest and open in the interview. We were asking her about her career, and working life.

Henna was in her early thirties at the time of the interview. She is a South Asian woman from a middle-class background, living in London and working in film and television. As well as her middle-class origin, she had a degree from a very prestigious university.

To the outsider's eye she had every possible advantage to 'make it' in her chosen cultural career. Yet she was blunt about the reality of working life:

> The UK film industry is not a meritocracy at all. It doesn't matter if you're intelligent or well-qualified or any of those things. What matters is who you know and who you've worked with. It's also massively to do with being a woman of colour … They would much rather hire the White dude, and they feel more comfortable with the White dude, than the bolshy brown woman who seems to have done things that they don't feel comfortable with. Of course. That's just the reality of it.

Henna tells us some of our reasons why we've written this book, and why we've given it the provocative title of *Culture is bad for you*. She gives us the starting point for why we should question some of the 'good news' about culture.

Henna was a successful filmmaker, with an international reputation. She was candid and blunt about her experiences in her cultural occupation. She reflected on the reasons that, despite her obvious talent and track record, she had not hit the same heights as some of her contemporaries.

'Who you know and who you've worked with' are how the labour market in film functions. The industry is risk-averse as a result of the huge costs of production (and of subsequent distribution and marketing), set against the uncertainty of success.

The issue of risk in the film industry is reflected in other cultural occupations. We may know a great deal about audience tastes, but we can never really be sure of what will be a hit. It is hard to be sure if investment in developing a new artist, a new musician, a new play, or a new novel will pay off.[14]

We would only get part of the explanation for Henna's frustration if we focused on how the labour market functions.[15] Finding it difficult because of not knowing the right people, of not having key networks and social resources, is understandable in a field with very fast schedules. Time, in film as in many other industries, is money.

This wasn't all that Henna told us. She told us her gender, and the colour of her skin, were given less value than those of her White, male colleagues. This was despite the claims by parts of the film industry, and by government policy, that film is open to any and all who are talented.[16]

This book tells the story of Henna's observation that film, and much of the rest of culture, is not a meritocracy. It is not enough to be talented and hard-working to make it.

We will see how the workforce in cultural occupations is deeply unequal, with class, race, and gender constituting crucial axes of inequality. Film and television occupations are hostile to women; museums, galleries, and libraries are

4

marked by their Whiteness. Publishing is 'posh'. The 'posh-ness' of specific cultural occupations, the absence of those from working-class origins, is not a new thing. It is a long-standing problem.

Inequalities in who works in cultural occupations are driven by several factors. Low and no pay are crucial in excluding those without financial resources from entering cultural jobs. At key points in careers, women face hidden, and not so hidden, discrimination. Childhood engagement in culture is important in getting a cultural career later in life. There are significant inequalities as people grow up. In many occupations the default image of a cultural worker, as Henna points out, is a White man from a middle-class background. People who are not part of that demographic group face substantial barriers to their success.

These are some examples of the dynamics that shape the sorts of culture we get. They shape the audience too. We will demonstrate how cultural consumption is highly unequal.

We sometimes think of culture as open to all. Government policy has made some museums free, and subsidised the cost of other artforms. Our analysis shows that engagement in many forms of government-supported culture are, at best, a minority concern. This is true whether we look at ticket sales or we survey people about what they attend.

Cultural production and cultural consumption are the two areas of focus for our story about culture and inequality. These two areas have seen a long-standing and rich set of research traditions and agendas associated with them.[17] We're contributing new data and new analysis to this already extensive academic work.

The *Panic!* project and partnership

Much of the new data and new analysis comes from two research projects. These were conducted by several academics, along with partners from the cultural sector. The focus of much of this work was raising awareness of what existing academic research was telling us about culture and inequality.

In 2015 Create London wanted to understand what they felt was a crisis for social mobility in the arts. Create's initial set of ideas created a research partnership. This brought Drs Sam Friedman, Daniel Laurison, Dave O'Brien, and Mark Taylor, along with support from Goldsmiths College, together with Create London and Barbican.[18] In the 2018 version Mark and Dave were joined by Dr Orian Brook, and Arts Emergency became a core partner with Barbican and Create London.[19] We were also lucky to work along with Drs Sara De Benedictis and Jordan Tchilingirian, Nikki Kane, and Bozena Wielgoszewska.

The 2015 project worked with the *Guardian* to survey cultural workers about their careers, as well as their values and attitudes. With help from trade unions and key individuals on social media we gathered 2,487 responses to that survey.

We then conducted interviews with 237 of those respondents, probing further elements of their cultural work and their cultural lives. We also used the interviews to double-check some of our survey findings.[20]

The survey and the interview fieldwork yielded massive amounts of fascinating data. The 2018 *Panic!* project reported on some of the findings.[21] It also allowed us to do more analysis of nationally representative datasets.

Using Census data and data from the government's Taking Part survey, which covers cultural activity in England, we were able to report new findings about culture and inequality. We also drew on work with other academic collaborators,[22] presenting findings from the Labour Force Survey and from British Social Attitudes, and British Election Study survey data, as well as the original *Panic!* survey data.[23]

These elements were brought together in the industry and public facing report: *Panic! Social Class, Taste and Inequalities in the Creative Industries*.[24] Along with the report, 2018 had an events and engagement programme driven by the arts partners, building on similar activities that took place in 2015.

Culture is bad for you is the third phase of these working relationships and that investigation into inequality and culture. *Panic!* showed how there was still a strong interest in our analysis, and we were keen to bring the stories from our interviewees into public debates. The *Panic!* project, and the book, reflects our contribution, but also some of the limitations of our expertise.

Orian worked in the cultural sector before training as a geographer: she has looked at mobility, broadly defined, and culture. Mark is a specialist in patterns of cultural consumption, primarily focused on class, race, gender, and education. Dave has written extensively about government policy on culture, as well as focusing on an intersectional approach to class issues in cultural jobs.

As a result, the book does not cover every axis of social inequality. Much more research is needed on, for example, the impact of disability in the creative workforce and in arts audiences, or the experience of LGBT+ individuals and communities. These are not areas in which any of us are experts, and it would have been inappropriate to claim such expertise. We are hopeful this book is a contribution to developing scholarship in those areas, as well as the more general study of inequality in society.

Thinking about inequality

Inequality is now an important subject for academic research. Much of this has been driven by economists and sociologists.[25] That work has tended not to look at cultural and creative industries. Cultural and media studies have done extensive research on the subject. We're aiming to situate our analysis between these fields.

There is extensive, and highly politicised, debate about the nature and extent of inequality.[26] This includes the extent of inequality *within* countries, as well as *between* countries.[27]

In the UK, along with countries such as the United States and France, the focus of research has been on inequality between the very 'top' of society and the rest of the population. The core argument here is that wealth inequalities are becoming greater. This is because profits from financial resources are outstripping growth in other areas of the economy, such as wages. This means that those who already have financial assets are getting richer faster than the rest of society.[28]

The setting for these economic changes is a decade of reduced levels of overall economic growth and reduced levels of government spending following the financial crisis of 2008. Just as the richest at the top of society are getting richer, social support for the poorest has been reduced.[29]

Economic inequality is only one part of the story. There are various other forms of division reflecting our unequal society.[30] We can see this in research showing the persistence of gender and racial discrimination, along with prejudice against other types of minorities.[31] Inequality is also, in the UK and elsewhere, seen in geographic divides, for example between London and the rest of England.[32]

We can think of these examples as social inequalities. These social divisions are linked to other sorts of resources beyond financial assets. These can include social networks and social connections.[33] Crucially, they have a cultural dimension. These sorts of inequalities are about what is valued and what is given worth.[34] This is the first part of our connection between inequality and the study of cultural production and consumption.

Social inequalities sit alongside economic inequalities. They also interact and intersect with each other. A useful example is the gender or racial pay gap.[35] We know women and people of colour are likely to receive lower rates of pay than their White and male colleagues, even where they are doing the same jobs. This reinforces their lower economic position, as well as reflecting a range of social prejudices.[36]

This example connects us to culture. Inequality reflects what is, and what is not, given value in society. This can be about financial assets or forms of labour. A good example is the way domestic work and childcare have low economic and social status, as compared with senior management positions.

What is valued in society is a much broader category than just economic assets. What is valued is much broader than objects too. What is valued includes people and social groups, as much as it does money. We can see this in how particular groups of people are afforded social status and social positions, while others struggle.[37]

The obvious contemporary example is found in the way immigration is discussed in contemporary politics. Immigrants are often demonised by contemporary media. Governments are keen to separate those with value to society and those they stigmatise[38] as 'not useful'. These divisions can be seen in discussions of people living in poverty, with long-standing discursive differentiation between deserving, respectable, and undeserving.[39]

This construction of worth and value is, at its heart, a cultural process.[40] It is highly dependent on culture, understood in a broad anthropological sense. It is also, in contemporary society, dependent on culture in a more narrow sense.

This is culture understood as the products of artistic and media practices. These can be state-funded, commercial, or more commonly a mixture of both. They can be fully professional, where everyone involved is being paid for their work, or they can capture the everyday activities of individuals and communities. Our cultural and creative industries, our media and arts occupations and institutions, are central to how value is afforded to individuals, communities, and even entire societies.

This is where we are focusing our attention. Inequality should not be conceived merely as an issue of income or even wealth. It is a cultural issue. We're going to focus on this cultural issue by looking at cultural production and cultural consumption.

Cultural production and cultural consumption shape what gets valued and given worth in society. In turn, what is given value and worth can challenge and change inequality. Or what is valued may reinforce and uphold the status quo.

What is a cultural job anyway?

We're going to analyse inequality in cultural production and consumption by looking at cultural and creative industries. Our focus is on a specific set of jobs within those industries. We're interested in cultural occupations.

Let's think about culture first. One view is that everyone, every day, is involved in making culture.[41] This understanding of cultural production is grounded in an *anthropological* view of culture. Here culture is the sets of signs and symbols, languages, everyday practices and activities, that constitute the social world.

This approach was refined and developed by cultural studies scholars. This intellectual project sought to destabilise and challenge hierarchies of high, legitimate, or elite culture. Cultural studies sought to include many of the practices of everyday life in our definition of legitimate culture. The contested cultural status of television[42] and the social importance of objects such as the Sony Walkman[43] are two useful historical examples.

This approach to the production and creation of culture is important. The academic tradition that was contesting cultural hierarchies was also the academic tradition that took seriously the idea that culture was an economic, or business and industrial, activity. Cultural producers were workers who make a contribution to the economy, in the same way as manufacturing, health care, or financial services.[44] In addition to being sources of jobs and growth in and of themselves, artistic and cultural organisations were seen as providing development and ideas for the wider economy.

That view of cultural production has a long, detailed, and keenly contested history. In government policies, especially in British and American cities, cultural activity came to be seen as an economic activity that could replace other, declining, industries.[45]

We can see the rise of creative industries is in these government policy approaches, along with academic work on economic measurement and classification. 'Creative industries' is a term that is quite familiar today.

It has not always been this way. Even now there are lively debates. These include debates over what constitutes a creative industry, if we should prefer the term cultural industries, and if the creative economy is distinct from cultural and creative industries.[46]

The category of creative industries is constituted by businesses and organisations, as well as jobs and occupations. It is important to note that *industries* and *occupations* are different categories.

Many uses of 'creative industries' tend to mix these two categories together, into a broad conception of the term. The categories of *occupations*, for example being an author and an actor, are usually intertwined with categories of *industries*, for example working in a bookshop or as an usher in the theatre.

The intertwining of *industry* and *occupation* initially seems to make sense. To give another intuitive example, jobs in cultural *industries* might be attractive to those seeking cultural *occupations*. We can think of the popular cliché of the aspiring author working in a bookshop, or the aspiring curator invigilating at exhibitions. The level of detailed subject or field knowledge that is part of entry to cultural occupations can make these staff excellent and outstanding retail workers. These examples also give clues as to the importance of making distinctions between *occupations* and *industries*.

Occupations refer to the sorts of activities or tasks people do in their jobs. *Industries* refer to what organisations or businesses do, for example the goods they make or the services they provide.

One of the key areas of research on creative industries has been how to define or demarcate these two categories. It is especially difficult where specific *occupations* are not solely based in specific *industries*. One example is actors, who work across film, television, radio, and theatre, as well as in

12

advertising, education, and other areas of corporate life, such as training activities.

Government and some academics draw a distinction between three different groups in the creative economy.[47] First are creative occupations working *in* creative industries. This is where we can find actors working in theatre and in film and television, or writers working in publishing.

Then there are creative occupations working *outside* of the creative industries. The most obvious example would be those with artistic occupations working within corporate businesses on things like branding and logos.

Finally, there are *non-creative and support jobs* in creative industries. This is where much of the confusion arises, for example retail occupations in museums and theatres, or cleaning and other sorts of semi-routine manual work in publishing or the music industry, as well as roles such as finance and accountancy within film and television.

The changing shape and nature of businesses means many of these 'non-creative' workers are in firms that are serving the creative industries. They are often no longer employed directly. The most recent government analysis of data on the UK economy in 2017 suggested these non-specialist occupations are around half of the employment in creative industries.[48]

These categories are very blurred in the lives of creative workers. For many of our interviewees, being a cultural worker was a vocation as much as a specific job or occupation.

We're interested in cultural occupations because of their very direct and central role in making culture. We are also interested in them because they allow us to have a focus for our analysis. As we will see in later chapters, they help us to interpret social mobility data, data about attitudes and values, as well as to see patterns in cultural consumption data. We're also linking our focus on cultural occupations to other, recent, studies of elite professional jobs.

For now, we're just going to think about the role of cultural occupations in making culture. As we noted earlier, inequality is bound up with the process of giving worth and value. This is a cultural process. Cultural occupations are the jobs at the centre of this process.

It is important to note that we're not saying everyday, anthropological, understandings of culture are irrelevant to the process of affording worth and value. Rather, we're highlighting the importance of formal cultural occupations within this broader anthropological view.

Cultural occupations shape which stories get told and which do not.[49] Which stories get told is a result of how cultural production is organised. Cultural consumption is a reflection, although not a direct result, of the organisation of cultural production.

One of the central elements of how cultural production is organised is who works in cultural occupations. This is not the only thing that matters, as funding, markets, technological change, and the overall political economy of culture are crucial too.

We'll see throughout this book that who works in cultural occupations reflects social inequalities. In turn, who works in cultural occupations shapes social inequalities too. The people who get to make and commission culture are not a diverse group. Certain groups are systematically excluded. The outcomes and products of cultural occupations are thus only a partial reflection and representation of our society.

Worse, the groups missing from cultural occupations are often misrepresented and caricatured, if they are seen at all. Women may only be the wives or mothers in male stories.

People of colour may be presented in cliched and racist ways. Working-class origin individuals may only ever be one-dimensional, in contrast to the complexity and depth offered to middle-class representations.

Class and cultural occupations

The last point, about representations of different social classes, prompts the final bit of ground-clearing before we can begin our analysis. Class is the central focus of inequality in this book. However, it is important to understand how we understand class.

The book adopts an intersectional approach[50] to social class. Throughout the book we'll try to think about how class intersects with other characteristics, primarily gender and ethnicity. Women and people of colour face barriers in addition to those associated with social class origin. As we'll see in Chapter 8, working-class origin women of colour face some of the highest barriers to success in cultural occupations.

As much as this book contributes to fields of sociology of culture, cultural policy, and creative industries, we are keen that class analysis, for example work on social mobility, takes seriously the need for an intersectional understanding.

'Class' is obviously a difficult and contested term.[51] This is especially so in Britain where it is one of the central axes around which society is divided and organised. It is important to individuals' and communities' identities, even where it is rejected or questioned.

This is not unique, as all societies have dividing lines around which they are structured and which shape individual and community identity. We can think of caste in India or race in the United States as good examples.

At the same time, class is a technical term used in academic research to understand how society is organised. If class is a complex subject for public discussion, it is equally difficult in academic work. There are disagreements over the definition, its boundaries, what 'counts' and what does not, for understanding class.

Even where there is agreement, for example that a useful way of understanding class is by looking at occupations in relation to the labour market, there are different traditions. Each uses different occupational schemes to equate to different, although often complimentary, analyses of society.

In addition to occupational approaches to class, there are traditions that seek to highlight cultural aspects of class. The most recent example of this approach is the BBC's The Great British Class Survey[52] (GBCS) project and the subsequent discussions.[53]

The GBCS was a reminder of the importance of taking cultural and social resources into account when understanding class. This is in addition to, and not instead of, economic and occupational elements of class.

Where do cultural occupations fit into these debates over social class? Cultural occupations, at least those in the UK government's definition, are almost always counted as professional and managerial jobs. They are what we would understand as 'middle class' occupations, as opposed to routine and manual work jobs that we might call working-class occupations.

It might seem strange to classify some cultural occupations as middle class. As we will see in Chapter 6, they can be very low paid and highly precarious. Yet they have a particular sort of social status. They also have the kinds of autonomy, along with occupational position in the labour market, that mark them out as middle-class jobs.

Cultural occupations are therefore, like many other middle-class professions, highly desirable. They are 'good' jobs. This is in addition to their role in shaping an individual's, a community's, and society's understanding of itself.

Cultural occupations are also important because they reflect another element of social inequality. This is the changing composition of the middle class.

In some of the literature we can see the argument that there is a difference or division within middle-class service jobs.[54] This is between technical and socio-cultural occupations.

Socio-cultural occupations include things like teaching and working in education, along with the sorts of cultural jobs we're discussing in this book. The dividing lines are around politics, along with values and social attitudes.

Across France, Britain, and the United States, analysis of political behaviour suggests the rise of a new fraction of the middle class. This new fraction is liberal, open, and tolerant. It reflects the sort of attitudes and values we're going to see from cultural workers in Chapter 3.[55]

At the same time, cultural and social theory has argued that we are seeing changes to what middle-class work is. Previously stable and secure middle-class professions may be becoming less secure and more precarious.[56] Cultural occupations are thought to be the leading examples of these sorts of changes, which may now be impacting more traditional professions.

So, we have the idea that a fraction of the middle class is distinct because of its values and attitudes. We also have the importance of cultural work as a potential 'future' for other middle-class jobs. There has also been a complimentary research tradition examining the sociology, and more particularly the economics, of artistic and cultural jobs. Finally, studying specific occupations has been a long-standing part of the sociology of work. This sits alongside the importance of studying 'micro classes' in American research on how society is stratified and divided.[57]

We can think of our cultural occupations as a 'micro class', a fraction within the middle class. Part of the analysis in the book is showing what brings cultural occupations together, for example a vocational commitment to cultural work. It is also about showing how even a shared vocation, and a shared solidarity, can contribute to the replication of social inequality.

Key themes and the structure of the book

We are going to begin the book by thinking about why culture is good for you. We'll see how research and policy documents make a compelling case for the positive impacts of culture.

There is also a compelling case for the value of culture in itself. This value is separate from any social or economic benefits it may offer to individuals, communities, nations, and the world.

Starting with the value and importance of culture allows us to think about some of the key themes that will run throughout the book. Our first is how the shared experiences of cultural workers hide significant differences. These differences reflect and replicate social inequalities.

We will see this in our discussion of the value of culture. We're using some of our middle-class origin interviewees to show how cultural workers are committed to the power and importance of culture in society. We use our middle-class origin interviewees because these are the social group that dominate most cultural occupations.

The dominance of those from the middle class is comprehensively demonstrated in Chapter 3. It analyses the labour force for cultural occupations. It presents five years of data from the Office for National Statistics' (ONS) Labour Force Survey (LFS). This shows how working-class origin people, people of colour, and in some cultural occupations, women, are absent from the workforce.

Chapter 3 also looks at how cultural occupations are held together, as well as being potentially closed. Using data on attitudes and values, as well as on social networks, we start to explain some of the inequalities we've seen in the labour force.

Cultural occupations are the most liberal, left-wing, and pro-welfare of any set of occupations, as well as being anti-Brexit. Survey data suggests the cultural workers in our research project recognise social inequality, but at the same time feel that talent and hard work explains success.

This commitment to meritocracy is at the root of our second theme. This is the way that cultural workers recognise structural inequalities in cultural occupations, as well as in society. The responsibility for these inequalities is, however, placed onto the individual. This is one reason why change is so difficult.

The other side to our analysis of inequality in production is inequality in consumption. Chapter 4 uses data from England to demonstrate that cultural consumption is highly unequal.

We will see that there is a minority of the population who are highly engaged cultural consumers. For the majority, *not* engaging in formal cultural activity is the norm. Almost every artform and cultural activity is marked by class and racial inequalities. There are also significant patterns of gender inequalities.

We contrast this with everyday forms of culture. In doing so we show the way that what counts, and what is valued, is a reflection of unequal cultural hierarchies.

Presenting the data on cultural consumption allows us to show another element of our cultural workers' shared experience. It also allows us to show another element of closure in cultural occupation.

Cultural workers are by far the most engaged of any occupational group. They are more culturally active than their middle-class professional colleagues. They are also totally unrepresentative of the patterns of cultural engagement in the working-class population.

The remaining chapters explain these inequalities by analysing key points in the life course of a cultural worker. They also continue the themes we've introduced earlier in the book.

Chapter 5 discusses the role of culture in our cultural workers' childhoods. It shows the role of individualisation of inequalities, along with the problem of *seemingly* shared experiences.

Many of the patterns of inequalities we've seen in production and consumption begin in childhood. We use survey and interview data to show how cultural resources, or cultural capital, are accumulated in childhood.

All of our interviewees highlighted the importance of culture when they were children. Looking at representative survey data from England we can see the importance of participation and encouragement in culture during cultural workers' childhoods.

This shared experience obscures the level of inequality in access to culture. Some of our workers grew up in homes that offered high levels of access to culture. Others were dependent on luck, perhaps having an encouraging teacher or access to local state-funded resources such as libraries or youth clubs.

The inequalities in access to culture profoundly shape how our cultural workers understood the possibility of a career in a cultural occupation. For some they were totally at home in cultural occupations. For others it was a revelation later in life that culture was something they could do for a living.

Making a living in a cultural occupation is hard. We know from existing research that cultural occupations offer big rewards, but also offer major risks for individual workers. Chapter 6 analyses the problem of pay.

Unpaid labour seems to be endemic to cultural occupations. We show how even this shared experience of working for low or no pay is differentiated by class and by age.

For our younger middle-class respondents unpaid work could be an investment in their careers. It could also be a chance for creative development.

For those from working-class backgrounds unpaid work was an unaffordable luxury. It was associated with exploitation and frustrating dead ends.

The sense of shared experience and solidarity obscures the different experiences of different social class groups. Shared experience of unpaid work hides class inequality in cultural occupations.

Unpaid work also reflects how risks are divided in cultural occupations. The individual is expected to have the economic resources, the economic capital, to support their creative career. If they do not, then the system of cultural production will not help.

Differences in experience by class were one axis of stratification of unpaid work. The other is age.

Age is important to our story of inequality in lots of ways. In the case of pay, our older workers told us of very different support mechanisms when they were starting their careers. This social safety net seemed to take responsibility for some of the risks and uncertainties of the cultural labour market.

This might suggest that inequality in culture is a recent phenomenon. In Chapter 7 we show how cultural occupations have been unequal for a long time.

The chapter discusses the idea of social mobility in cultural jobs. It presents the first ever analysis of ONS's Longitudinal Study to show that cultural occupations were just as exclusive forty years ago as they are now.

Of course, there have been major social and economic changes since then. Changing and challenging inequality in our cultural occupations has been slow, and there seems to be little progress.

In the early 1980s the chances of someone from a working-class origin making it into a cultural occupation were much lower than the chances of someone from a middle-class origin. In current data we see those chances have remained at a similarly low level.

The broad patterns of social mobility, as shown in the quantitative analysis, reveal that cultural occupations have long-standing issues of inequality. These issues exist because of barriers like unpaid work, and closed social networks. They also exist because of more subtle (and sometimes not-so-subtle) forms of exclusion.

In Chapter 8 we analyse the experiences of those who are socially mobile into cultural occupations. We try to foreground the experiences of working-class origin women of colour. They are most likely to be absent from cultural occupations.

By doing so, we show that cultural occupations have a 'somatic norm' of White, male, middle classness. Social mobility, along with diversity and inclusion, policies have not addressed this structural problem. Our individual workers still have to bear the burden of responsibility for cultural occupations' failure to welcome and support them.

We see this again when we look specifically at gender inequality. Chapter 9 presents new analysis of the ONS's Longitudinal Study. This shows the dynamics of gender inequality in the cultural labour force.

The decision to start a family is crucial to gender inequality. We lay bare the relentless hostility to women with caring responsibilities. This is especially important in accounting for gendered exclusions from the top of creative occupations.

Caregiving, much as unpaid work, cultural taste, or access to culture in childhood, obscures important inequalities. Class matters in who manages to overcome the barriers associated with cultural occupations' refusal to support women with children.

Sadly, we also see how our interviewees take responsibility for these structural problems onto themselves, as individuals. Again, this may account for why inequalities in cultural occupations seem to change so slowly.

Thinking about class also reminds us that parenting and caregiving is not the only explanation for gender inequalities. This point has been at the centre of the academic work in this area, but does not seem to be reflected in policy responses to inequality.

Our final substantive chapter reflects on the slow pace of change. It also provides a contrast to women's experiences highlighted in Chapters 8 and 9.

In Chapter 10 we hear from the 'somatic norm' of cultural occupations. These are men who are in senior positions within their organisations or artforms.

These men all have political and moral commitments to addressing the problems of inequality in the sector. They see the problem of inequality. In some cases they offer us detailed analyses of structural sexism, racism, and class-based forms of inequality.

Recognising the problem does not solve it. Our 'senior' men narrate their careers through luck and self-effacement. According to their stories, structural inequalities did not seem to help them become successful. This leaves them, in their own careers, unable to challenge or change these structural inequalities. This is despite their faith in the idea that culture is good for you.

We have focused on making this book an overview of culture and inequality. It is primarily written from a sociological standpoint. Sociology can do much to show the regular patterns of inequality in our cultural occupations. It can hopefully show the social mechanisms that help us to explain inequality in our cultural occupations.

Yet sociological study is only one part of the story. We are hopeful that this book will contribute well beyond sociology, particularly to those disciplines in the humanities that address both cultural objects and the future cultural workforce. The problem of social inequality, and how to address it, is not the preserve of one academic subject. It is also not the preserve of academia alone.

Our second hope for the book is that it will contribute to discussions within cultural occupations. We are hopeful that public and policy discourses will see clearly the problem of inequality in our cultural occupations. We are also hopeful that the solutions they devise will be mindful of the long-term and structural nature of the issues we have researched.

The conclusion to the book reflects on the prospects of success for these efforts to challenge and change inequality. We reflect on our four themes: the individualisation of risks; how shared experiences actually obscure structures of inequality; the reflexivity and self-awareness of our cultural workers; and the long-term nature of the problems.

This latter point suggests inequality is, and will continue to be, dynamic. It is not something that has one single solution. There will not be a magic bullet. As strategies emerge to address inequality, the powerful will adapt. They will adapt practically, as we see in our discussion of unpaid work and the development of cultural capital in childhood. They will also adapt discursively, as we see in senior men's 'inequality talk'.

To understand the dynamic nature of inequality we need to better theorise the relationship between inequality and culture. Developing the overall story presented in the book, we suggest the need to think about *weak* and *strong* theories of the relationship between culture and inequality. Both are valuable.

The former connects to the necessary project of incremental reform to make cultural production and cultural consumption open to all. The latter is more pessimistic about culture's role in reinforcing the unequal structures characteristic of our contemporary society.

Article 27 of the Universal Declaration of Human Rights states that 'everyone has the right freely to participate in the cultural life of the community, to enjoy the arts and to share in scientific advancement and its benefits'. At present we are a long way from that right being realised.

Cultural occupations must change. They must change if society is to freely enjoy the benefits of culture, and participate fully in cultural consumption and production. As our interviewees tell us in Chapter 2, cultural occupations are crucial to making the world a better place. At present cultural occupations are not doing this. They are, in fact, part of the mechanism by which society continues to be unequal. Culture is bad for you.

2

Is culture good for you?

Introduction: Michaela's story

I distinctly remember one of the first times I went to a contemporary gallery; I can't remember which one it was. I was 17. I walked in the door and I was made to feel like a piece of shit. Like, really, it was disgusting, the way that people behaved towards me, but I had determined that, as I was going to live a life that was, for me, unprecedented; I didn't know anyone else who was doing it, that I would have to find a way to be comfortable in any room I was in, otherwise there's no point in me doing anything. I think certainly at that early stage I had those feelings of discomfort all the time, whereas now I don't. I don't think that's entirely due to changes in the art world, although it has definitely shifted. I think it's also changes within myself, and a kind of decision to not prioritise other people's perceptions of me.

We are starting our discussion of inequality in cultural and creative occupations with Michaela. A Black British woman from a working-class background, she was in her late thirties when we interviewed her. She had found success in the art world, as a curator and creative practitioner. However, her reflections on her experiences of an art gallery as a teenager suggest the art world had not been welcoming to her.

Michaela's experiences connect directly to her drive to be successful in the art world. Her experiences also give us insights into the structural inequalities that she faced in order to be successful. These inequalities are the core subject of our book's analysis.

We will see in Chapter 3 that there is an absence of people of colour and those from working-class origins in museum and gallery occupations. We'll see in Chapter 4 how the demographics of visitors to galleries and museums have similar patterns of inequality to those of the workforce.

Michaela's story is a story of being out of place in the gallery, and out of place in the art world. This feeling of being out of place is not only because going to a gallery was a novel or first-time experience for her. It is also because of her experience of outright hostility from individuals in that place.

Versions of this story will be repeated throughout the book, irrespective of the cultural or creative occupation in which the individual is working. We'll see the importance of understanding how class, gender, and race *intersect* in experiences of inequality. We'll also see, from our White, middle-class origin cultural workers, very different stories of culture in childhood.

At the same time, Michaela's narrative is one of resistance and refusal to be excluded. This shows her commitment to the importance of the art world, and the importance of her presence within it. Michaela tells us that she would be doing something 'unprecedented' to feel comfortable in the world of cultural institutions.

Her story is about how *individual* and *individualised* resistance and refusal can be. She describes how she, herself, has changed.

Struggling to feel comfortable places demands on the individual to adapt to structural inequalities, even as individuals challenge and perhaps change these structures.

It is clear she believes that struggling against the hostile environment she encounters in cultural spaces is something worth fighting for. Culture is something that is so valuable that it was worth changing *herself*. This change was in order to ignore hostile perceptions from others in the cultural world.

Michaela's struggle with the art world, and her sense of having changed, indicates the *value* of culture. It reminds us how working in a cultural occupation, and feeling comfortable in cultural institutions, is something that is profoundly important. Its importance is especially vital to cultural workers.

We're starting with Michaela because we want to make it clear that inequality is a problem. In Michaela's case it is inequality in the art world, but it could be in the music or film industries, in theatre or television.

We are also starting with her because we want to make it clear that culture matters and has value. Part of the motivation for our focus on inequality, and the idea that 'culture is bad for you', is the way that the *good* and positive elements of culture are not evenly distributed throughout society.

Understanding Michaela's experience of inequality is not possible without establishing why culture is so important to people who work in cultural jobs. The value and importance of culture to our interviewees helps us to understand how they keep going in the face of structural inequalities. The value of culture is sadly also part of the reason why *structural* change is so difficult.

The value that culture has for cultural workers, and their commitment to their cultural occupations, also points towards the positive contribution culture makes to society. We're going to discuss that positive contribution, the idea that culture is good for you, in this chapter.

First, we're going to give a flavour of contemporary policy and research on the benefits of culture to society. We're then going to develop the insights from policy and research by looking at what our interviewees thought about the value of culture. We'll see that our interviewees shared a commitment to cultural work, irrespective of the cultural occupation in which they worked.

We are, emphatically, not denying the value of culture. But this value also requires us to reflect on what is lost because of the relationship between culture and inequality. If there are systematic exclusions of some parts of society from commissioning, making, and participation in culture, what are the consequences? We come back to this question in the conclusion to the chapter.

Making the case for culture

There is a long history of arguments over the benefits, and the potential hazards, of engagement with culture.[1] These positions manifest in different ways, and come from different traditions and perspectives. The benefits range from moral, emotional, social and civic, to economic growth, urban regeneration, and tourism.

In some traditions the very idea of culture is associated with personal and social transformation. Here there are complex and controversial lines of thought, most notably Victorian conceptions of the role of cultural institutions in addressing issues deemed to be social problems.[2] This role for the gallery or museum is grounded in the idea that culture might 'civilise' those who, in the eyes of the ruling elities, were seen as having moral or personal failings.[3]

The transformational role of culture is still with us today, albeit more rarely expressed in the same sort of judgemental and hierarchical language. The potential of culture as a resource goes beyond the individual to include social movements, political movements, visions of citizenship, and, crucially, economic development.

One version of this is that exposure to the best that has been thought and said will make individuals 'better' people. Another is that engagement in culture will help society in terms of health and well-being, reducing crime rates, and developing social cohesion. These ideas have come to be known as the 'instrumental' benefits of culture. They have a long history.[4] Others question justifying funding, or giving social status, to culture based on impact. Instead they see the value of culture not in the *consequences* of engagement or participation, but rather in culture itself.[5]

This perspective, often described as the idea of 'art for art's sake', has a similarly long history. Here the artistic value of culture alone, over and above any associated benefits, justifies a special social status for those making culture.[6]

We can see this in arguments for the importance of the artist,[7] or the auteur filmmaker, or in the value of music.[8] This special social status sits alongside funding and institutional support.

The latter point brings us to where discussions about the benefits of culture have been most prominent. In public policy the question of which activities should be funded (and why) is crucial. This has led to a range of policy research considering the benefits of culture. Some of this has been to aid decision-making, while some has been so that the cultural sector can advocate for resources.[9]

In order to distil this vast literature, we're going to focus on recent research and policy work that has considered the value or benefit of culture. We'll give an overview of the public policy questions and the existing research. Our focus is on recent interventions that connect with the problem of social inequality.

Three recent documents have comprehensively summarised the value and benefit of culture from a variety of perspectives: Geoffrey Crossick and Patrycja Kaszynska's *Understanding the Value of Arts & Culture*,[10] which summarises a major project on cultural value funded by the UK's Arts and Humanities Research Council; *Changing Lives*, the UK Parliament's Digital, Culture, Media and Sport Select Committee report about its inquiry into the social impact of participation in culture and sport;[11] and, finally, *Creative Health: The Arts for Health and Wellbeing*,[12] which is the report from the All Party Parliamentary Group on Arts and Health's work on health impacts.

Taken together, these three reports show the complexity, but also the importance and value, of culture. We'll use each of them as a lens to see the particular perspective on the benefits, and value, of culture that they contribute.

One thing that they all have in common is that they point towards the settled and uncontroversial position that culture is good for society, in a variety of different ways. These include the social and economic benefits of culture. They also try to focus on the specifically *cultural* aspects of the value of culture. This is subtly different from previous eras' insistence on art for art's sake, or the debates over the 'intrinsic' and 'instrumental' value of culture.[13]

Changing Lives: The Social Impact of Participation in Culture and Sport

Social impact is a crucial element in debates over the value of culture in contemporary society.[14] It has a very long history, which is well-covered in academic literature, for example in Eleonora Belfiore's work on cultural policy.

In the UK, since the 1980s and 1990s, both arts policy and cultural organisations have been adapting to systems of public management and measurement.[15] During this period both Conservative and New Labour administrations demanded evidence for government decision-making.

Initially the economic impact of culture dominated the evidence base.[16] This attempted to render visible activities such as jobs created, tourist spending, and investment into local areas or national economies. Economic impact research was about highlighting the importance of cultural organisations to the economy.

This approach was influential beyond the need for just data to inform policy. The research making the economic case for culture was conducted at a time of industrial decline, when cities and towns were keen to find new sorts of jobs and industries.[17] Some roots of the idea of cultural industries as a sector of the economy can be found in the 1980s, the initial era of economic impact research.[18]

There were, and still are, numerous critiques of economic impact. Many reject the idea that culture can be narrated through numbers of jobs, businesses, or financial contributions to the economy.[19]

In part, these critiques are technical. They focus on the accuracy of some of the estimates of culture's economic impact and importance. This line of thought often argued that the economic impacts of culture had been exaggerated.[20]

Perhaps more important is the objection that the point of culture is not to make money.[21] Although 'art for art's sake' has become a rarer position in current discourse about culture, there are various activities where the benefits of organisations, participation, or engagement go beyond jobs or spending.

By the 1990s, artistic traditions associated with community activity and social practice were becoming influential.[22] They gathered a similar status to the demand for new forms of economic activity in towns and cities. Ways of understanding *social* impacts were established as both counterpoint and complement to economic impact.[23] These social impacts included educational attainment, community cohesion, lower crime rates, and health and well-being.

This brief flavour of the roots of 'impact' frameworks for culture inevitably glosses over methodological and ideological struggles that have characterised the past forty years. What this summary does is help to situate *Changing Lives: The Social Impact of Participation in Culture and Sport* and its articulation of the benefits of culture. *Changing Lives* is a report from a British Parliament select committee inquiry. Select Committees invite written and oral evidence from interested parties to help with their work. The opening sections of the report are clear that from the evidence submitted and the work of the inquiry 'there is no dispute about the positive social impact of participation in culture'. Later sections highlight that 'cultural and sporting organisations are having positive impacts on their communities every day of the week'.

These positive impacts occur across several areas of public policy and social life. They include crime and criminal justice, education, health and well-being, and regenerating communities. It is worth focusing on two in particular, education and regenerating communities.

In education the report uses several examples. One is Feversham Primary Academy, a school in Bradford in the North of England. At Feversham the headteacher embedded arts provision, in the form of drama, music, and the visual arts, into the everyday life of the school. The headteacher spoke of this commitment to culture for education as a major reason for the improvement in academic standards and in attendance rates.

Culture in education is connected to the development of social skills, along with enhanced confidence and motivation. Contact Theatre, another of the examples in the report, is cited as being an important provider of these activities. They develop young participants as leaders and decision-makers, with a particular focus on those from areas characterised by high unemployment and low educational attainment.

Yet these benefits are not entirely divorced from our overall focus on inequality. While highlighting these benefits, the report also notes how many award-winners and people in key arts occupations were privately educated. This inequality sits alongside the uneven distribution of access to cultural education for children in the English school system. This is a key point that we'll discuss in more detail in Chapter 5.

In terms of regenerating communities, *Changing Lives* draws on a long-standing policy tradition that art and culture can have place-based benefits.[24] The primary example in the report is the city of Hull's designation as UK City of Culture in 2017. The programme leveraged funding, provided events designed to increase both local and tourist interest in the city, increased local pride in place, and changed external perceptions.

The report also notes how the bidding process for UK City of Culture can be beneficial. Although Coventry was awarded the designation for 2021, Sunderland's evidence to the Committee discussed how the bidding process opened up a conversation about the priorities and directions of the city, facilitated by the bid for a year-long cultural festival.

These examples are in the wake of perceived regeneration success in Liverpool, which was European Capital of Culture in 2008.[25] They also follow longer-term developments of cultural infrastructure in regions such as the North East of England.[26]

This is controversial territory, with a long-standing academic tradition critical of the appropriateness and effectiveness of the use of culture for place-based transformations. The effect of regeneration may be to squeeze out poorer residents of communities.[27]

Nonetheless, for the organisations submitting evidence to the Digital, Culture, Media and Sport Committee's inquiry, the power of culture for remaking localities, and the beneficial social impact of participation in culture, are settled questions. The perspective in the report is that cultural organisations have moved beyond debates over whether arts and culture *can* provide social benefits. Now these benefits are one of the core purposes of culture.

The rich variety of case studies and evidence submissions are broad enough to indicate that cultural organisations are united around the benefits of participation in their programmes. Culture is about *changing lives*. This is a view that our interviewees strongly support.

Changing Lives complements much of the economic rhetoric associated with creative industries that we discussed in the introduction to this book. This line of thinking is further developed, and nuanced, when thinking about arts and health, and cultural value.

Creative Health: The Arts for Health and Wellbeing

Changing Lives also contains significant discussion of the relationship between culture and health. Much of this discussion was based on a project which connected researchers and politicians in the All Party Parliamentary Group for Arts, Health, and Wellbeing. This was a cross-party group of MPs and members of the House of Lords. The results were published as *Creative Health: The Arts for Health and Wellbeing*.

We can see interest in the relationship between culture and health as a result of several developments. It can be situated in the tradition of advocacy and research associated with social impact. There has also been a long-standing academic area of study on health impacts.[28] This has been given increased prominence in relation to specific problems, such as mental health, and new types of intervention (whether for efficiency or cost reasons in the context of increasing social spending on health policy).

There is now also greater research interest in the social basis and determinants of good health outcomes. Culture and health has also seen increased interest as governments have thought more about the happiness and well-being of their citizens.[29]

Finally, there has been interest in new research methods to provide high-quality evidence. These include using creative methods to interrogate health interventions, and using methods from health sciences to understand the relationship between culture and health.

Creative Health: The Arts for Health and Wellbeing makes three points. It argues that arts and culture can keep people well, aid recovery, and support longer lives; that arts and culture can be used to meet complex challenges to health, such as those associated with ageing, and chronic and long-term conditions, including mental health issues; and that arts and culture can save money for health and social care services.

The report is grounded in a social view of good and bad health. It is explicit about the way social inequality affects health, and sees a place for the arts in the context of unequally experienced social determinants of health. Crucially it suggests that the use of arts for health is a way to address some of the unequal patterns of cultural engagement. We discuss these in Chapter 4.

The social view of health allows the report to take in a wide range of health effects. It looks across the life course from birth to old age and death, and at place and community level effects. It has a broad view of culture, citing the theorists Raymond Williams[30] and Pierre Bourdieu[31] to establish an anthropological take on culture grounded in cultural engagement and experience. It is similar to *Understanding the Value of Arts & Culture*.

Overall, *Creative Health* is unequivocal. Arts and culture are good for us. They are good for us as children, as working-age adults, and as we get older. More support and investment will change society for the better. Arts and culture will not only make us healthier and help us to live happier lives, they will also have a profound social impact, changing our built environment, and saving money that would otherwise be spent on health-care budgets.

The take up of the report, for example the numerous references to it in *Changing Lives*, indicates health impacts may become the dominant mode of thinking about the benefits of culture. Yet this mode of thinking is still framed by the idea that culture can have an *impact*. This is distinct from recent engagements with the idea that we should understand the *value* of culture, rather than its *impact*.

Understanding the Value of Arts & Culture: The AHRC Cultural Value Project

The literature on arts and health is a logical evolution of attempts to establish and demonstrate the benefits of culture. These attempts have taken place alongside work focusing on the *value* of culture.

This work often contests simplistic notions of impact. The *Understanding the Value of Arts & Culture: The AHRC Cultural Value Project* report is the clearest example of this, synthesising over seventy funded research projects along with the two authors' own work.

Value is a complex term with a complex history. Even the specific idea of *cultural* value is contested, with various meanings depending on whether the 'value of culture' or 'cultural value' is under discussion.[32] Sometimes these two areas are used interchangeably, which has only added to the complexity of the subject.

Academic disciplines treat 'value' differently too. For many economists, value is at the core of their research. Here value is about individual utility and preferences, which are often expressed in prices. Even where particular goods or services don't have prices, such as clean air or museums that are free to enter, economists are interested in the value of these things.

For humanities, and some social science traditions, value is more complex. Political science, psychology, and sociology have an interest in *values*, which here relates more closely to moral, social, and political attitudes.

When thinking about culture, 'value' is also used in the sense of evaluation and value judgements. This understanding is common in the humanities, and some parts of social science research. This sense is important in two ways.

The fact people make judgements about what they like or dislike establishes a certain value for culture. It establishes what matters and what is given worth.[33]

Some of these judgements are formalised and have specific social status, such as reviews of concerts, theatre, or novels. Unequal status is given to particular individuals' judgements, whether as critic, audience, or commissioner.[34]

The unequal status of judgements points towards the second way evaluation and value are important. This is the way that judgements are contested and struggled over. One example might be the distance between critical and audience acclaim, which can manifest in both avant-garde or 'cult classic' cultural forms.[35]

Culture as a site for struggle and competition matters in several ways. In the first instance it highlights the relation-ship between judgements of taste and social inequalities. Inequalities shape who gets to make judgements. Critics are a useful example here. Recent work from USC Annenberg's School for Communication and Journalism suggests serious gender inequalities in film criticism, where between 2015 and 2017 80% of American film reviews were written by men.[36]

In the United States (and elsewhere) it is difficult to get films made that centre women as protagonists, or are directed by women. Those that are made receive fewer industry awards. Even if we don't know the direct *causal* relationship between gender inequality and film production, they are very clearly and obviously related.

This struggle manifests in policy and funding regimes. What is given money, what states, governments, and thus societies choose to *formally* support, is afforded particular status above other cultural forms.[37]

Even what counts as culture for the purposes of surveying people's tastes is subject to these status struggles. We'll see much more about this in Chapter 4.

Second, there are potentially great consequences for the struggle over cultural value. These consequences stem from the way that specific representations may depict individuals, communities, and social groups in ways that are positive and inclusive. They may also have negative and harmful depictions. There is extensive academic work devoted to demonstrating this relationship.

A nuanced example is Melissa Terras' work on commercial publishing.[38] She explores the depiction of scientists in children's books. Hundreds of books, over a century of publishing, share a set of stereotypes of professors as White, male, middle-class individuals, whether kindly teachers or evil madmen.

These depictions have important consequences in terms of who is seen to be a professor, and who is *represented*. These depictions can be connected to struggles over practical issues such as gender balance in academic or scientific professions, pay gaps, and racial discrimination. Even where we are discussing a relatively privileged professional occupational group, we can see how struggles over what counts in a canon can quickly be connected to social consequences.

At the other end of the social spectrum are television programmes focusing on the lives of people claiming benefits. Programme makers argue these shows fulfil their responsibilities to inform audiences. Researchers have characterised them as inaccurate and unethical, offering reductive and stigmatising representations of poverty.[39]

A lack of diversity in the people commissioning and creating these programmes is seen as a key cause of negative or stigmatising images. This lack of diversity is also influenced by the costs of media production and the changing political economy of television. We will see more about the lack of diversity in the cultural workforce in Chapter 3.

This is the frame for *Understanding the Value of Arts & Culture.*[40] Its starting point is with the *experience* of culture and the arts. This experience, whether good or bad, joyful or upsetting, is the important element of cultural value. This perspective was shared by many of our interviewees, as we'll see later in this chapter.

The AHRC Cultural Value Project categorises many facets of the value of culture, some of which have been discussed already. We will highlight two particular areas of focus for the report, *the reflective individual* and *the engaged citizen*.

These two areas of focus highlight the ability of arts and culture to offer individuals better developed understandings of themselves. Arts and culture also give better understandings of other individuals, and other communities and societies.[41]

That empathetic element has also been the subject of recent arguments from policy-makers, who see this as a core reason for arts and cultural policy. For Crossick and Kaszynska the cultural experience combines affective, emotional, and cognitive elements. This combination is at the root of its value.

Good, or great, cultural experiences here are not just the preserve of specific canons or venerated aesthetic traditions. They are not just about happiness and joy. Rather, great cultural experiences are those that combine emotional and cognitive aspects to generate personal reflection. Personal reflection has the capacity to stimulate personal growth and empathy for others. Our responses to culture give us an opportunity to 'practice our moral responses'.

The process of emotional responses shaping our understanding of ourselves and others is demonstrated by a range of examples. Rates of imprisonment and reoffending changed as culture helped prisoners conceive of alternative futures beyond incarceration and crime. Better health outcomes followed the recognition of patient needs and experiences by care and health professionals who had been through arts programmes.

Perhaps the best example of the personal and social enmeshment of our responses to culture came from a report on the value of poetry. The authors noted that poetry is experienced in many everyday contexts. These include social situations, for example in schools, at weddings, or on the radio. Poems allow us to make sense of the world, as we make personal meaning through the social and cultural resources available to us. Poems can be a mediating artefact between individual and community.[42]

This leads us to consider culture as a space for shared *reflections*, and thus community cohesion or participation. Culture can also be a site, or space, for shared *information*. It can foster campaigning or social movements.

Campaigning and social movements come in a variety of forms. They can be in response to large-scale social crises, such as in post-conflict societies. They can also focus on more localised participation in civic life. Participation is defined widely. It includes traditional forms of action, such as local politics and campaigning. It also captures cultural expressions that challenge misperceptions or misrecognitions of marginalised groups.

Reflections and information were two key starting points in our interviewees' discussions of the value of culture. Culture influences people. It changes the world for the better. It is a right that people should have access to culture.

Not only is there a reflective and informative value in culture. *Working* in cultural occupations was given high value in and of itself. We'll return to this theme in Chapter 6.

The value of culture, as demonstrated in *Understanding the Value of Arts & Culture*, is a crucial idea to keep in mind throughout this book. It is part of the reason why cultural workers are committed to cultural occupations. This commitment is in the face of the inequalities that are characteristic of cultural and creative work.

The power of culture

I think the one thing about working in the arts, it can be hideously, hideously moribund and stale and it's White and it's middle-class and all these sorts of things, but it is essentially led by people, and it's people that work in there tend to have a social mission, they have a set of values and they have a set of ethics, and that's quite a powerful thing to be working within.

I wouldn't be still doing this after fifteen years if I didn't believe in what I'm doing. I do believe that culture changes society. I think there's a far wider impact and you can see it in – I don't mean it in the way that the arts always seem to think that they can cure everything like poverty and cancer and things like that. I mean, actually, that there is – I grew up with a very big cultural life and I know that's how – that's influenced me massively. The things that I read, my thinking, my politics, it's been influenced by a cultural activity around that. The art that I like, the theatre that I go and see. And the thought of actually not either working in that or actually being exposed to anything cultural is just anathema, I can't imagine it.

This long comment by Meena echoes the ambivalence about the cultural sector that we saw in Michaela's story. Meena was in her early forties when we interviewed her, a middle-class-origin British Asian woman with a long career in a range of cultural occupations.

Meena is explicit about her frustrations with a 'moribund' White and middle-class cultural sector. Despite this, her faith in the arts is clear. She wants to share and open the arts up. She can't imagine not having access. This is because culture has a profound, positive, influence on people. Meena is explicit. This positive influence changes society.

The policy and research documents we discussed earlier in the chapter shared this sense that culture changes society for the better. We're going to see how this commitment to the positive value of culture plays out for our interviewees.

In doing so, we'll set up a juxtaposition. This is between cultural workers' commitment to the importance of culture, and the inequalities we demonstrate throughout the rest of the book. These inequalities in cultural production and consumption limit the potential value and impact of culture.

The commitment to culture was a dominant story for our cultural workers. This was irrespective of the sector, cultural practice, occupation, or artform they were working in. They saw culture as something that positively changes the world and that influences people. For some interviewees, culture was intertwined with a sense of explicit social activism. For others, the importance and power of culture, whether state-supported or commercial, gave rise to more subtle attachments to social change. They were united in the belief that culture should, and must, be open to everyone.

The right to culture

The idea that culture should be open to all is a prominent struggle in almost every part of the cultural sector. We can see it in the most commercial cultural forms, with online campaigns such as #OscarsSoWhite that aimed to challenge on- and off-screen representation in the film industry.[43]

The idea that culture should be open to all is there in discussions over gender in the music industry,[44] in questions about who headlines music festivals, and about who wins literary prizes.[45] We can also see it in cultural forms that are associated with government funding, such as campaigns to ensure museums decolonise their collecting and institutional practices.[46]

Let's look at Gerald's story. A White man from a middle-class professional social origin, he was in his mid-fifties and working in a very senior role in a major cultural institution at the time of our interview.

He gives us an example of the drive to make culture open to all. He's playing down the sense of activism or social change that we'll see from some other interviewees, but he is also open about being an 'evangelist', wanting other people to like art:

> I was always a bit of an evangelist. I was always, you know I was always slightly socially motivated I suppose, but not in anything beyond learning, not in a social change sort of way, but I thought I have got to really like this stuff and I would like other people to like it.

Gerald's motivation to have people share, and share in, his liking of culture was a similarly important trait in many our interviewees. It is a foundational commitment that motivates cultural workers, irrespective of their occupation or sector.

At the same time, the right to consume culture was matched by interviewees' commitment to representation. Michelle was in her twenties at the time of interview, a White woman from a professional middle-class background, who was working in publishing. She told us about the need for particular social groups to be represented in commercial literary culture, and how this motivated her work:

> To know that people who don't have access to queer voices will finally be able to go into their local bookstore, pick something up and think, 'Oh look, someone is like me. Someone has written something that I can relate to and I can feel better about myself because it is out there in the world.'

For Michelle, culture could give representation to marginalised individuals and communities, as well as creating a positive sense of identity. In this way, as for many of our interviewees, the power of culture was about changing the world for the better.

Influencing people and changing the world

The ability of culture to change the world, by influencing people, was captured neatly by Howard. Howard was in his early seventies, a White man from a middle-class clerical background. He had enjoyed a long and successful career in television, and reflected on his motivations, along with the joys of his work.

He told us how he felt that culture affects people, even if he only came to realise this later on in his life:

you are in an amazing unique place … To be able to do what you want to do and to influence people. You may not know that it's an influence if you see what I mean. In retrospect you suddenly realise perhaps what you were doing has been an influence.

Howard, along with Gerald, can be contrasted with Michelle. For our men in senior roles, struggles over representation, and the politics of who is included and excluded from culture, were not at the forefront of their thoughts. Rather, it is a more general sense that culture has a positive impact.

Howard and Gerald's shared narrative about culture will be extremely important later on in the book. As we will see in Chapter 10, the way men in senior positions think about cultural occupations is part of the reason that inequalities persist.

For now, we can just note the sense of impact and influence of culture. This is present even when our cultural workers were not making a direct connection between social causes and their cultural work.

We have seen our interviewees talking about some of the commitments that drive their cultural work. We've highlighted some of the impacts of culture, such as influencing people and representing communities. We've also seen how our interviewees wanted culture to be shared with, and open to, all.

We will elaborate on these ideas by introducing Matt and Henna. They give a more detailed sense of the power of culture to change the world.

Matt was a Black British playwright and poet, and was in his early forties when we interviewed him. His parents worked in traditional middle-class occupations and he grew up in London. He attended fee-paying schools both in the UK and internationally.

Matt's upbringing clearly afforded him advantages and opportunities. It was rich in the sort of resources and capitals we'll be discussing in Chapters 5 and 6.

Matt is an excellent example of the power of culture enunciated by many interviewees. He shows how even the most privileged we spoke to discussed the importance of changing the world. Matt's narrative of what success means as a cultural worker was about making a difference to individuals, and to their communities:

> I think success is also how you can make a difference in the communities that you pass through. I have an opportunity to pass through many different types of community; artistic communities, social communities. I think a marker of success is the difference that you make to those people. Once we've done what we've done and we've shared what we've shared, they're like, 'Wow, you really helped this child', or, 'After somebody saw what you did, they decided to ...' or, 'Wow, this person sat in your workshop and now they've won this award or they've changed their life around.'

We can see many elements of social impact in Matt's comments. They are exactly the sort of social impacts we saw in the *Changing Lives* report. We also see the *commitment* to social impact that was explicitly made by many of our interviewees.

In this context we can think back to Meena's comment that opened this section. We are also reminded of Michaela's words at the very start of the chapter.

Both women were explicit about cultural workers' social mission. This sat alongside a set of values, and a set of ethics. This social mission is an extension of the commitment to give access to culture. It is driven by faith in the power of culture to change society.

From these narratives the purpose of culture is clear. Its purpose is to change the world. However, underpinning these discourses is a sense of the inequalities that mean culture is not open to all. These inequalities stop culture changing the world in the way Matt, and many other cultural workers, desire.

To develop this point, we're going to hear from Henna. She will help to conclude our discussion, and introduce the book's core point about the potential consequences of inequality.

We met Henna in the introduction to the book. She was a very successful British Asian filmmaker from a middle-class background. In spite of her apparent success in the film industry, she had experienced barriers. She continued to struggle, as a result of her gender and ethnicity.

She was candid about her motivations for working in film. She also highlighted how her presence could have a positive social change. That potential social change gave her a sense that her cultural work was a form of activism.

Her work was also coming at a cost. She was uncertain, despite her success, about continuing a career in film. This was despite the importance of her presence in the film industry. She was explicit that she was part of making the creative industries, and thus the world, a different and better place:

> I don't want to be making, like, worthy films about diversity. I just want to be telling stories. That need is really strong, and it's really the only reason that I haven't left the film industry, because I really want to tell different stories. I think it's important. I think it's important if my name is on a film poster or on the front credits and people are like, 'Oh, wow, that's not a name that I usually see associated with film.' I think it's really, really important, and I hope things are changing. I hope I can start making the kind of movies that I want to make, but I don't know. I don't know how long I can survive in the industry, with the way it is. I really don't know.

She clearly has opportunities and networks that support her. Nevertheless, the film industry was more likely to offer 'worthy films about diversity' to her, rather than affording her the autonomy that would go to filmmakers deemed less 'risky'. Again, we see how individuals are given, or refused, value.

Henna had a need to tell different stories, just as Michelle had a need to improve queer representation in commercial publishing. Henna recognised the price of this need. She saw the importance of being visible as a filmmaker in order to demonstrate the importance of diversity in the film industry.

This recognition was balanced by her fears over 'surviving' in the industry. Earlier on in the interview she was explicit about loving her job. She told us how it had fulfilled her ambitions, and how it had given her both a subjective sense of achievement along with more objective markers of success:

> I love being in the film industry and I love what I do right now, 100% ... I feel that I've succeeded in a lot of things that I've wanted to do in life. I've worked in four different continents. I've studied at a great, amazing institution. I've got a privately-backed company. I made a film that came out all over the world.

We can see the force of her commitment to working in film. Her language is explicit. It is a language of 'love', 'success', and of '100%'. This commitment is often highlighted in research on cultural work. It is sometimes ambivalent, whereby the commitment, the love, for working in culture, is intertwined with exploitation.

Henna recognised that changing the cultural and creative industries, and changing the world, is hard. It is hard because of the structural inequalities we're going to demonstrate throughout the rest of this book.

It is also hard because the burden seems to fall onto individuals. We return to Michaela's comments at the start of the chapter. She noted how she'd had to change *herself*, as much as the art world had changed with her.

This burden of change reflects the unequal distribution of power in cultural occupations. Those who have the most insight into the problems are often given the least power. As we will see in Chapter 8, those with the most experience of inequality often have the least value attributed to their perspective.

The idea that value is attributed to some perspectives and not others is an important concluding point for this discussion. We can show this by reflecting on the choice of interviewees in this chapter. We began with Michaela, a Black British woman from a working-class background.

The rest of our interviewees in this chapter were then chosen very deliberately. They all came from middle-class social origins. This is despite the differences in their age, gender, ethnicity, and cultural occupation.

Our selection of middle-class origin cultural workers is not a result of who we interviewed. We chose their comments to highlight how cultural occupations are dominated by individuals from middle-class social origins. As we'll see in Chapter 3, cultural occupations have a serious class problem. This is in addition to exclusions based on gender and race.

Conclusion

In this chapter we have shown how cultural workers are invested in the transformative power of culture. We've shown that there are different ways this manifests itself, whether as making culture accessible, influencing people, or more direct forms of changing the world. We've also contextualised our respondents' commitment to culture, using recent policy and research work. The three documents we've discussed offer differing perspectives on the social impact of culture, the health benefits of culture, and on cultural value. The reports and our interviewees are united in a shared commitment to the importance of culture.

Our interviewees, along with the policy and research documents, also introduce the problems that the book analyses. These are the problems of inequality and the production and consumption of culture.

We can conclude the chapter with Catherine. She illustrates some of the problems of culture and inequality.

Catherine was in her thirties, working in theatre and writing at the time of the interview. Catherine's mother was a clerical worker when she was growing up. She told us she worried about the consequences of the middle-class domination of drama production. She was especially worried about the representation of those who were not part of the middle-class world of drama:

> I am quite concerned with class when I read work and portrayals of working class people I guess, because, even if I don't identify that way myself, I think of the people around me that I know that do and ... I feel uncomfortable if I see even well-meaning representations of working class people as sort of being, you know, horrific mothers or any of the other stereotypes ... where plays ask you to look at sort ... of middle class jokes about working class people's decisions ... all those things make me really uncomfortable.

Catherine expresses her concern about the *consequences* of middle-class dominance of drama as a feeling of being personally uncomfortable. She also identifies the inaccuracies and stereotypes that might result. Finally, she notes the impact on those she is close to who are working class.

We can theorise Catherine's narrative as a threefold problem. Social inequality shapes who gets to produce culture. Social inequality also shapes cultural consumption. The culture that is produced and consumed shapes representations of people and communities. These representations exclude the perspective of those that are not present as workers in cultural occupations.

These three aspects of the relationship between culture and inequality are likely to feed into and to reinforce each other. We'll see examples throughout the rest of the book.

What this means is that the commitment to changing the world, and the power of culture discussed by our interviewees and demonstrated in policy and research documents, can never be fully realised. We'll see in Chapter 3 that if culture is good for you it is clear that, in terms of who works in culture, it is only good for a restricted and in some cases very narrow section of society. In Chapter 4 we'll see the same problem repeated in terms of who goes to formal cultural activities.

In the context of deeply unequal patterns of consumption and production, culture will never be good for *all* of us. The consequences of the inequalities in consumption and production mean that culture may, in fact, be bad for you.

3

Who works in culture?

Introduction: Meg's first job in theatre

I spoke to a youth worker, and she advised me to go and work as a receptionist. Because I knew I didn't want to go to university. Her thought was if I start as a receptionist, or an administrator, I will get in an organisation, and then I can see how it works, and then I can think about what I want to do. I applied for two receptionist jobs, one in a gym, one in a law firm, and then an apprenticeship at a local theatre. I had never heard of [that] theatre before … It was incredible, but it was really hard. The first three months I felt completely alienated … Because some people did look down on me. Some people would talk to me like I was stupid in the beginning. And I've never been stupid. I just didn't have the articulation or the language, the tools to say what I was thinking.

When we interviewed Meg she was working in a major arts institution as a creative producer, where she primarily focused on new work. In her mid-twenties, a working-class origin mixed-race woman from a single-parent family, she told us about how she had struggled in her first job in theatre. Meg is important in many ways. We'll meet her again in Chapter 8. There we explore the *experience* of the patterns of workforce inequality that we demonstrate in this chapter.

In this chapter, Meg's story matters because she is an outlier in many ways. As a mixed-race, working-class origin woman, she was unlike many of her colleagues when she started working in theatre. Her story is one of discrimination and feeling alienated. Later in her career she would see incredible success, moving from having an apprenticeship to being a producer at a major institution in London.

As we are going to see in this chapter, she is *not* typical of those working in cultural occupations. As a result, she didn't know a career in theatre was possible; she felt alienated and that colleagues looked down on her; and she believed she didn't have the language to say what she was thinking in this environment.

Her class origin is important here. In later chapters we're going to explain how social origins influence some people's feelings of belonging in cultural occupations, and others' feelings of alienation; we're going to look in detail at how class, race, and gender intersect to make cultural careers harder for some than others too.

It is worth keeping in mind that Meg is an unusual success story. We encountered more 'typical' cultural and creative workers at the end of Chapter 2. We closed that chapter by reflecting on the class origin of the interviewees we had selected to discuss the power and importance of culture. As we shall see, the class origin of that selection indicated a problem within cultural and creative occupations. Our selection gave clues about the dominance of middle-class social origins in cultural jobs and in the cultural sector. It hinted that culture has a class problem.[1]

Cultural and creative occupations' class problem sits alongside well-known issues for women and people of colour when they try to get in, and get on, in cultural occupations. Class, gender, and race all intersect, meaning over-representations of some demographic groups, and the absence of others.[2]

These patterns are the focus of this chapter. We're going to explain who works in cultural and creative occupations, and how the workforce for culture is not representative of the rest of the population. We're going to see how those from middle-class origins dominate most cultural occupations; how people of colour are absent from the creative occupations associated with major cultural institutions; and how women are missing from key commercial cultural occupations such as those in the film industry.

We are also going to begin to explain some of these workforce patterns. We're going to show how cultural and creative occupations have a shared set of attitudes and values, and a shared understanding of what explains success. These shared values help build a sense of professional identity. At the same time, the shared values may also be alienating and reduce the chances that the workforce inequalities we're going to discuss will change.

We concluded Chapter 2 with a problem. Who works in cultural occupations, who produces culture, is one of the most important aspects of culture and inequality. As we will see in Chapter 4, there are clear inequalities in how cultural consumption is patterned. If women, people of colour, and those from working-class origins (and particularly individuals from the intersection of those demographic groups) cannot get in and get on in cultural occupations, what does that mean for culture more generally?

The inequalities we're going to discuss are the foundation for what media and cultural theorists have identified as poor and misrepresentative depictions of women, people of colour, and the working class in contemporary culture. These representations then feed into broader social inequalities. The cultural sector's inequality problem is thus society's problem too.

Who works in cultural and creative occupations?[3]

We noted in the introduction that much of the work on cultural and creative industries, and their associated occupations, has been shaped by policy definitions. As with the other parts of our analysis in this book, we are using the Department for Culture, Media and Sport's (DCMS) influential definition. DCMS's well-known formation of creative industries covers nine occupational clusters: advertising and marketing; architecture; crafts; design (product, graphic, and fashion design); film, TV, radio, and photography; IT, software, and computer services; publishing; museums, galleries, and libraries; and music, performing, and visual arts.[4]

These nine clusters are constituted of around thirty groups of occupations, for example music, performing, and visual arts is constituted by: artists; actors, entertainers, and presenters; dancers and choreographers; and musicians. As we've discussed in the introduction, we're primarily interested in a core set of cultural occupations, which we discuss in more detail later in this chapter.

In the UK the best source of data on the workforce is the ONS's LFS.[5] The LFS has information on the gender, race, and class origin of workers across a range of occupations. The LFS uses the National Statistics Socio-economic Classification (NS-SEC),[6] which is what we're using as our measure of social class.[7]

NS-SEC clusters occupations together into eight groups, from I (higher managerial and professional, which includes doctors, CEOs, and lawyers) to VII (routine occupations such as bar staff, care workers, and cleaners), while VIII is those who have never worked or who are long-term unemployed. Cultural and creative occupations are almost all found in the NS-SEC I and II categories. NS-SEC II (lower managerial and professional) includes jobs such as teachers and nurses, representing skilled professional work, if not high salary or social privilege. This means we can think of creative jobs as 'middle-class' jobs, even though they may be low paid and precarious for many people working in them.

Since 2014 the LFS has asked people about their class origin. They do this by asking what the main income earner in their household did for work when they were fourteen.[8] Knowing if someone had a parent who was a doctor (NS-SEC I) or a cleaner (NS-SEC VII) gives information about a worker's class origin. Using information on parental occupation means we can add class origin to information the DCMS publishes every year about gender and ethnicity in the creative workforce.

Sociologists used the 2014 data to sound the alarm about a class crisis in cultural occupations.[9] In this section, we're going to use 2019 LFS data to show how this class crisis continues today. We're also going to begin to think about how inequalities persist over time, looking at the patterns between 2014 and 2019, and setting up Chapter 8's analysis of longer-term trends.

Figure 3.1 shows the class, ethnicity, and gender profile of creative occupations according to the 2019 LFS. It also shows the same class, ethnicity, and gender profile for all occupations overall, to give a sense of how our creative occupations compare to the rest of the workforce. As we can see, there are a range of inequalities in creative occupations.

Who works in culture?

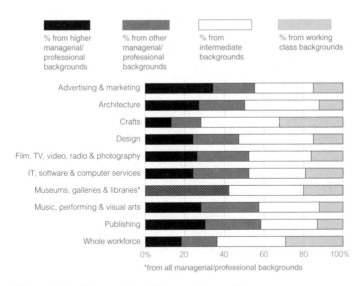

Figure 3.1a Composition of the creative workforce.

We can see that most of our cultural occupations employ individuals drawn from 'middle-class' origins. Below, we'll see that there are low levels of people of colour in most creative occupations. In some occupations there are also very low levels of women in the workforce; others see an absence of men.

It is worth noting how different many of the occupational sectors are from each other. IT, which is dominated by IT consultancy while also including game development, has a good representation of those from minority ethnic backgrounds, but has a very low number of women and people from working-class origins in its workforce.

In contrast, key arts occupations are not ethnically diverse. The LFS suggests about 87% of the overall workforce are White. Music, performing, and visual arts seem to have a good

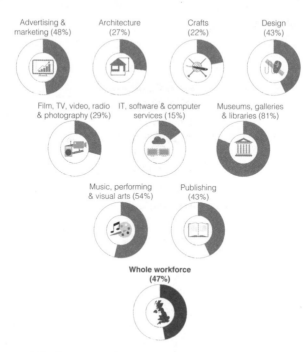

Figure 3.1b Percentage of women in the creative workforce.

representation of people of colour, as does advertising and marketing. The 2019 LFS data suggests people of colour constitute just 5% of publishing occupations, a serious issue for equality and diversity in this sector. Film, TV, radio, and photography, and design also have fewer people of colour than we might expect if they were representative of the workforce more generally.

The sample size in the 2019 LFS does not allow us to comment on race and ethnicity in the museums occupations, although we know from 2014 and 2015 LFS data that there is an under-representation of people of colour.

Who works in culture?

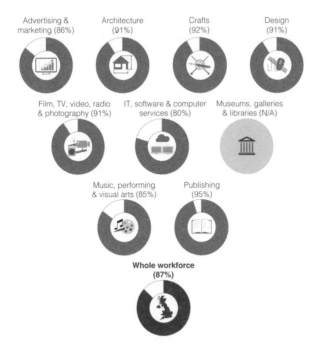

Figure 3.1c Percentage White in the creative workforce.

We see similar inequalities in gender, with only music, performing, and visual arts, and museums, galleries, and libraries having more women than men. As with race and ethnicity we need to be cautious with our museums data, as it is the smallest set of the LFS's creative occupations, and so may be less precisely representative than the data for larger sectors such as IT or advertising.

These two sectors also remind us that while occupations as a whole might present a particular pattern, specific roles, such as very senior leadership in prestigious institutions, or who wins music awards, might still be skewed away from the general pattern.[10]

In 3.1a we cluster together groups of occupations into Managerial/Professional, Intermediate, and Semi-routine/Routine (or 'working class'). This allows us to demonstrate how the story of social class is a story of exclusion. Every sector apart from craft has an over-representation of those from middle-class social origins, with those from working-class origins making up a much smaller proportion of the workforce.

In publishing the situation is especially grave, with almost 60% of key occupations coming from managerial or professional occupations. When we look in more depth, we see nearly 30% come from NS-SEC I, the higher managerial and professional origins. This is in contrast to those, most privileged 'middle class', origins only constituting 18% of the overall workforce in the 2019 LFS dataset.

We see this over-representation of the managerial and professional origin middle class for every creative occupation aside from the occupations constituting crafts. Moreover, for those occupations for which we can report the data, we see consistently that around one-quarter or more of the workforce are from NS-SEC I, the higher category of the managerial and professional middle-class origins.

Those from semi-routine and routine, 'working class', origins are underrepresented as compared to the number of working-class origin individuals in society overall.

Our working-class origin individuals constitute around 29% of the workforce overall in the 2019 LFS data. The numbers of working-class individuals in specific creative occupations, aside from craft, do not come near to this figure. In the 2019 data we see only 13% in publishing, 12% in music, performing, and visual arts, 16% in film, TV, video, radio, and photography, and 20% in museums, galleries, and libraries.[11]

Moreover, people from managerial and professional origins dominate many creative occupations compared to those from working-class origins. Working-class origin individuals are also under-represented. In every creative occupation we see those from managerial and professional origins dominate the occupations, as compared with those from working-class origins. Where we have the data, we also see the dominance of those from the higher professional and managerial middle class as compared to those from working-class origins.

Creative jobs are thus highly exclusive. Culture has a class problem. This class problem sits alongside the other, well-known, problems of gender and racial exclusions in cultural and creative occupations.

When using large-scale, nationally representative datasets, the numbers of people working in specific creative occupations can be small. While there are large numbers of workers in IT and computer services occupations in the economy overall, there are fewer writers and fewer curators. We can bring together several waves of LFS data, collected between 2014 and 2019, to look in a little more detail. This also allows us to see how consistent these class exclusions have been in recent years. It also sets up our longer-term analysis of fifty years of ONS Longitudinal Study data presented in Chapter 7.

Figure 3.2 shows the changing levels of class origins in our cultural occupations from 2014 to 2019. As with Figure 3.1, we've kept our clusters of Managerial/Professional, Intermediate, and Semi-routine/Routine (or 'working class').

What should be immediately striking is the consistently low level of working-class origin individuals in every set of creative occupations apart from craft. While there are annual

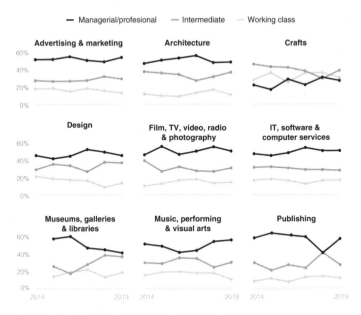

Figure 3.2 Class origins in creative occupations.

fluctuations, the story of class in creative occupations seems to be a continuing story of exclusions.

In Chapter 7 we explain how the overall class structure of British society has changed over time. The numbers of working-class occupations, and associated working-class origins, have declined in the economy overall.

We also, over the longer term, need to think about how cultural and creative occupations differ from other sets of managerial and professional occupations. In some ways the story of culture's class crisis is the story of a more general set of consistent, long-term inequalities in social mobility into Britain's professions.

The LFS data offers a picture of cultural and creative occupations that are not diverse, nor representative of the population.

Moreover, even where we cannot comment in detail for specific occupations, such as museum curators, we know from previous analysis that they too have under-representations of those from working-class origins and people of colour.

The situation is especially acute for those at the intersection of these demographic categories. As Sam Friedman and Daniel Laurison suggest in their analysis of the 'class ceiling' in key professions, working-class origin women of colour also face the most serious pay gaps compared to their White, middle-class origin, male co-workers.[12] In Chapter 8 we will see how working-class origin women of colour's experiences of working in culture can help to explain the labour force patterns we have presented in Figures 3.1 and 3.2.

Who works in cultural and creative occupations: attitudes and values[13]

Cultural and creative occupations are, based on current data, not diverse. There are important under-representations of particular individuals and communities. The demographics of cultural production seem quite exclusive. Many professions have class, gender, and racial inequalities. In some ways cultural occupations are just like other middle-class professional occupations, as we see debates over class, gender, and race in top professions such as law, medicine, and accountancy.[14]

As we noted in the introduction to the book, who makes culture matters. As we saw in Chapter 2, culture can be good for you. Based on the demographics of the workforce, the benefits of cultural work are limited to specific social groups. The benefits of engagement and consumption are also likely to be shaped and constrained by these workforce inequalities. The joy of working in a cultural occupation, which we will see in Chapter 6, is also similarly limited.

Alongside the demographic inequalities, we can see patterns of inequality reflected in occupational attitudes and values. This is another way of understanding the exclusivity of cultural occupations. By looking at attitudes and values we'll see that cultural occupations have specific characteristics that make them especially interesting for study.

These characteristics contribute to the exclusivity of the cultural workforce. They also raise questions in the context of creative workers' role in creating representations of individuals, communities, and society as a whole. This was Catherine's fear, which we saw at the end of Chapter 2.

We can see this tension in the work of one of the key, but highly critiqued, theorists of cultural and creative work. Richard Florida,[15] writing about what he called the 'creative class', identified shared ideological values that bound together occupations from science and technology through to the arts.

For Florida these values were individuality and nonconformity, openness to difference and the embrace of diversity, and meritocracy. These values sat alongside the creative class' rejection of wealth as a means of judging themselves and their lives. These values were also expressed in place and space, with this 'creative class' attracted to urban and city living.

Florida's work has seen extensive criticism,[16] and the idea of a coherent 'creative class' that covers artists as well as scientists and tech workers is too broad. Yet the idea of occupations having shared cultures, although not unique to Florida's work, is useful for thinking about cultural occupations. The focus on creative and cultural occupations having specifically liberal values that bind them together as a class resonates with our analysis.

Of course, there are contradictions and ironies in these shared values. The notion of meritocracy potentially reinforces and naturalises existing, social structural, inequalities. Openness and tolerance is potentially only in terms of a diversity of elites.[17] There are limitations to a creative class monopolising resources as they cluster together in cities and urban areas.

In our study of cultural occupations we are not arguing for a 'creative class'. Rather, thinking about values and attitudes shows some of the shared positions that bring people together in cultural occupations, and some of the contradictions which result from these shared values.

In Britain's cultural occupations we can see a coherent set of values and attitudes that are liberal, left-wing, and in favour of welfare and social security interventions. Cultural occupations seem to be the most committed to these positions of any set of occupations. British Social Attitudes (BSA) survey data demonstrates these commitments. BSA data shows that of all the industrial groups measured, people working in cultural and creative industries have the most left-wing, liberal, pro-welfare values.[18]

We can use other datasets to see the differences between people working in cultural and creative jobs and the rest of the population. Here we're going to draw on data from the British Election Study shown in Figure 3.3.[19] Using this data, we can see the left-wing, liberal, pro-welfare values of our cultural occupations. We can also see information about political behaviour, such as civic engagement, protesting, and voting choices.

We have identified six key characteristics of our cultural workers' attitudes and values. First, whether they were happy with the result of the 2016 referendum on whether to leave the

European Union, and how strongly they identify with Remain, on a scale of 0–10.[20] Second, we've looked at voting in the 2016 referendum.

Third, we have looked at people's responses to how left- or right-wing they think they are. We've also looked at how liberal or authoritarian they think they are. These are two axes that are most traditionally thought of as dividing lines in UK politics.

Finally, we've included analysis of their non-electoral participation. This includes activity such as writing letters to their MPs or attending different protests. These results show the distinctiveness of creative workers in managerial and professional occupations.[21]

They are more strongly pro-Remain and less happy to be leaving the EU than other groups, even after adjusting for variables known to be associated with these attitudes like educational attainment.[22] They're also much more liberal, though they're not as radically more left-wing as is sometimes made out. Finally, they're more highly politically engaged, and far less likely to have actually voted Leave.

These shared attitudinal positions are important. We are not using them to make a definitive argument as to a wholly coherent 'creative class', as Florida did in his work. We are more interested in these shared values and attitudes as a potential manifestation of social closure in cultural occupations.

As we have seen, cultural occupations are exclusive in terms of their demographics. Here we've seen that they have a specific set of social attitudes, identities, and behaviour, that are different to many other occupational groups. In turn, these attitudes may have consequences for who works in cultural occupations.

To illustrate this point, we can move from national level representative datasets to more bespoke work. As part of the *Panic!*

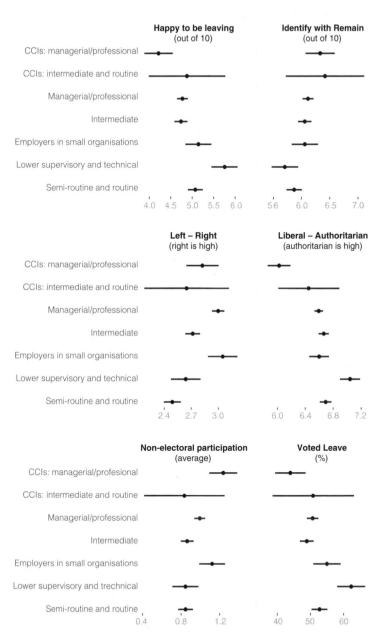

Figure 3.3 Analysis of British Election Study data.

project in 2015[23] we collected data from almost 2500 creative workers. Within this, we asked specific questions about their explanations for success in their creative occupation.

We use responses to a standard set of questions about getting in and getting on at work to understand perceptions of fairness in the sector.[24] We asked respondents: 'Looking at your creative occupation as a whole, how important do you think each of these is in getting ahead?' This question, and the range of responses, is used in standard surveys in lots of countries. It has been well validated as a good way of exploring people's attitudes.

In our analysis we grouped the responses along three lines. First there are responses associated with 'meritocracy'. These include talent, ambition, and hard work. This cluster of responses suggests individuals get what they put in, or deserve, from the sector, irrespective of background or privileges.

Our second cluster reflects what social scientists call social reproduction explanations, such as networks (who you know), family background and wealth, along with gender and ethnicity. These explanations point to barriers in the cultural sector, so that no matter how talented or hard-working someone is, they will still struggle if they aren't the 'right' class, race, or gender.

Finally, there are responses associated with education – people's own, and their parents'. These responses didn't fit closely with either responses around meritocracy, or around social reproduction. Research shows a strong relationship between someone's level of education and their career success, but also finds that privileged groups have better access to elite educational institutions.

Looking at the axes simultaneously, at the top left-hand corner we find those respondents (30%) who most strongly

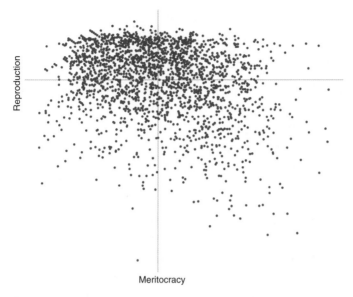

Figure 3.4 How responses cluster around meritocracy or social reproduction.

think that talent and hard work explains getting in and getting on in creative jobs, and do not agree that class and knowing the right people are important. These respondents narrate the sector as 'meritocratic'.

By contrast, those respondents clustered in the bottom right-hand corner (21%) were most likely to suggest 'social reproduction'. These respondents emphasised social exclusions or advantages, rather than talent or hard work.

The top right corner clusters those (34%) who emphasised both social reproduction and meritocracy: those believing hard work and talent are essential, but acknowledging the roles of barriers and exclusions.

Finally, those respondents in the bottom left corner (16%). They emphasise neither, implying that success in the creative industries is more-or-less random.

As we can see, the majority of respondents are in the top area of the plot.[25] This suggests the prevailing opinion in our survey respondents was towards a belief that the sector is meritocratic. Some respondents recognise the influence of social factors, such as class, age, race, and 'who you know'.

The majority of respondents believe that hard work, talent, and ambition are essential to getting ahead. Levels of agreement with these explanations of 'getting in and getting on' in the sector were similar across the demographics of our respondents, with a parallel story told by women, working-class origin people, and by ethnic minorities.

There is one group that stands out. This was the people who were most highly paid. These respondents, who are in the most influential positions in the cultural sector, believe most strongly in the meritocracy account. They are also most sceptical of the impact of social factors, such as gender, class, or ethnicity, on explanations for success in the sector. The best-paid hold these attitudes irrespective of their starting point in life.

It seems, from our respondents, once people have achieved major success within the sector they become most committed to talent and hard work as explaining that success. This attitudinal position helps to explain some of demographic patterns we see in our data about the workforce. However, it also raises several questions about how this plays out in terms of hiring and commissioning decisions. We come back to this point in Chapter 10's discussion of men's attitudes and understandings of inequality.

Who works in cultural and creative occupations: social networks

Attitudes and values are one part of the story of understanding both the exclusivity of cultural occupations, and understanding how they might form a coherent and closed cultural sector. Another way of seeing this is by looking at social networks. This adds to the LFS data suggesting a closed set of cultural occupations.

Who do creative workers know? This question is important for two reasons. First, we know that getting creative work is highly dependent on social networks, especially for projects that can happen very quickly at short notice.

Second, there is the question of representation, about the impact of who creative workers know on their ability to tell stories and accurately depict individuals and communities with which they have little or no contact. We'll see more about this issue in our discussion of consumption inequalities in Chapter 4 too. It was crucial to the conclusion in Chapter 2.

To understand the social networks of creative workers, we're again drawing from the *Panic!* project. We asked our respondents if they knew individuals in a range of different occupations, both as friends and as family members. Again, this is a fairly standard social science question, and was used in one of the biggest studies of cultural tastes and social exclusion in Britain in the 2000s.[26] We're looking at a subset of the data here, from the second part of our *Panic!* project. This involved interview fieldwork with over 200 creative workers, about 10% of the survey respondents.

Figure 3.5 shows how *Panic!* respondents were most likely to know other cultural and creative workers. This is as expected given the nature of their occupational networks. In contrast,

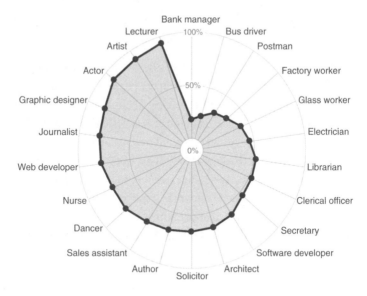

Figure 3.5 Who do our creative workers know?

they tended to be less likely to know people working in more traditional 'working-class' occupations. Our *Panic!* respondents seem to know other creatives, rather than knowing factory workers, bus drivers, or solicitors. This is one way these jobs are 'socially closed', meaning it is difficult to enter without these sorts of networks.

This may reflect the fact that those in professional or managerial occupations tend not to know many people in working-class occupations,[27] either as friends or as family members. It may also reflect the smaller numbers of traditional 'working-class' occupations in society, the changing composition of the economy, and the growth of middle-class occupations. We discuss this point in more detail in Chapter 7.

Conclusion

In some ways our creative and cultural workers reflect the social closure of professional occupations in general. This is directly connected to struggles over social mobility as the expansion of top professions has slowed in many societies. This is the centre of Chapter 7's analysis. For now, we're just going to note that although the closure of cultural occupations echoes trends in other professions, there are dynamics, and consequences, specific to cultural occupations.

We have mentioned the consequences in the introduction to the book, and at the end of Chapter 2. Of course, we need a more diverse and open set of senior professions. It matters if doctors, judges, accountants, and executives are all drawn from a narrow section of society. This really should not be a controversial point. In the cultural sector there is an added, if distinct, incentive for diversity.

Who makes culture has consequences for the way individuals and communities are represented. In television, for example, we see a huge distance between commissioners of particular genres,[28] such as reality television focused on welfare and poverty, and the subjects of those shows. This genre is very popular, but it has been criticised for its sensationalist, distorted, and unfair representation of working-class communities.[29]

This example points towards more general consequences of inequality in the creative economy. We can see these consequences when we consider American research on hiring in top professional occupations. Here there is a process of 'hiring as cultural matching'.[30] This is not about having high, traditional, or elite cultural tastes. It is about displaying the sort of interests in, and ways of consuming, culture held by employees already working in these professional organisations.

To return to cultural jobs, we can see from American research how being a consumer of a range of different cultural forms, and showing knowledge and enthusiasm across genres and activities, is crucial in this process of cultural matching for creative work.[31] These hiring practices are part of the explanation for the patterns of inequality we've seen in the cultural workforce. Yet they are only *part* of the explanation.

Cultural matching during the hiring process draws attention to inequalities in patterns of cultural consumption. It raises the question of how tastes are patterned, particularly how tastes are patterned within cultural occupations. We're going to explain how, just as with social networks, attitudes and values, and workforce demographics, there are distinct characteristics that differentiate cultural occupations from the rest of society. These characteristics are the next element in the story of culture and inequality.

4

Who consumes culture?

Introduction: Becca goes to the opera

> By saying I have been to and go to opera that puts me up in kind of an elite class, which having spent my career really trying to push against that, and try and make arts and culture much more accessible, I suppose I find it a bit depressing that it is still seen as an elitist activity, and that I would therefore be associated with that.

Towards the end of our interviews, we asked about our participants' perceptions of inequality in contemporary society. Becca, a White woman in her forties, from a middle-class origin, was working as a freelance arts manager at the time of interview. She told us of her frustration at the relationship between inequality and the arts. She focused on her trips to the opera, depressed that her engagement with that artform would mark her out as part of a social elite. Indeed, the frustration was linked directly to her work in the arts, where she aimed to make culture accessible.

Becca's frustration echoes what we heard in Chapter 2, about our interviewee's faith in the power of culture. Her commitment to her work was bound up with the drive to open arts and culture to all. Yet she is also keenly aware of the relationship between social inequality and the arts. It is a relationship she is pushing against, and fighting to change.

Part of Becca's desire for change is because of the possible benefits from engagement in culture, as we saw in Chapter 2. More important is her desire to strip away the social hierarchies that are attached to arts and culture. Sadly, as we are exploring, culture is closely intertwined with inequalities.

There is a long tradition of research[1] demonstrating the close relationship between our unequal social hierarchies and cultural tastes. Culture and inequality also manifests in the way we think about categories of art and culture.[2] Inequality is present in the language of elite and mass, avant-garde and popular, low-, middle-, and high-brow. Culture and inequality is institutionalised in what states fund and support, and what they leave to markets, communities, and individuals to sustain.[3]

This chapter asks about these relationships. Becca was, in many ways, right to be depressed. As social scientists have long demonstrated, there is a clear relationship between people's cultural consumption and more general social inequalities. We can show this with England as our example.

In England, on average, someone in a high-status job, with a degree, in the higher managerial or professional category, who is female, and living in the South of England, has particularly high engagement in culture. Those in working-class occupations, ethnic minorities, and those without wealth, have significantly less *formal* cultural engagement as compared to their wealthy, White counterparts.

From our analysis we will see that *not* being a heavily engaged cultural consumer is the norm for much of the English population.

To develop our discussion of inequalities in the workforce, in cultural production, we're also going to take a detailed look at people working in cultural occupations. We'll see how cultural workers are very highly engaged, both in terms of their attendance and in terms of the range of artforms they are interested in. Just as with networks, attitudes and values, and the class, race, and gender basis for the workforce, the consumption patterns we see for cultural workers show another side to the social closure of cultural and creative occupations.

How is cultural consumption patterned? Evidence from England

To understand cultural consumption we are going to use data from the UK government's Taking Part survey. This survey interviews around 10,000 people every year about their cultural habits. Taking Part is nationally representative for England, and has run each year since 2005/2006. The government uses Taking Part to report good news about culture in England, that 78% of the population have engaged with the arts at least once in the past year.[4]

Underneath that headline good news is a more complex story. We're going to visualise this story in a series of figures. Our first, Figure 4.1,[5] is broken down into individual artforms. It shows the percentage of the English population aged sixteen[6] and over who attended each artform at least once in the previous twelve months.[7]

Seeing a film at the cinema is the outlier in Figure 4.1. Every other cultural form is attended by a minority of the population. 'Other live music' is the category that covers genres such as pop, rock, metal, and rap, and doesn't include classical, jazz,

Culture is bad for you

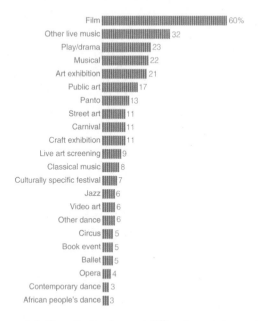

Figure 4.1 Overall attendance at different events (percentages).

and opera. Just over 30% have attended at least once in the past year, which is perhaps surprising given how popular these musical genres are.

Just over 20% of people had been to a play or drama, a musical, or an art exhibition. Fewer than 10% of people had been to any classical music; fewer than 5% had been to ballet, opera, or contemporary dance. Becca's worries that arts and culture might not be accessible are, unfortunately, realised in this data.

Attendance is one way of understanding cultural consumption. Participation, being actively involved in a creative activity, is another. That data is visualised in Figure 4.2. This reports the

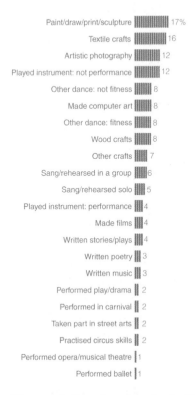

Paint/draw/print/sculpture	17%
Textile crafts	16
Artistic photography	12
Played instrument: not performance	12
Other dance: not fitness	8
Made computer art	8
Other dance: fitness	8
Wood crafts	8
Other crafts	7
Sang/rehearsed in a group	6
Sang/rehearsed solo	5
Played instrument: performance	4
Made films	4
Written stories/plays	4
Written poetry	3
Written music	3
Performed play/drama	2
Performed in carnival	2
Taken part in street arts	2
Practised circus skills	2
Performed opera/musical theatre	1
Performed ballet	1

Figure 4.2 Overall participation in different forms (percentages).

percentage of the English population aged sixteen and over participating in a range of cultural activities.

These numbers are even smaller than the attendances shown in Figure 4.1. The two most popular categories are both in creative visual arts, painting, drawing, printing, or sculpture, and textile crafts, with 17% and 16% of people participating in each of these two categories. These numbers are still a minority of the population. Twelve per cent of people have played an instrument for their own pleasure (as opposed to for an audience); about 8% of people have danced; the numbers for opera, musical theatre, and ballet are at about 1% each.

Understanding everyday participation

In the introduction to the book we noted that what counts and is classified as culture is itself the subject of struggles and social inequalities. Social surveys about cultural attendance and participation reflect these struggles. For example, attending and participating in opera is given a formal category in surveys about arts attendance and participation. Other everyday activities, such as listening to music on the radio, are not.

Figure 4.3 shows a range of activities that are a much closer reflection of the majority of the population's pastimes. Within the Taking Part survey these are classed as 'free time activities' rather than cultural attendance or participation. For some cultural forms there is a clear connection to attendance

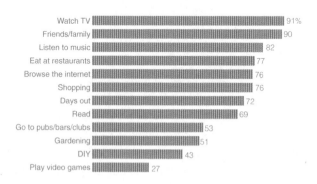

Figure 4.3 Overall participation in different free time activities (percentages).

and participation, for example with music. Yet the levels of the population engaging in listening (over three-quarters) is much higher than those attending or participating.

About 90% of people say they watch television, and spend time with friends and family; about three-quarters of people say they listen to music, eat at restaurants, browse the internet, and spend time shopping. This isn't just about going out and staying in. Three-quarters of people go to restaurants, two-thirds go on days out and about half go to pubs, bars, and clubs. Even playing video games, at just over a quarter of the population, is more popular than attending or participating in most of the cultural forms in Figures 4.1 and 4.2.

Our three visualisations tell the first part of our inequality story. England has a population that clearly have rich cultural lives. Unfortunately, the sort of things produced by cultural workers, for example in theatres and galleries, form a minority of the population's rich cultural life.

Who goes to culture? Class, gender, ethnicity, age, and geography

The sharp differences in levels of engagement suggest specific cultural forms are a minority activity in England. We might see this as a problem because of the relationship between state support and levels of engagement. Opera, for example, sees comparatively high levels of state investment, but attracts a minority in terms of attendance and participation.

There may be good reasons to support this minority interest, particularly if the artform would struggle to exist without funding. At the same time, two of the largest interests, film and watching television, benefit from a mixed economy of state support and commercial income.[8] The problem really emerges when we examine the relationship between cultural activities and social inequalities.

We're visualising one element of this relationship in Figure 4.4. It shows how the same activities shown in Figure 4.1 vary by social class.[9] The different coloured bars in the figures show our three groups. Black for managerial and professional, darker grey for intermediate, and lighter grey for semi-routine and routine.

Looking at the graph we can see that for some artforms the bars are similar lengths, meaning consumption is at a similar level irrespective of the class of the household. Where our bars are different lengths, it means we're seeing differences in cultural consumption relative to class.

Figure 4.4 shows that attendance at different cultural events is heavily stratified by class. For almost all activities, the managerial and professional group are more likely to attend than the intermediate group. In turn, the intermediate group are more likely to attend than the semi-routine and routine groups.

These differences aren't identical across the activities. While the differences look biggest for going to a film at a cinema, that's largely because it's the most popular activity; about 69% of people in the managerial/professional group attend, compared with about 49% of the semi-routine and routine group.

We can see the dominance of managerial and professional individuals as attenders at other cultural forms. For going to a play/drama or to an art exhibition they outnumber people in the semi-routine and routine group by about 3:1. In classical music, opera, book events, and contemporary dance, the figures are 4:1, or even higher.

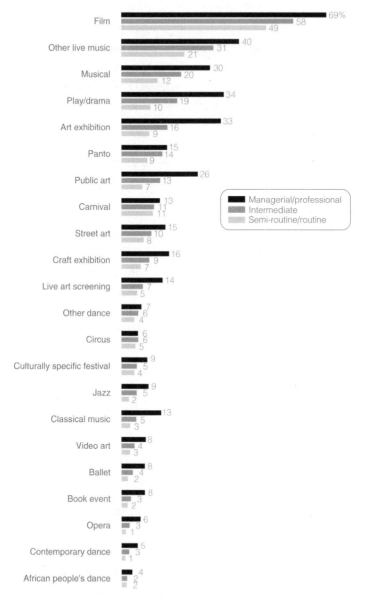

Figure 4.4 Attendance at different events, by social class: percentages within each group.

We have to be cautious in these cases because the numbers of people attending are small. In particular, the numbers of people in the semi-routine and routine groups are very small.[10] Yet it is striking how stratified by social class these activities are.

Even with the class differences, it is important to remember that *not* attending is the norm for the English population. Even for our managerial and professional group, only about 13% go to classical music, and only 5% of them go to contemporary dance. The numbers of professional and managerial attenders are far larger than for other groups. Yet even for managers and professionals, attendance at these events is still unusual.

Social inequalities don't just consist of class inequalities. This book approaches inequalities in an intersectional way, thinking about other major categories of race and ethnicity, and gender. Figure 4.5 looks at gender.

Compared with class, attendance by gender is less unequal, but still important. Most events are attended by more women than men, particularly those that take place in theatres (plays, musicals, panto, and different forms of dance).

At first glance it seems as if class is a bigger factor in shaping attendance than gender. What about race and ethnicity? Figure 4.6 shows rates of attendance at these events for White people, and people of colour.

Figure 4.6 shows that there are some big differences. White people dominate attendance in some key artforms, such as film, art, and theatre. This is even true of artforms that should have mass appeal. White people are nearly three times more likely to attend a panto than people of colour.

It is only with artforms that reflect and represent specific communities that we see this pattern reversed. For African people's dance and Chinese dance we see 3.5 times the proportion of

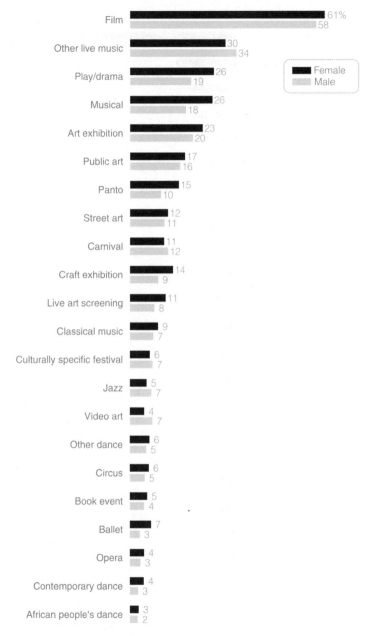

Figure 4.5 Attendance at different events, by gender (percentages).

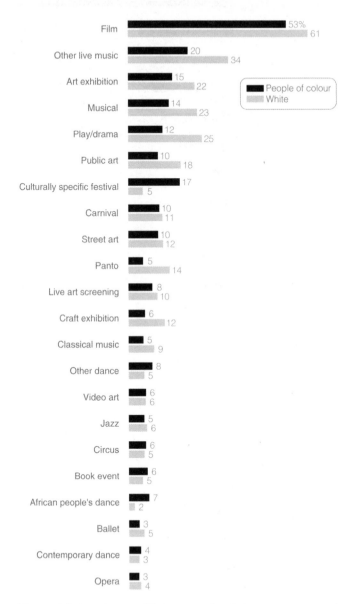

Figure 4.6 Attendance at different events, by ethnic group (percentages).

people of colour attending, relative to the White population. It's similar for culturally specific festivals, such as Vaisakhi and Mela.

Other activities are more mixed. Roughly equal fractions of White people and people of colour attended contemporary dance, opera, live art screenings, carnivals, and street art. Carnivals might come as a surprise, with the most high-profile carnivals in England being associated with minority ethnic groups; this indicates that, while those might be the most high-profile cases, other carnivals have larger proportions of White audiences.

We have seen significant differences by class, gender, and race in attendance at culture. Age is also important to inequality, as we'll see in Chapters 5 and 6. The interaction between age and other demographic characteristics such as class, gender, and race also matters as we start to think how they intersect with each other. For example, the ethnic minority population is younger than the White population.[11] Figure 4.7 shows rates of attendance for people in different age groups.

Differences in attendance across age groups are very substantial at some kinds of events, while very small in others. Attendance by the oldest group tends to be the lowest of all for most categories. This makes intuitive sense, particularly for artforms such as other live music, but there are exceptions to this trend, such as attendance at craft exhibitions and at classical music.

Leaving aside those aged over seventy-five, patterns of attendance by age vary across our artforms. There are some clear patterns: activities associated with traditional forms of high or elite culture, such as opera, ballet, theatre, and classical music, have higher rates of attendance by people aged forty-five and older. This is also true for most forms of visual art.

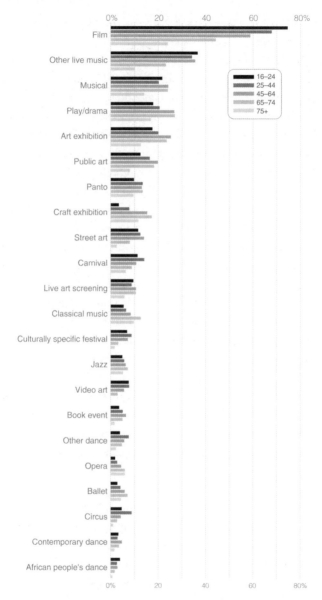

Figure 4.7 Attendance at different events, by age group.

Film has a very different gradient, with people aged under twenty-five being the most likely to attend. Other live music – a category likely to be dominated by popular music – has roughly equal rates of attendance among the 45–64 age group as it does between the 16–24 and 25–44 age groups, suggesting a shared love for attending this artform across the generations.

Our visualisations have focused on attendance, but participation follows similar patterns. People in managerial and professional households are far more likely to participate in arts, as well as to attend them. The biggest differences are in playing a musical instrument, which is heavily stratified by class.

By contrast, activities like playing video games, shopping, and spending time with friends and family see almost no class differences. Everyday cultural activity is something the English population shares; the more traditional types of artistic participation are the site of significant class inequality.

Differences in cultural participation between ethnic groups are small, though with a few exceptions: people of colour are much less likely to engage in textile crafts and wood crafts and go to the pub, but much more likely to participate in dance.

The biggest difference of all is the gender difference in textile crafts – such as knitting and sewing – with about 35% of women and just 5% of men participating. Women are also much more likely to dance, while men are more likely to engage in wood crafts. The other big gender differences are that women are more likely to read and shop, while men are more likely to do DIY and play video games; other activities, like eating at restaurants and browsing the internet, are similar for both women and men.

This section has been descriptive, highlighting how cultural attendance and participation differs by key demographic categories of class, age, race, and gender. However, we've also undertaken analysis of how attendance differs between people who do and don't report a disability, and people living in different parts of England.

The fractions of disabled people attending different cultural forms are consistently around 75% of the corresponding figures for people who don't report disability. This isn't the case across the board. A slightly larger fraction of disabled people attend craft exhibitions than people who don't report disabilities. The difference is also larger for attending live music events, but the patterns are largely consistent.

This analysis doesn't allow us to compare people with different kinds of disabilities, and it's likely that people with disabilities associated with mobility issues and with energy levels are disproportionately less likely to attend different kinds of events.

Cultural funders are often criticised for the large fractions of their spending that go to organisations based in London.[12] In fact, the rates of people attending different cultural events in the different regions of England are surprisingly similar. Again, there are exceptions to this, with people in London particularly likely to attend visual art exhibitions, but also particularly unlikely to attend panto, craft exhibitions, and live music. Other than these, the fractions of people in different areas attending different kinds of events are more similar than you might expect.

These descriptions have treated each of these activities as if they're independent of each other. Given what we already know, it's likely that there's a lot of overlap, with our audiences for particular niche cultural forms also attending other niche cultural forms. Because of our suspicion about this overlap, our next step is to see how these different activities fit together.

Who goes to culture? Explaining the patterns[13]

To look at how different activities intersect we've combined several years' data from the Taking Part survey. This gives a total of around 117,000 different people's answers. We use a technique called multiple correspondence analysis[14] to analyse this data. This lets us identify whose patterns of attendance are most similar and whose are most different. Instead of looking at several different activities separately, we use this technique to attempt to identify the underlying structure in the data.

For each activity, each person is classified as either having attended or not attended. The analysis clusters similar answers together. So, for example, if people who attend contemporary dance are also likely to attend ballet, those two categories will be clustered close together. We can then make a 'map' of cultural activity in England.

Our analysis combines the formal cultural activity we discussed at the start of the chapter with the free time activities we saw in Figure 4.3. We've brought these two forms of cultural activity together to see if there are distinctive patterns to how people spend their cultural time.

Figure 4.8 is in two parts. Figure 4.8a shows the results of the multiple correspondence analysis for cultural activities.[15] Figure 4.8b then places occupational groups into the picture.

Figure 4.8a shows the way particular artforms, such as opera, contemporary dance, and ballet, cluster together. This is because people who go to the opera are also likely to go to contemporary dance, and ballet. It also shows how people who garden are also likely to do DIY, and go on days out. They are less likely to be heavily engaged in opera, contemporary dance, and ballet.

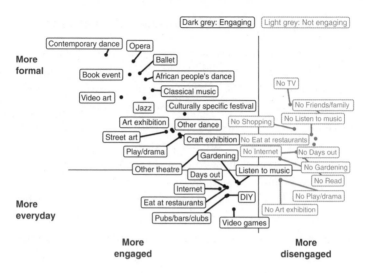

Figure 4.8a Multiple correspondence analysis of how people spend their time (cultural activities).

Figure 4.8b shows how social classes, as well as specific occupations, relate to these patterns of taste. It shows where occupational categories, such as professional or routine occupations, are positioned in relation to each other *and* in relation to artform interests. We've highlighted cultural occupations too.[16]

What do Figures 4.8a and 4.8b tell us? On the x-axis, running left to right, we can see *activity* distinguished from *inactivity*. Left-to-right also shows high numbers of people to low numbers of people. The story of Figure 4.8 is a story that most people say they do *not* attend culture. This axis represents the main way in which categories are most similar, or most different from each other. Attending and not attending is the main way in which activities are distinguished from each other.

How does this work for formal cultural activity? We saw in Figure 4.1 that attendance at most art and cultural forms is a

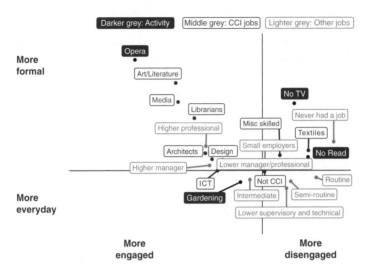

Figure 4.8b Multiple correspondence analysis of how people spend their time (occupational groups).

minority activity. Film was the major outlier, with a majority of the population going to see a film at least once in the last year.

Figure 4.8 re-presents these patterns. The activities on the left-hand side, such as opera, ballet, classical music, contemporary dance, video art, book events, are attended by small proportions of the population. What's more, the fact that these activities are closely clustered together indicates that there's a large amount of overlap in who attends these activities. We can see a heavily culturally engaged minority in England.

Many of the categories on the left-hand side of Figures 4.8a and 4.8b will look familiar from Figure 4.1, which we discussed earlier in the chapter. These are the activities that the smallest numbers of people attend. Activities such as attending film and live music are closer to the centre of the Figures 4.8a and 4.8b, consistent with the fact that more people are attending.

The majority of the English population is clustered together on the right-hand side of Figure 4.8a. The overall story is that the bulk of the population are clustered around *not* attending, while a minority attend many different artforms. The division in England is between *not* attending, the norm for the English population, and a highly culturally engaged minority.

What about our everyday cultural activities? The activities classified as 'free time' look rather different. These activities are situated closer to the centre of the graph. This reinforces the point from earlier that these activities have far more people spending their time on them than on formal arts activities. This cluster of activities can be very clearly distinguished from attending formal culture.

The y-axis, running bottom-to-top, deals with differences in genre, and is closer to the distinction between what might have historically been described as 'highbrow' and 'lowbrow'. We've called this formal culture and everyday participation.

While this axis also explains a large part of how categories are similar or different from each other, it's not as crucial. It's still important, but not as important as the axis running left to right. The formal versus everyday culture division can be seen on the right-hand side of the graph. On the right-hand side we can see how *not* doing formal culture, for example not attending opera, dance, or ballet, clusters together.

By contrast, we can see differences between free time activities more vividly. Not watching television is the highest up of any of the categories of people not doing everyday things. This suggests there is still cultural cache in not watching television. Figure 4.8a tells us about patterns in cultural interests. Figure 4.8b allows us to tell a story of inequality by social class. The axes in Figure 4.8b are the same. More to less engagement runs from left to right, and formal to everyday culture from top to bottom.

People in managerial and professional jobs attend the widest range of different events, compared with people in other occupational groups. We can almost draw a straight line onto Figure 4.8b, a social gradient, in cultural attendance. This runs from left to right, connecting higher professional, higher managerial, lower managerial and professional, intermediate, small employers, semi-routine, lower supervisory and technical, routine, and never worked.

This social class gradient in cultural attendance is clear. People in higher class groups attend a wider range of activities. However, there's a much less clear gradient in terms of whether engagement skews more formal or more everyday. *Most* of our different class groups, understood by occupations, cluster around the middle of Figure 4.8b, between formal and everyday culture.

The exception to this is people in higher professional jobs, who include university lecturers, doctors, and lawyers. People in this group not only have the highest engagement in culture in general, but they also skew disproportionately towards formal culture.

As a result, the middle class isn't homogeneous in terms of its cultural consumption. The higher professional group is different from the higher managerial group. CEOs and senior finance officers are less heavily engaged, and less heavily 'highbrow'. This reflects the discussion of changing patterns within the middle class that we saw in the introduction to the book.

Part of that discussion suggested that cultural occupations are especially interesting. We can see that in Figure 4.8b. People working in artistic and literary occupations, and in the media, have high levels of engagement with formal culture. These levels are clearly higher than any other occupational group, even the top middle-class professions.

Artistic and literary occupations have a particularly distinctive pattern of engagement. They are the most engaged in the formal cultural activities that Figure 4.8a showed are of interest to the smallest minority of the population.

Librarians and archivists are moderately more highly engaged than the higher professional group, while other groups of creative workers, such as those working in architecture, design, and ICT are more like the rest of the professional middle class.

People working in craft occupations seem to have similar levels of engagement to people in working-class occupations. This is a reflection of how craft occupations are classified alongside working-class occupations, rather than as middle-class occupations like the rest of the creative industries.

The differences we have demonstrated in Figure 4.8 persist even when we take other factors into account. In Figures 4.4–7 we've seen some of the differences by class, gender, ethnicity, and age. Even when we think about the relationship between gender, age, ethnicity, or things like geography, the divisions we've seen in Figure 4.8 remain.[17]

What has this told us? We've learned that the main way in which people's cultural engagement differs is by amount of consumption. Whether someone attends lots of cultural activity versus little or none is a crucial dividing line in England.

This division is driven by a range of factors, all of which relate to social inequalities. We've also seen how engagement differs by type of activity. This is whether activities are 'highbrow' or formal cultural activity, or more everyday forms of participation. This analysis reinforces the findings of a long tradition of academic work looking at these patterns.[18]

Crucially some of our cultural workers, particularly those in artistic and literary occupations, and in the media, are outliers. They're attending a far wider range of activities than the rest of the middle class. Even things like their level of education do not account for how high their rates of engagement in formal cultural activities are.

The unique taste patterns of cultural workers extend Chapter 3's discussion of how cultural workers might be different or unusual. It also reminds us of the question of *why* cultural occupations are unequal. As we shall see in Chapter 5, cultural taste is important to who gets into cultural jobs. It is also closely related to inequality in childhood.

Who goes to culture? Evidence from box offices[19]

Our analysis so far has used survey data that asks people to recall their cultural habits from the past year. There are other ways to understand how cultural engagement is patterned. To round off our analysis we're going to look at patterns of consumption using a different set of data.

It is important to offer a second reading of inequality in consumption for several reasons. As we saw in the introduction to the book, culture is a site of conflict over value, values, and hierarchies, none of which are static. The way that categories in survey data reflect divisions between formal cultural activity and everyday participation is an example of struggles over hierarchy and (cultural) value.

So, we might object to our analysis because key artforms are missing from the survey we use.[20] We might also wonder if nationally representative surveys are the right frame for thinking about culture.[21] In particular we might worry about under-representations of specific communities. Finally, it may also be the case that people lie or misremember, particularly if their one trip to a cultural event wasn't memorable.[22]

Survey data on attendance captures what people *say* they have been to. Ticketing data, on the other hand, tells us about actual transactions. Ticketing transactions are in contrast to self-reported attendance seen in surveys. This is because in *most* cases, the people booking tickets for events do attend them.

Obviously, there are limitations to this data. If someone books four tickets, we don't know about the three other people they go with (or indeed the four people who end up going if they've bought tickets for friends and family). Even with this note of caution, ticketing data provides an alternative perspective, particularly for those sceptical of nationally representative surveys. As we shall see, it shows almost the same patterns of inequality seen in surveys.

The transactions we analyse come from the Audience Finder dataset.[23] This consists of transactions at over 800 venues in the UK (although most are in England) for a wide range of different artforms, including theatre, music, dance, and film. It's a total of about thirty-four million transactions.

We classify transactions into first-tier and second-tier categories. For example, 'dance' is a first-tier category, while 'contemporary ballet' is a second-tier category. We've grouped the second-tier categories so they are comparable with the categories from Taking Part.

We do not have the same amount of data from each ticket purchase as we do for each survey respondent. We know things like when the transaction took place, when the performance took place, how many tickets were purchased and for how much. On its own this information doesn't help in understanding the dynamics of social inequality.

What we do have is people's postcodes. We can combine this with data from the 2015 Index of Multiple Deprivation (IMD), which is a location-based measure of deprivation. IMD is based on seven dimensions, including income, employment, and health deprivation and disability. Not everyone living in an area of higher deprivation is more deprived themselves, so there are very important notes of caution.[24] However, using IMD helps us to understand broad patterns.

We combined data from Audience Finder with the IMD data, to make a 'map' of ticket transactions across different groups of IMD areas. The IMD brings together places in England into ten groups, deciles, according to the level of deprivation, running from least to most deprived. When we look to a parliamentary constituency-level analysis,[25] this means that constituencies like Middlesbrough, Preston, and Tottenham are in the most deprived decile, Wokingham, York Outer, and Richmond Park are in the least deprived decile, and Hove, Chingford & Woodford Green, and Southport are around the middle.

We can compare and contrast Taking Part and Audience Finder using this geographical approach. There are more notes of caution here. First, there are several categories with relatively low numbers of transactions in Audience Finder, including attendance at craft events and circus. These activities should be treated with an accompanying level of uncertainty. This is in comparison to distribution across IMD deciles for theatre, where we are much more certain.

Second, Audience Finder includes data on ticket sales for types of events that are not usually ticketed, for example, people visiting art exhibitions. While there are several transactions associated with art exhibitions, these only capture attendances which are ticketed. In England there is a policy that some national museum collections are free, and not ticketed at all, to enter. Moreover, many people showing up to art exhibitions haven't booked. This means that there are some activities that we *should not* expect to look similar across the two datasets, because we know the ticketing data is only capturing part of the story.

It is also important to note that the activities in Taking Part with very low rates of attendance – for example, contemporary dance and dance associated with communities from different parts of the world – have high levels of uncertainty associated with them. If only 2% of people attended, we're drawing conclusions about the distribution based on about 200 people's responses. This means, again, we should be cautious about our comparisons.

We can see how ticket sales vary in Figure 4.9. The key is to look at whether the percentages attending from each decile are different. If the percentage of attendance is higher in the *most* deprived decile then that cultural activity is disproportionately attended by those from the poorest areas. Likewise, if the percentages are higher in the *least* deprived decile, that indicates that those activities are mainly attended by people from less deprived, more affluent places. If there are identical percentages in each decile, that means attendance at the art form in question isn't socially stratified.

We then follow this up with Figure 4.10. Here, we show the distributions of ticket sales broken down by the IMD side-by-side with the equivalent figures from Taking Part. This means we can compare the distributions from the two datasets. The activities are ordered so that the ones that Taking Part records as being attended by the most people are at the top left.

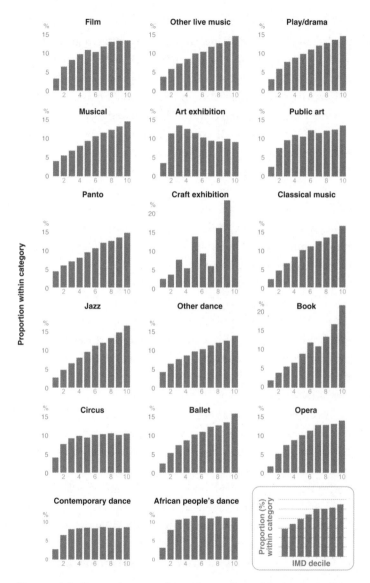

Figure 4.9 Comparing attendance figures from ticketing and survey data.

Figure 4.9 shows that most of the events that are highly attended, and mainly ticketed, show similar patterns to our earlier analysis. Plays/drama, classical music, and ballet all show a pattern where there are larger fractions of people attending from less deprived areas than from more deprived areas.

Other activities don't show this pattern. In some cases, this might be because of issues with using ticketing data. For example, because all national museums are free to attend in the UK, as are several other museums and galleries, ticketing data on attending art exhibitions is likely to be unrepresentative of all attendance at museums and galleries. We can see that art exhibitions display a very different pattern from these other activities, with the peak coming in some of the more deprived areas of the UK, in deciles 3 and 4.

Figure 4.10 contrasts this ticketing data with survey data derived from Taking Part. The bars in grey are from the survey data, while the bars in black are from the ticketing data. If the grey and black bars are at identical heights throughout, that means that the story from the two different datasets is identical; if the heights differ, that means that there are some discrepancies between the two.

When we return to those activities that are mostly ticketed and are well attended, such as musicals, we see very similar distributions across both Audience Finder and Taking Part. Earlier in the chapter we saw that attendance at the theatre, at ballet performances, at classical music concerts, and other formal cultural activities, was marked by clear social class inequalities. Here we can see attendance is also marked by inequalities by area-level deprivation, and in similar ways. This is regardless of whether we're looking at data from survey responses, or data from actual ticket sales.

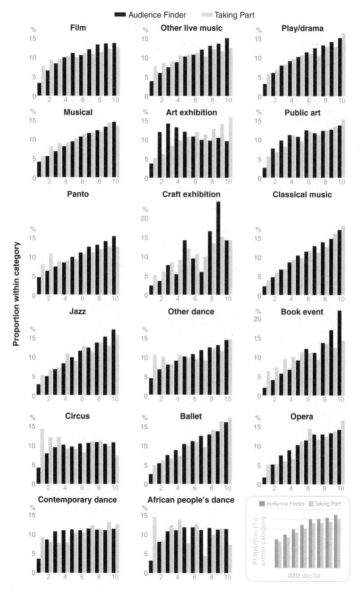

Figure 4.10 Distribution of ticket sales and self-reported attendance by Index of Multiple Deprivation.

This should put any scepticism about the numbers from survey data to rest. People may be sceptical about survey data because of who's participating in surveys, or what happens when they answer questions. In fact, the numbers look very similar when we're using actual tickets sales to look at patterns of inequality.

We can distinguish these patterns from two other categories: activities which are widely attended but not widely ticketed, such as attendance at art exhibitions; and activities that are generally ticketed but not widely attended, such as contemporary dance. For both film and live music, attendance is slightly higher for people in less-deprived areas in Audience Finder than in Taking Part. Social inequalities in attendance at these activities are sharper in the Audience Finder data than in Taking Part. This is largely because of the kind of data that Audience Finder holds.

Audience Finder is not an exhaustive dataset covering all venues, instead focusing more heavily on venues supported by the Arts Council. The audiences showing up at a Vue cinema, or at an O2 Academy live music venue, are not captured. These audiences are large enough that there are likely to be genuine differences between our culturally engaged minority in the Audience Finder dataset, and everyone else in the population.

The most striking difference is in art exhibitions. In Taking Part, less deprived areas have more people attending art exhibitions, while in the ticketing data, it's more common for people living in more deprived areas. As discussed above, it is likely that this is because of the kinds of art exhibitions for which tickets are sold.

Finally, there are the activities towards the bottom of the figure. These are activities for which events are often ticketed, and take place in the sorts of venues included in Audience

Finder, but where there are large discrepancies between Audience Finder and Taking Part.

Taking Part shows the most deprived 10% of areas attending more contemporary dance than the subsequent two deciles, while Audience Finder shows this decile to be by far the one with the fewest transactions. In these cases, the issue is likely to be with Taking Part. The numbers of attendances are so small that the uncertainty around estimates of the fractions of attendances in each decile are very large.

Overall, the activities we expect to look similar across Taking Part and Audience Finder do. The activities we expect to look different do.

This analysis in no way challenges what we already know about social inequality in cultural consumption. Instead, it provides even more support for our argument.

We have tried to understand social inequality in culture using area-level deprivation rather than social class. We've also used ticketing data, rather than survey responses. We still draw the conclusion that the activities that are most stereotypically associated with the 'high arts' are marked by pronounced social divides.

Conclusion

We have used this chapter to introduce a problem. This is the distance between the perception of policy-makers and practitioners about culture, and the reality of attendance and participation. In some ways this is old news for academic researchers, even though we're presenting new analysis.

Academic discussions about culture and inequality take for granted that engagement in culture is unequally distributed throughout society. The debates are more technical in the academic literature debating the exact explanation for these inequalities, for example social class or status,[26] age,[27] education,[28] ethnicity,[29] or gender.[30] Yet there is a very well settled consensus that the story of cultural consumption is a story of inequality.

We have presented two sets of new analysis, of Taking Part data and Audience Finder ticketing information, to make it clear that what has been a long-standing fact in the literature is still an issue today. This is, thanks to our comparison, irrespective of whether you're looking at people's behaviours, through ticketing, or their recollections, via face-to-face survey data.

Telling the story of inequality, as we have done in this chapter, matters for several reasons. It reinforces the distance between much of what our cultural occupations produce (and what the state funds) from a majority of the population. It shows how unusual our cultural workers are, in terms of their taste patterns, reinforcing the analysis in Chapter 3. Taken together, these two chapters, and these two points, suggest a disconnection between cultural production, cultural consumption, and whole swathes of the population. This is especially true when we think about the intersections of class, race, and gender.

Why is culture, both in production and consumption, so unequal? Part of the explanation lies in the *relationship* between consumption and production. Chapter 3's analysis suggests only a certain type of person gets to work in cultural occupations. The norm of who gets to make culture starts at a very early age. It starts with cultural consumption. We'll see how this works in our next chapter.

5

When does inequality begin in cultural workers' lives?

Introduction

> I love dance. I'm quite close to dance, because my children are dancing, and so they're into contemporary and ballet, and I take them to see some performances, but yes. It wouldn't be exactly what I would choose, sometimes.

Tasha, a White woman whose parents worked in craft occupations when she was growing up, was in her forties at the time of our interview. She was working as a curator. Tasha talked in detail about the way her cultural participation and cultural tastes changed when she had children. In some ways she had two cultural lives, one as a curator within the art world, and the other at home.

Tasha noted how her tastes had adapted, with much less time for film, theatre, and music, all of which she was passionate about. Dance had become an important element of her tastes, driven in part by her children and her desire to support their participation and their interests.

We quote from Tasha for two reasons. First, her patterns of engagement have changed because of parenthood. The impact of children on creative careers is the central issue for Chapter 9. We're commenting here to note that it is not just in terms of careers, but even things like tastes are changed by parenting. Parenting has wide-ranging impacts.

Our more substantive point from Tasha's comment is the powerful impact parents have on their children's connection to culture. This point is grounded in extensive academic literature demonstrating the important role parents play in supporting cultural engagement.[1] In Tasha's case the pursuit of her own cultural interests is inhibited by the responsibilities of parenthood. Instead her personal cultural participation becomes expressed through supporting the cultural interests of her children.

At the end of Chapter 4 we commented that the patterns of inequality in cultural consumption in the adult population start from a young age. We're going to use this chapter to explore this, and in addition to show how some of the patterns of inequality in cultural production are related to people's experiences growing up.

Tasha's support for her children gives them particular advantages. These advantages are especially important if her kids would like to follow their mother into a cultural and creative occupation. In Chapter 4 we saw how unusual our creative and cultural workers are because of their tastes, as compared to the rest of the population. That difference stands out in the patterns of their cultural activity as children.

Childhood experiences of culture are not equal. Within the education system, as we shall see, there are important inequalities. These inequalities are then related to access to elite institutions and occupations later in life. As the American academic Lauren Rivera notes, hiring in top firms is a process of 'cultural matching'.[2] In creative occupations, as Sharon Koppman has demonstrated, the way you express your cultural tastes and interests is a way of showing you'll be a good fit, over and above your talent or willingness to work hard.[3]

We cannot go as far as to say that high levels of cultural engagement are a *cause* of getting in and getting on in cultural work. We can say there is an important relationship, and that inequality in cultural engagement begins early in life. We're going to start with some analysis of Taking Part data, and then back this analysis up with evidence from our interviewees.

Our interviewees all stressed the importance of culture in their childhood. In turn, the importance of culture to their childhood underpins their commitment to culture in adulthood, which we saw in Chapter 2.

Why culture matters in childhood

In this chapter we are going to draw on American sociology that has sought to highlight the role of culture in upholding social inequality. In particular, we're using Annette Lareau's[4] work on unequal childhoods,[5] and Shamus Khan's[6] discussion of social elites' relationship with culture. Both authors see the importance of 'cultural capital' as a part of how we account for social inequalities.

Cultural capital helps to explain how some social groups are better than others at navigating our highly competitive and complex social world. This is especially true in those parts of the social world constituted by elite educational and professional institutions. These include schools and universities, or specific occupations such as law, medicine, accountancy, and, of course, cultural occupations.[7]

There is a huge literature on cultural capital.[8] It is a term that has been subject to debate and scrutiny since it was brought to mainstream academic discussion in the work of French sociologist Pierre Bourdieu.[9] Bourdieu saw the social world divided up into different parts, or fields, in which different sets of resources, or capitals, were influential in determining an individual's success.

Two of Bourdieu's capitals are straightforward to understand. Economic capital is associated with monetary wealth. Social capital is associated with networks and contacts, especially those networks and contacts in important or influential positions.

Cultural capital is a more slippery idea, and some have questioned its coherence and usefulness.[10] For some researchers it can be as broad as being familiar with, and participating in, whatever art and culture is dominant in society.

Cultural knowledge has been shown to 'pay off' later in life.[11] This can be because of the link between forms of cultural engagement and entry to professional occupations as a result of a 'cultural match'.[12] It can also be because of a potential association between income levels and particular patterns of taste.[13]

Another tradition has looked more closely at specific institutional settings, for example pupils in school whose knowledge of their society's dominant, 'legitimated' culture means they are *perceived* to be smart or talented. This version has been tested in British educational research, to see whether just knowing about what is seen as culturally legitimate or culturally dominant is enough to get higher test scores.[14] In this educational setting parental influence is crucial.[15]

Discussing these definitional debates is a book in itself. For now, we would like to think about cultural capital in two ways. First is how it has been used by Lareau and her co-authors. Cultural capital here is not only knowledge of facts or familiarity with art and culture. It is also knowledge of, and familiarity with, organisations and institutions.

This approach is useful because it suggests that what matters about cultural capital isn't just knowing about particular art or cultural forms. It is how that knowledge is deployed and the context in which that is made meaningful.

For Lareau this was about individuals knowing the 'rules of the game' of institutions. This is accompanied by a sense of entitlement about how institutions and social situations should best respond to their individual needs.

This is akin to debates in academia about first-generation university students. The ability of someone to get the grades to enter an elite educational institution does not mean that they also have the tacit knowledge about the norms and implicit rules that are crucial in such places.[16]

The rules of the game can also be seen in policing of behaviour of certain audience members in performing arts venues. For example, when it is appropriate to clap or laugh[17] is a struggle for control of the performing arts space. Who feels entitled to make such a judgement, and who they feel should be subject to their judgements, is of course classed and racialised.

Cultural capital also helps to understand data from interviewees whose parents worked in cultural occupations. They were at ease in the competitive and complex world of cultural occupations. They knew the 'rules of the game', as much as they knew about art and culture. This understanding is also crucial to understanding Chapter 8's discussion of how some people seem to fit easily into cultural jobs, while others feel out of place.

We would also like to connect back to Chapter 4's discussion of taste patterns to note how cultural capital can change. What is a dominant or legitimate set of art and culture, and the way in which that is consumed, discussed, and known about, can change over time.[18] To make this connection we can draw on Khan's work on American elites.

Looking at the education of elites in the United States, Khan highlights the importance of arts, humanities, and cultural education. This is not in order to make the children of elites love classical music or a venerated literary canon. Spielberg's *Jaws* is afforded the same status in the cultural hierarchy as *Beowulf*.

Young elites are given time and resources, within the education system and within extracurricular activity, to explore arts and culture widely. This breadth of cultural engagement has shifted patterns of elite tastes. Now, being engaged in lots of cultural forms, being open, and being able to articulate that range of interest is a key characteristic. In the European setting Laurie Hanquinet has written about this new dividing line, between open and eclectic and more limited and closed taste patterns, as reflective of emerging cultural capital particularly associated with young, urban life.[19] We can also see these changes reflected in how elite media, such as broadsheet newspapers and literary magazines, treat culture.[20]

For Khan, being afforded time and resources, and having a sense of openness and curiosity validated, is the preserve of very elite educational institutions. It is in contrast to much of the rest of the US education system, where Khan sees a focus on less creative and much more didactic, test-based teaching. It is not difficult to see the parallels with the UK.

In the UK, the rich cultural offer of many fee-paying schools may be producing similar kinds of elite ethos and ethics that pay off later in life. This pay-off is access to elite universities and then access to elite professional destinations.

The importance of cultural capital to understanding and explaining social inequality is one of the reasons we gave such a detailed discussion of taste patterns in Chapter 4. In the context of childhood cultural engagement, we can see the importance of cultural capital in debates about art and culture within the education system.

Recent work by the UK government's Social Mobility Commission has drawn attention to just how unequal access to extracurricular activity is for young people. Household income is a key driver of participation for children, and music lessons seem especially socially exclusive. Attendance at fee-paying schools offers 'unparalleled breadth and range of activities compared to state schools'.[21]

Childhood cultural life is thus highly unequal. We should be unsurprised by research that draws attention to the most successful parts of key cultural professions, such as acting, being dominated by those from independent schools.

Access is also an issue for a range of professions, not just those in the creative economy. It suggests the importance of access to culture in childhood for access to any of the major professions, let alone making it in the cultural sector. Access seems dependent on parental wealth, whether spent directly on the costs of extracurricular activity, or via school fees.

The divide in resources for culture between state and fee-paying schools draws attention to larger issues within the education system. Much of this debate has been focused on England, where curriculum reform has had controversial results. In 2018 analysis of Department for Education figures conducted by the Cultural Learning Alliance (CLA)[22] suggested a crisis for arts education in schools.

The CLA estimated a decline in the hours of arts teaching by 21% between 2010 and 2017, and a 20% decline in arts teacher numbers. Design and drama were singled out as having been hit particularly hard. Much of this, according to the CLA, was grounded in a reorganisation of the curriculum to focus on a set of core subjects for secondary school exams that did not include art, drama, or design.

Analysis by the All Party Parliamentary Group for Music Education[23] found a similar crisis in music since 2014, even when smaller cohort sizes over the period were taken into account. The decline in music GCSE exam entries went hand-in-hand with a decline in teacher numbers. Those most likely to be discouraged from taking music were found to be those living in deprived areas.

Subsequent academic research indicates that even where those from the most deprived backgrounds are getting access to arts education, they received the weakest programmes, positioning them as passive learners with little creative control.[24] The contrast with the sorts of experiences highlighted in Khan's study of US elite fee-paying schools is clear.

Creative workers' childhood cultural consumption

Access to culture in childhood, it seems, reflects a range of inequalities. How does this play out in practice for our cultural occupations? In Chapter 4 we saw how cultural and creative workers have unusual patterns of taste when compared to the rest of the population. They are much more engaged in culture than any other set of occupations in society. This is even in comparison with people working in other professional jobs.

We can say that cultural and creative workers have high levels of cultural capital. As our previous section has shown, cultural capital is closely related to people's experiences growing up, for example their family or school. We're now going to look at those experiences, to see how cultural capital is developed for our creative workers. The story here will, again, be how they are different to the rest of the population, even to their middle-class peers. We'll see this from two sets of data.

First, we are going to look at Taking Part again. It asks about people's cultural consumption when they were growing up.[25] As it's a nationally representative survey, we can use it get a sense of the impact of cultural engagement on later careers. In the section on their childhoods, respondents in the Taking Part survey are asked if they did cultural activities such as going to libraries and galleries, playing musical instruments, reading books for pleasure, and drawing and painting.[26]

Figure 5.1 shows the proportions of people working in creative jobs, and in more general sets of occupations, who said that they'd participated in various cultural activities. These are the same categories we saw in Chapter 3. Our creative workers are highlighted in black, while more general categories of occupations are in grey.

This graph highlights important distinctions between the cultural activities that we've combined in Figure 5.1. It shows us that there are big differences between occupational groups when people report their youthful cultural engagement. There are also huge differences depending on which activities we're looking at.

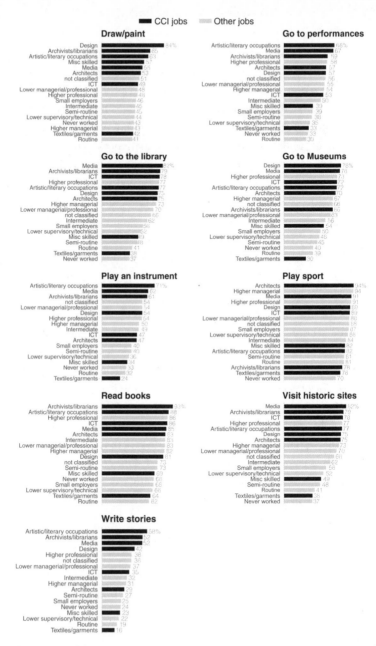

Figure 5.1 Reported participation/attendance in different activities while growing up.

Sport is a key category for childhood activities. It is an almost universal experience, with every occupational group reporting high levels of engagement. Reading books is also common. Although archivists and librarians are the group most likely to have done this when growing up, the differences between the most and least engaged groups are not large.

For drawing and painting, we can see that designers are by far the most likely to have done this as children. At 84%, this is some distance from the 65% of archivists and librarians in second place. Among most other occupational groups, only between 40% and 50% had done this as children.

This isn't necessarily surprising. Children who loved drawing and painting might have stuck with it through childhood, and this might have motivated them to become designers.

This pattern is echoed in writing stories and in playing an instrument. Groups in cultural and creative industries are by far the most likely to have participated. Fifty-eight per cent of people working in artistic or literary jobs wrote as children, compared with just 38% of people working in higher professional jobs. In turn there are big differences between managerial and professional jobs and other sorts of jobs. The fraction of people in routine jobs who wrote stories as children is half of that of those people in higher professional jobs, at 19%.

For performances, there are two things we can see. The first is that, again, some cultural and creative workers are far more likely to have gone than anyone else. These are those working in artistic and literary occupations and those working in the media. We can also see that there are big differences between people in middle-class jobs and people in working-class jobs.

There are echoes of these patterns in several other activities: going to historic sites, going to the library, going to museums. Among all these activities, a cultural and creative occupational group comes top.

Overall, the big differences are between managerial and professional occupations (including those in the cultural and creative industries) and those that we might classify as intermediate and working-class jobs. The occupational class differences we saw in adult cultural engagement seem to be mirrored in recollections of childhood activity.

These patterns look almost identical when we look at which activities people were encouraged to do when they were children, rather than the activities that people actually *did* do. It's tempting to interpret Figure 5.1 as an argument for providing more opportunities for children from all sorts of different backgrounds to draw, paint, and play an instrument in schools. However, further data from Taking Part shows very similar patterns of whether people in different occupational groups were encouraged to do these same things by their parents when they were growing up. Once again, we can see the distinctiveness of our cultural workers, over and above what you might expect from people working in other professional jobs.

Remembering culture in childhood

During our interview fieldwork the importance of participation and engagement with culture was clear in the life histories of our participants. Yet we do have to be cautious with the data from our interviews and from Taking Part. Although we are confident both are a good representation of key cultural occupations, discussions of art and culture in childhood may be skewed in two ways.

First, as part of our interview we asked specifically about their cultural life when they were growing up. This was because of the importance of cultural capital that we have shown earlier in this chapter.

Second, these are individuals in cultural occupations, and as a result may overstate the importance of art and culture to their lives. The interviews were a discussion of their career in cultural and creative industries. They took place against the backdrop of continuing debates over arts funding and arts education. Cultural workers may have felt the need to stress how crucial childhood access and experiences are, in order to defend both funding and education.

It may also be the case that individuals outside of cultural and creative occupations do not place the same levels of importance on childhood cultural activity and thus forget much of it, raising questions about the Taking Part data. You can imagine someone who thinks of herself as a creative adult concluding that her childhood creative activities must have been significant.

These caveats are important. As we will show, our data goes beyond these notes of caution to make a powerful case for the relationship between childhood cultural engagement and working in a cultural occupation. Across our dataset demographics seemed almost irrelevant; all of our interviewees attached importance to childhood cultural life and no one told us art and culture were absent.

In keeping with the rest of our discussions in this book, this seemingly coherent and consistent story revealed different experiences. Even within the 'norm' of a rich cultural child-hood for creative workers, we can see the process of broader social inequalities at play. We'll see this again when we discuss pay, and when we discuss parenting. Shared experience hides significant, unequal, difference.

Cultural activity in school and in the home

Home and school are crucial as sites for childhood engage-ment in culture. We did see some nuances within our inter-viewee data, between men and women, older and younger interviewees, and differing cultural occupations. Despite these differences, the story was overwhelmingly clear. All of our inter-viewees saw culture as a key element in their childhood and had rich cultural lives.

For a minority of interviewees these rich cultural lives were about everyday culture, with little or no school or parental support. Sean, an artist in his thirties, recollected no specific parental or educational figures encouraging him during his working-class childhood:

> They didn't encourage or discourage. They just wanted me to do what I wanted to do, really. I was always into art. I was always drawing, and always reading, so it would have been … yes, the books, art, and football were the three things, I think.
>
> I don't think there was any particular teacher that, sort of, did any of that, to be honest. No, I guess the main influences were just through media, newspapers, TV. I had Sky TV from a very young age, so I think that was a big influence.

Sean was unusual in our dataset. Yet even without school or parental encouragement he still had a rich cultural life. A more representative example is Carys. She provides a good starting point when we think about cultural workers' childhoods.

Carys shows the importance of school teachers as well as parental commitment. A White woman in her late fifties, an artist and arts manager from a working-class background, her story is essentially of luck at an early age:

> There was a teacher when I was eight who, when I look back now, I see that she must have really valued creativity. I was good at drawing and I was good at making things and I used to make all my dolls' clothes. I used to make things when I was at home. She said I think to my parents once, 'Oh you should send [Carys] to art school.' So my parents, they didn't know but they enquired and they thought I could go then when I was eight. Then they found out I wouldn't be able to go until I was 18. I think it was from then on I thought this is something I could do, I could do art. This is what I really like. I think it sort of came about like that really. I didn't know that you could be an artist. I had this thing in my mind then that I could go to this place where I could just do art. That was what got me through school really, that goal.

Having the right teacher instilled a lifelong love of the subject, and a belief in herself as having a special affinity for art. In the context of her parents not knowing about the art school system for school leavers, Carys might not have pursued a career in the arts without the influence of her teacher. She was not discouraged from an interest in the arts as a child, but the household 'had no reading material'. Her father 'ended up taking us to the library once a week and I just read every fairy tale book in the library. I really got into reading, it opened up another world. It was like I had another life apart from school.'

Even where parents had little or no formal cultural interests or knowledge of how cultural institutions worked, they were still encouraging of Carys by taking her to the library. Her story is of a rich cultural life.

The importance of parental support

Carys illustrates the dominant narrative from our interviewees. Parents were supportive of our interviewees' engagement in artistic and cultural activities. This was the case irrespective of connections or resources.

These parents took our interviewees to classes, even when they did not fully understand what happened there; they took them regularly to the library; and they responded positively to suggestions from teachers, both in school and in extracurricular classes. This was true even where parents seemed totally disconnected from or uninterested in formal, legitimated arts. Farida, a working-class origin British Asian woman in her twenties recollected a disconnection between her work in theatre and the absence of this artform in her childhood:

> We weren't a theatre-going family or anything like that, just because it doesn't really exist in our … Well, back then, it didn't.

Yet her family's cultural life was very, very rich:

> but things like music were very important to us, obviously. So, we'd go to festivals where there were always music and musicians and dancers entertaining us. Yes.
>
> Films were very important to us as well, I guess. Just getting together and going to the cinema and stuff like that.

Farida's mother was especially important in encouraging her, for example through reading:

> We lived opposite a public library. I remember my mum saying that she bought the house she did just because it was opposite the library and it would be good for us to read. I think I had an ambition of trying to read every single book there.

Farida's mother's comment can be complemented by looking at Camille, a thirty-year-old White woman, working in the classical music industry at the time of interview. Camille's family background is more traditionally middle class, coupled with growing up in rural England rather than London or a major regional city. She recalled a distance between her parents' cultural interests and her work in classical music, in a similar way to Farida's story about theatre. Reading was also important to her:

> I certainly wasn't taken to concerts or anything, or the theatre as a child, because my parents, they don't really do it themselves. But in other ways, say for example the library, I was taken to the library from being a baby. My mum is obsessed with books and so I'd be, in terms of books and reading and stories that was around from the word go. My mum was very, very keen that I read.

At this point we can begin to introduce the importance of social class differences in the comparison between Farida and Camille. Camille's mother was not initially interested in classical music. Just like Tasha told us at the start of the chapter, Camille's mother responded to her daughter's cultural interests. As her daughter showed aptitude and interest, Camille's mother was not only encouraging but also invested considerable time to support her. She shifted her own interests and tastes to facilitate that support:

> But then of course, the minute I started to do the music and actually my older brother was playing the piano as well, there was,

certainly from my mother there was this kind of total, 'Well if the kids are into music, I'm going to get into it.' Then she started buying all the CDs and coming to all the concerts.

She would sit with me while I was doing my practice and she would quiz me on it, she would ask me my scales, because that's just who she is, she's very giving in that way, so she completely got into the music.

We are going to see more of this difference later in the chapter when we look specifically at the advantages our middle-class origin interviewees described to us. These advantages are in contrast to those from working-class starting points. Again, it is important to stress, Farida and Camille are both telling stories of their own engagement and commitment as children, matched by parental support.

Yet Camille's mother was, in some ways, more engaged and able to offer a type of support that shifted her own, and the family's, tastes and practices. Farida, by contrast had support from the family's existing cultural practices of cinema and their interest in music. This is a subtle but important difference that becomes clearer as we think about our interviewees' perceptions of what was, and was not, a rich cultural childhood.

What is a high level of engagement anyway?

We mentioned a note of caution about the interview data, as a result of the importance of culture to cultural workers. It would be strange if our interviewees did not mention that art and culture was important to them; it would be especially strange given what we would expect to see based on our analysis of Taking Part.

We did encounter a paradox from some interviewees. They initially described low, or in some cases non-existent, levels of engagement with arts and culture as children. Yet, when they went on to give specific examples it was clear they were describing very high levels of activity. Their engagement was especially high when compared to the rest of the population.

What is especially interesting here is how this was articulated. Chloe is a good example of how some interviewees, usually those with access to the *greatest* cultural and economic resources, saw their cultural engagements. They described what they thought were, at best, ordinary, or even quite low-level cultural engagement. Chloe recalled her mother reacting to a poetry performance:

> She had always told us we're not creative, and actually, after I did – I perform poetry – my first performance, I called her, and she said, 'But why did you do that? You're not creative.' It's this kind of understanding that if you're creative, you paint, or, if you're creative you play gigs, or whatever it is.

Chloe was working across several arts organisations in a variety of creative and management roles when we interviewed her. A White woman in her mid-twenties, her story of growing up was of her clerical mother and business-owning father's slight suspicion of things 'creative'. At the same time they were very encouraging:

> My mum, I mean every time she walked past a charity shop she'd buy five books, and I would just consume them and I would read and read and read.

And her cultural life was very rich:

> Fiction, love fiction, poetry. Writing poetry from about twelve. Anything to do with literature. Cooking as well; cooking all the

time. Cooked a lot for my family from a very young age. Making things … a bit of drawing, but nothing very exceptional. Piano; I used to play the piano, learn it. I used to learn saxophone and guitar as well.

Yet she felt it this cultural life wasn't about 'great' arts or a particular cultural canon:

Nothing like that exposure to like, 'This is a great artist, and this is a great piece of work', or, 'This is a great poem.' It wasn't like that kind of education, it was just like, 'Here's a load of stuff, go and read it and enjoy it.'

We know from existing research and policy work that class origins are important in shaping children's cultural experiences. We also know this is patterned differently according to gender, with young women more likely to be engaged readers.[27] For Chloe, this level of support, as a reader, and intense engagement in learning musical instruments was part of her everyday cultural life. It was 'a load of stuff' rather than a conscious engagement with 'great' art, coupled with maternal suspicion of the 'creative'.

We can contrast this to Gavin. He was thirty-four, a White man working in theatre, with several directing and management roles behind him. He was raised by his mother who did a secretarial role for a large business. He was much more circumspect in his discussion of his cultural childhood:

I cannot remember ever going with them to a museum, or a performance, or anything that I do now in my leisure time. I never did that with my parents and so it's kind of really … I can't put a finger on why I've ended up in this world, because, like you say, it wasn't encouraged, it was never … There was no kind of positive modelling of: 'We're going to take him here and then he's going

> to enjoy this', and so forth. No, there was nothing like that; it was mainly, like I say, sport, watching sport, and watching TV.

Part of this is grounded in the gendered differences researchers find in fieldwork interviews. Moreover, we might expect a young man to have less interest in the sorts of cultural life Gavin discussed and perhaps be more engaged with sport. As recent work by Victoria Cann has shown,[28] young people's cultural tastes are very clearly differentiated by gender, and gender plays an important role in reinforcing taste differences.

Gavin wonders how he ended up in theatre. In the interview he reflected that he 'only started engaging in the arts at sixth form' and found inspiration and a love of theatre via the education system:

> there was a theatre and dance teacher who was kind of interesting. Again, that was the space where you were able to express a level of independence and individuality, whereas obviously in a lot of the curricula it's about rote learning and memory rather than actual education.

As we saw with Carys' comments about a teacher encouraging her and her parents to think about art school, the education system is crucial for those who do not have the same sort of cultural resources in the home.

It is a fair assumption that Gavin would not have taken a theatre degree, nor worked in theatre, without this. However, even within the education system there are important differences in levels of resource and support. When reinforced by parental resources, whether economic, social, or cultural, these can make an important difference to getting in and getting on in cultural jobs.

'Everybody went to art classes as a child, didn't they?'

At the start of the chapter we noted how all of our interviewees told a story of some form of cultural engagement as children. This matches what we've seen from our analysis of Taking Part. We also noted how the coherence across these narratives and numbers might hide important differences. As we're going to see in the next chapter's discussion of unpaid work, even where the headline data suggests shared experiences, there are often important inequalities beneath the surface.

We have seen a little of this in the comparison between Chloe and Gavin. As our final analytical point, we're going to look in detail at the childhood cultural life of our respondents whose parents were cultural workers. This was, obviously, a minority of the sample. They are worth highlighting for two reasons.

The first is they are the most extreme examples of how resources can accumulate to give advantages for getting in and getting on. In this instance social networks and cultural knowledge are foregrounded, although economic resources matter a great deal.

Second, the children of creatives are perhaps most at home and most at ease in the world of cultural work. Existing research on cultural occupations highlights how many young people don't see a cultural career as something 'for them'. Moreover, a lack of knowledge of the range of possible cultural careers was identified by British public policy as a key reason for the lack of diversity in creative jobs.[29] While this book demonstrates that there are many factors explaining the narrow social basis of the creative workforce, growing up 'knowing' the world of arts and cultural jobs matters.

Isabel offers perhaps the richest example, and is worth quoting from at length:

> My mum is a singer, and during my childhood my dad was also a musician, so yes, I guess I grew up in a musical household … I always was interested in acting; I went off and did performing arts classes and stuff on Saturdays. I always did it, but it was never really something – I never really thought about that as a career. I guess I never really thought about a career in general. It wasn't like I was really particularly was, like, 'I'm going to be a famous actor.' I just went to a performing arts class, they had an agency attached, I ended up doing this series, and I was, like, 'All right, this is kind of fun', it kind of just happened.
>
> My dad is friends with this actor, who sort of got me an agent; he basically suggested to his agent that I come on her books, after I'd done that series. That was a very good foot in the door. He was very encouraging, but it's not like he was a mentor or anything.

Isabel was a successful child actor, before moving into a range of creative practice and management work aged twenty-three. We see a similar modesty to Chloe, normalising what was a very culturally well-connected childhood. In doing so, Isabel shows the importance of feeling at home in culture. For her it was 'never really something' to act as a child, and success 'just kind of happened'.

In Chapter 10 we're going to raise the problem of misrecognising or playing down privileges by interviewees who end up in senior roles. Here the focus is different. What Isabel shows is how the right mix of resources can make a cultural career seem like the norm, despite the immense struggles that others face.

This is not at all to criticise Isabel, nor to play down her talent or the inevitable hard work that her modesty may be obscuring. Rather it is to show, much as with the experience of unpaid work we'll see in the next chapter, that the experience of a rich cultural childhood is differentiated according to parental occupation.

Having a creative worker as a parent thus offers social and cultural resources, as well as the feeling of being at home or in place in the cultural world. Isabel is a unique case in some ways, given she was in a television show. What then of other children of creatives? Here we see narratives that have less obvious immediate success, but show an equal wealth of resources.

Lydia is our example here. She was an artist and working in theatre, in her late twenties at the time of interview. Both of her parents had traditional professional middle-class occupations during their lives, but Lydia's mother had a creative career during Lydia's childhood.

Certainly, school would have been very encouraging. I was never short of colouring pencils and god knows what else. And art classes. I'm sure I went to art classes. Everybody went to art classes as a child, didn't they? Something to do on a Saturday morning … Didn't we all? Didn't we all do papier-mâché at some point in our lives? I did piano and horse riding. But yes, lots of books, lots of art materials, lots of trees, lots of animals. All of it, just all of it. Very, very fortunate. Oh gosh, we went to the museum weekly … An awful lot of things. I mean, I consider board games quite cultural given the right context. And there was always music playing. Yes, just the stuff you kind of imagine everybody else does as a child, but maybe they don't. I don't think so. I think it was more just a steady progression of influences and support, or nice comments or something. Just lots of small, steady progressions as opposed to one massive thing. There probably was one massive thing but it seems I had quite a busy childhood.

Again we see the sense of immersion in culture, a sense that this is the norm, coupled with a reflexive recognition that perhaps her 'busy' childhood was different.

We started the discussion of our interview data with Sean, who told us about drawing, reading, and television, and with Carys' recollections of the importance of a teacher pointing her towards art school. Culture was obviously important to both of their childhoods, as it was to almost everyone we interviewed.

This importance also shows up in our analysis of Taking Part. What is clear though is how the importance of culture obscures the differences in access, whether in school or in the home.

Lydia's assumption that everyone did art classes, along with her moment of doubt that 'maybe they don't', illustrates the uneven distribution of resources and the sense of the taken-for-grantedness of a rich cultural life. The broad definition of culture, including board games, museums, music, and art, is reflective of the cultural omnivorousness we observed in the taste patterns of our cultural workers in Chapter 4. It also reflects what Khan describes in terms of elite tastes in the United States.

From Lydia's recollections it seems the omnivorous orientation starts very young. In Lydia's case it was shaped by the context of growing up in not only a middle-class,[30] but also a cultural worker's home.

Conclusion

The sense of being at home in cultural occupations is an important factor in accounting for who gets in and gets on. It is no surprise that there is a close relationship between who gets to accumulate cultural resources, cultural capital, in childhood and inequalities of parental class. We can then add on to this the sense of knowing the 'rules of the game' that children of cultural workers may gain.

We have obviously been concentrating on cultural occupations in this book. The sorts of issues we've outlined in this chapter are a useful moment to connect culture to more general inequalities in the workforce. Just as the American literature on childhood and cultural capital was useful to frame this chapter, it's worth restating the US literature on hiring that we mentioned at the start of the chapter.

We made this point at the end of Chapter 3, but it is crucial here too. Both Sharon Koppman[31] and Lauren Rivera[32] have shown the importance of the right sort of cultural cues in getting jobs. For Rivera hiring at top firms represents a form of 'cultural matching'. This process isn't just about having shared tastes. It is about who is seen to be worth supporting, fighting for in the interview room, and investing time and resources in developing.

Koppman shows similar patterns in creative occupations. She shows that potential employees need the eclectic omnivorous mode of consumption to appear 'different like me' in the eyes of commissioners and hirers. We have noted this eclectic sense of omnivorousness seems to start very young for our cultural and creative workers.

Both of these authors reflect the US tradition of asking how specific occupations – 'micro classes' – replicate themselves. It is difficult to do this in the UK, for cultural and creative occupations, as the scale of high quality, nationally representative, data is smaller.

What we can say, from Isabel and Lydia's stories, and the contrast with Carys and Farida, is that cultural resources, cultural capital, matter a great deal in getting access to cultural occupations. The accumulation of cultural capital starts young. It is part of the reason that some feel at home in cultural occupations. By contrast someone like Meg, who we met at the start of Chapter 3, did not have this sense of being at ease and included.

We have shown how these inequalities begin in childhood. As a result, inequalities in the workforce will be hard to change in the short term.

The long-term nature of these inequalities suggests they are *social structural* problems as much as they are to do with pay, conditions, or qualifications. It is not just that there is an over-supply of candidates for some cultural occupations. It is that there is not an even playing field. Some have a vast head start over others, when it comes to the cultural resources, the cultural capital, which is crucial to success.

Cultural capital is only the first part of the story. Getting in and getting on is difficult if you don't have the money to support yourself, as we will see in Chapter 6. We will also see how shared experiences of low and no pay, like shared experiences of culture in childhood, hides important inequalities.

6

Is it still good work if you're not getting paid?

Introduction: Emily doesn't get paid

I did an internship … that would have been completely unpaid and I probably got expenses. I did another internship that was completely unpaid straight after that. Two internships completely unpaid … So I have got, so over a period of about six months it was three internships, actually four because I started two simultaneously, but the second one, the second one of that simultaneous time was paying me and so then I was like wow, and that felt very unusual like I was getting £50 a day.

Every year in the UK the DCMS publishes figures outlining the economic performance of creative industries. The most recent figures,[1] for 2017, suggested creative industries as a whole were contributing over £100 billion to the economy, with remarkable growth since 2010. The cultural sector, as a distinctive part of the creative economy, contributed almost £30 billion. While there are complexities underpinning the relationship between individual firms' profitability, workers' wages, and overall contribution to the economy, it is fair to say there is money to be made by making culture.

Yet this does not seem to be the story for many workers. Academic and industry research reports significant differences between a small number of high earners and a much larger number of much lower earners.

Emily was in her early thirties, working in the music industry when we interviewed her. She grew up in a single-parent family in London. This gave her the advantage of having family located in the hub of Britain's music business. This meant, in very basic practical terms, she had somewhere to live when facing the demand from the industry that she work unpaid.

At the time of interview she was leaving music, to work in another creative occupation where she could use her management skills. When she got her first paid position she remembered thinking 'I just couldn't believe I was allowed to do something that I wanted to do involving music that would pay me.'

There are many depressing things about Emily's experience of having to work for free. We could highlight the relentlessness of unpaid work she describes, having three unpaid positions over a six-month period just to get a foothold in the music industry. We could note how she 'couldn't believe' she was eventually paid for a job working in music.

It can be a cliché to make comparisons with other professions and occupations. Unpaid internships or low-paid apprenticeships exist in other areas of the economy. Nevertheless, we do not associate other occupations with disbelief that one might be paid for one's work. We could also emphasise how a quirk of parental geography, her mother living in London, had enabled her to participate in the music business without pay.

What is perhaps most depressing is that this is an unsurprising story about getting into the music business. It is *not* a shock that Emily's experience was of several internships, and that these were also unpaid. In 2017 the Institute for Public Policy Research[2] singled out creative industries as one of the sectors most dependent on internships for routes into work. Alongside this policy research, academics have repeatedly demonstrated that unpaid work is a long-standing, structural problem in creative jobs.[3]

In this chapter we are going to build on that existing research base to think about the problem of working for free. We're going to demonstrate that although unpaid work has been the subject of high-profile campaigning[4] and attempts at regula-tion,[5] it remains an important part of how creative labour markets function. Our data echoes the existing research suggesting working for free is a dominant and inescapable experience for our creative workers.

At the same time, we are going to build on an idea we intro-duced in Chapter 5. Even where the same conditions confront all cultural workers, they are experienced very differently across key demographic groups.

Working for free is not experienced equally, nor are its conse-quences the same for every creative worker. For older workers, secure in their careers, unpaid work can be a choice. At the start of their careers unpaid work took place in a very different social context. There was support from the state via the social security system. There were also a very different set of labour market pressures. We'll see more about how things have changed in Chapter 7.

For our younger respondents there is no such social safety net. Their experience is clearly marked by social class. This chapter explores the intersection between age and social class, and how class origins insulate some from the worst elements of unpaid labour.

For those from middle-class, affluent origins, unpaid work is affordable. It can be an investment that pays off artistically and in terms of access to a creative career. For those from working-class origins unpaid work will often lead nowhere. It is experienced only as exploitation and certainly not as an opportunity for creative development.

Our younger middle-class respondents spoke of the ability to take a show to Edinburgh, to take a long internship at a publishing house, or to avoid taking a second job while developing a first exhibition. These examples contrast with the dead ends that those from working-class origins are more likely to run into.

The consequences of this go beyond just the obvious barriers to those who cannot afford to work for free, and who cannot afford the additional costs of subsidising their free work in London, where housing and living cost are very high. They also go beyond the moral questions of exploiting people in industries that are very comfortable trumpeting the huge amounts of money that they contribute to the British economy.

The experience of unpaid work, differentiated by age and social class, is an important driver of a false sense of social solidarity for our cultural workers. Earlier in the book we discussed the shared attitudes and values, and the shared childhood experiences, of our cultural workers. In the case of unpaid work that shared experience takes on a distinctly negative aspect. This negative aspect, which we address in the conclusion to the chapter, helps to explain how culture connects to more general inequalities, beyond the class and age inequalities we're about to demonstrate.

Good work?

By highlighting the way unpaid work is stratified, and the insecure forms of solidarity that result, we raise the question of why people persist in trying to break into creative occupations.

There is a long-standing academic research interest in creative work as good work.[6] It can be fulfilling, offering chances for self-expression, freedom, for work to be a source of joy and love. This is not confined to, or unique to, creative industries, as many other occupations generate similar sorts of commitment, pride, and vocational worth.

The juxtaposition of unpaid work with narratives of joy and love is how we start our analysis in this chapter. It points to a defence of creative labour even in the face of, for many, exploitative conditions preventing them from gaining access to creative jobs.

Foregrounding unpaid labour can obscure how creative workers also love and enjoy their occupations. The story of work in cultural occupations is not only the story of no pay, precariousness and exploitation. It is important to remember this point. It connects to themes we've already seen in the book.

The positive experiences of work sit alongside creative workers' sense of the positive and beneficial impacts of culture. Their commitment and love of their jobs is difficult to separate from the sense that culture can make the world a better place. We've seen this already in Chapter 2. For now, it is worth keeping in mind that for all of the problems the book discusses, there is still a strong commitment to working in creative occupations.

Our workers loved their jobs! They told us this, often explicitly using the word 'love', and framing work in ways that made this commitment clear. Work was 'a labour of love' (Maura), that gave 'a lot of pleasure' and 'the best feeling' (Richard). One interviewee, Holly, told us that she was 'one of those annoying people that really loves their jobs'.

The love of work goes hand-in-hand with the range of positive aspects afforded by cultural jobs. For some this was the sense that their interests were totally aligned with their work:

> Well I suppose I go to a lot of museums and galleries because it's what I do for my job and it's also my hobby. I'm lucky to have a job that is also my hobby to some extent. I do spend a lot of my spare time doing that.

Lauren, a White, middle-class origin woman in her twenties was working in a museum at the time of interview. She told us work was her hobby, and that it reflected her friends who were similarly committed to artistic and cultural occupations.

Key theorists of cultural work have noted that while working in occupations that elicit happiness and fulfilment is a good thing, the blurring of life and work, of jobs and hobbies, has potentially negative consequences.[7] We'll see some of this later in this chapter, and in Chapter 8. It is worth noting the blurring of life and work mentioned by Lauren, as it is part of a more general sense of vocation.[8]

The joys of cultural work were generally stressed across our interviews, along with a nuanced recognition of some of the problems. Stefano, a White male director in his thirties, from a working-class background, is a perfect example:

141

> I have really enjoyed everything that I've done ... I have gotten
> to do some amazing stuff with brilliant people and I have worked
> in some jobs for money that were not nice and this is a nice job
> even if it is paid poorly that is very, yeah it is a rewarding job. It
> is a challenging job. It is creative, you know there are far worse
> out there.

The end of Stefano's comment is crucial, and exemplifies a
dominant trope in how our interviewees narrated the joys of
cultural work. Not only is working in a cultural occupation full
of fulfilling, good work, but it is also defined in contrast to other
sorts of work.

We see this in Finn, a White, middle-class origin man in his
twenties, working as a producer at the time of interview. Finn
highlighted the positive elements of his occupation, contrasting
them with the idea of being in an office, and being surrounded
by people who are not passionate about their work:

> But most of the time, you meet loads of different people, you
> go to loads of different locations, and you interact with so many
> different kinds of people and cultures. It's a lot more interesting
> to me than sitting in an office, at a desk, with people who are just
> there to work ... Everyone's really passionate and driven, who
> I've met in the creative industry, anyway. No one's just there, just
> ambling along.

This contrast between creative and office or desk work is an
important part of the story of love of work and commitment to
the vocation.[9] It adds another layer of nuance and complexity
to how creative work is defended.

Many interviewees used this sort of comparison, between
'working for a bank', wearing 'a suit', not wanting 'to do something boring' and work in a cultural job. For Deb, a White,

working-class origin producer in her fifties at the time of interview, being a cultural worker was part of rejecting what she perceived to be a boring life:

I knew I didn't want to do something boring. I knew that I would rather have an adventure. I didn't want the house, the family. I ended up with the house and the family and everything like that, but I set out to do something interesting. So the choice of courses at university was, 'Do I do something that I could do but it feels a bit dull? Or do I do the thing that's more interesting and exciting? Do I go for the adventure?'

In some ways Deb's language suggests a choice between becoming a creative, via university, and a more traditional route and more traditional work. For some of our interviewees this choice came later in life, but was still seen as a choice. Matt, who we met in Chapter 2, was actually working for a bank before committing full-time to his artistic and cultural practice:

So I remember, it wasn't the best circumstances but I remember sitting at the bank and thinking, 'Is this where I want to be? Is this who I want to become, this person just handling other people's money and stuff?' I mean, it has some kind of beauty to it or some kind of prestige, but it doesn't fulfil me.

The language of beauty, prestige, and fulfilment points us towards the way in which, for many, cultural work is not actually something they have chosen. Rather, it is who they are. Our interviewees told us things like they 'couldn't see myself living any other way' (Erica) and that their work 'is a state of being' (Sasha). The state of being meant, for Emma, she explicitly rejected the idea of 'being a normal grey Joe on a bus going to an office job'.

The *need* for beauty and prestige is balanced against the risks of leaving full-time work to the more precarious labour market for poetry, art, and theatre. In Matt's case his willingness to take the risk was shaped by education and class. This is a point we've seen already in Chapter 5, and we'll keep seeing throughout the book.

Matt's decision was supported by the social, cultural, and crucially *economic* resources at his disposal. We're now going to turn to the role of those economic resources, or capital, in the rest of this chapter.

Precariousness, pay, and cultural work

Growing up I always said, 'When I grow up I am going to be a writer. All I am going to do is write books and that is going to be my job.' I still aspire to that, it is just facing the realistic implications of what that means has been a little bit of a struggle, but we will get there.

The determination to not be a 'normal grey Joe' and the inability to see oneself 'living any other way' mean many creative workers will try to cope with poor pay and conditions in the hope of making it into a more secure, or at least better paid, position. This is where we can see the importance of comments like the one from Alex, a White, middle-class origin journalist in her twenties.

Alex's 'little bit of a struggle' matters in two ways. It leads us to ask what this 'struggle' has consisted of and how it has been experienced. And it also leads to the question of how this 'struggle' is stratified. Is Alex's 'struggle' experienced equally by all, or do some find it easier to make it as compared with others? As we show throughout the book, the struggle to make it in cultural occupations is closely related to the intersection between one's race, class, and gender.[10]

These two points are reflected in how academics have thought about work in the creative industries. Cultural work is often seen as an exemplar of precariousness.[11] Within this, unpaid or free work stands out as a core characteristic of precariousness.[12]

Our interviewees told us many positives of their jobs, for example the blurring of work and life because of artistic or creative vocations. These are also negatives when it comes to important issues such as getting paid, being seen as a worker, having workplace rights, and developing a work–life balance. We'll see more of these issues in Chapter 9.

We can see unpaid work as an important element of what makes an occupation precarious. Guy Standing is perhaps the most prominent theorist who has tried to define this idea.[13]

Standing suggests precariousness is characterised by unstable labour conditions, a lack of occupational narrative, high levels of unremunerated work (including work preparation and re-training), high levels of education relative to the job, low levels of non-wage benefits such as holiday or sickness pay, high levels of debt and associated financial uncertainty, and a reconfigured form of citizenship rights with regard to access to both benefits and public services.

Precariousness has been a controversial concept. The cultural theorist Angela McRobbie has cautioned for the need for context.[14] She notes how many non-creative jobs are just as precarious as creative jobs, if not more so. Occupations such as care work and cleaning are not only precarious, but they are more likely to be staffed by people from marginalised groups, for example women, people of colour, and migrants.

The uneven distribution of what characterises precariousness between different sorts of occupations, means we have to be cautious when using the term. Often cultural jobs exhibit strong senses of occupational and vocational identity. This can take the form of specialised and specific work in film or television, or the more general sense of self and identity that derives from working as an actor or an artist.[15]

An understanding of precariousness focused on creative occupations comes from the communication studies scholar Greig de Peuter.[16] He understands precariousness as 'existential, financial, and social insecurity' made worse by the demand that workers be flexible with their time. 'Freelancing, contract work, solo self-employment, temporary work, and part-time jobs' are the usual forms of employment relationship.

These contractual relationships go hand-in-hand with passionate work and exploitation, low pay and internships, and being 'always on'. Pay, or more accurately lack of pay, is central to understanding the meaning of precariousness in cultural and creative jobs. Pay is also, in our analysis, intimately related to the idea of economic resources, or capital.

There are, of course, lots of different varieties of unpaid work. This ranges from the sort of free labour we might do every day as part of our activities on social media platforms (which benefits their owners and advertising companies), through to formal positions that are not remunerated, for example unpaid internships. We're concentrating on the latter, more formal, forms of unpaid labour.

Is everyone working for free?

Figures 6.1–6.3 summarise how many of our interviewees had worked for free in various different ways. In the original survey, we asked people whether they'd ever worked for free at all. We also asked about the varieties of free work, such as whether

Age

18–29	93%
30–39	93
40–49	98
50+	92

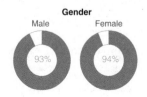

Gender

Male — 93%
Female — 94%

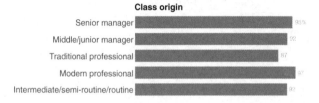

Class origin

Senior manager	95%
Middle/junior manager	92
Traditional professional	87
Modern professional	97
Intermediate/semi-routine/routine	92

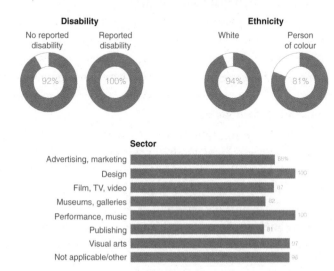

Disability

No reported disability — 92%
Reported disability — 100%

Ethnicity

White — 94%
Person of colour — 81%

Sector

Advertising, marketing	89%
Design	100
Film, TV, video	87
Museums, galleries	82
Performance, music	100
Publishing	81
Visual arts	97
Not applicable/other	98

Figure 6.1 Fractions of interviewees having ever worked for free.

they'd done an unpaid internship, and whether they'd been paid for all the hours they'd worked in the previous month.

These figures are broken down by several demographic factors: age group, ethnic group, social class origin, whether they report having a disability, gender, and which part of the cultural and creative industries they work in.

These results make it clear that working for free is endemic across our interviewees working in creative jobs. There are some small differences, but the story is clear. Importantly, almost identical fractions of respondents from different age groups reported having worked for free at some stage. This is an important point to keep in mind for the rest of the analysis in this chapter.

In contrast, while there are very few differences in whether the people we interviewed have worked for free at all, there are some systematic differences in whether they have ever done unpaid internships, as detailed in Figure 6.2.

The key difference is by age, with 52% of the under-thirties having done an unpaid internship, compared with 5% of over-fifties; however, there are also large gender differences, with far more women having done unpaid internships than men. The other main difference is by sector; a majority of respondents working in film, television, and video have done unpaid internships, while only a small fraction of respondents working in visual arts have done so.

There are some differences by social origin. Those from senior managerial and modern professional backgrounds are far more likely to have done unpaid internships. This is perhaps because they are most likely to have economic capital and be able to afford unpaid internships.

This final set of graphs in Figure 6.3 shows the distribution of having not been paid for all hours worked in the last month.

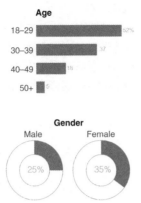

Age

- 18–29 — 52%
- 30–39 — 37
- 40–49 — 18
- 50+ — 5

Gender

Male — 25%
Female — 35%

Class origin

- Senior manager — 37%
- Middle/junior manager — 23
- Traditional professional — 24
- Modern professional — 43
- Intermediate/semi-routine/routine — 22

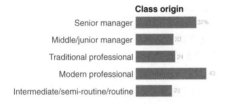

Disability

No reported disability — 31%
Reported disability — 36%

Ethnicity

White — 33%
Person of colour — 33%

Sector

- Advertising, marketing — 44%
- Design — 35
- Film, TV, video — 52
- Museums, galleries — 32
- Performance, music — 30
- Publishing — 29
- Visual arts — 17
- Not applicable/other — 29

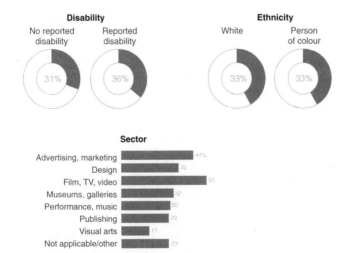

Figure 6.2 Fractions of interviewees having undertaken an unpaid internship.

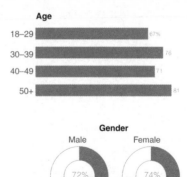

Age

18–29   67%
30–39   76
40–49   71
50+   81

Gender

Male   Female
72%   74%

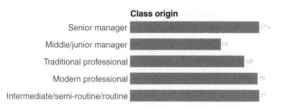

Class origin

Senior manager   77%
Middle/junior manager   64
Traditional professional   68
Modern professional   76
Intermediate/semi-routine/routine   77

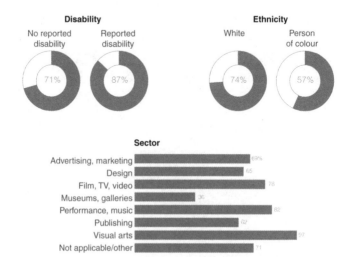

Disability

No reported disability   Reported disability
71%   87%

Ethnicity

White   Person of colour
74%   57%

Sector

Advertising, marketing   69%
Design   65
Film, TV, video   78
Museums, galleries   36
Performance, music   82
Publishing   62
Visual arts   97
Not applicable/other   71

Figure 6.3 Fractions of interviewees not having been paid for all hours worked in the last month.

The key difference here is that those sectors where relatively few respondents have done unpaid internships are those sectors where workers are most likely to have worked unpaid in the last month. This indicates different varieties of unpaid work across cultural occupations.

There is again an interesting difference by age in this data. Figure 6.2 suggested our younger respondents are far more likely to have done unpaid internships than our older respondents. In Figure 6.3 we see that 81% of respondents aged over fifty report having not been paid for all hours worked, compared with 67% of under-thirties. This raises questions around whether this reflects genuine inequality in hours worked and hours paid for, or whether the older respondents are more aware of the hours for which they have not been paid.

The survey results from our interviewees suggested that, on the surface, working for free, and thus an associated form of precariousness is a common experience for this sample of creative workers. This is what much of the research on creative work suggests we should expect to find.

A useful example of this research comes from Neil Percival and David Hesmondhalgh,[17] looking at unpaid labour in the film and television sectors. In their survey work, they found differences in attitudes towards free or unpaid labour between those who were established, long-standing workers and newcomers to both sectors. Newer entrants to film and television work were either more ambivalent or more willing to highlight the benefits of unpaid labour. More established workers had a very negative view of unpaid work.

Age and career stage are therefore crucial, grounded in the 'acceptance on the part of young workers of what they feel to be an inevitability'. This acceptance is related to the identification of the non-financial benefits of unpaid labour, contrasted with older and more established workers' resistance and critiques of the practice.

Our analysis develops this by adding another layer of stratification, that of social class. The seemingly endemic nature of unpaid work masks the important role of social class in shaping the experience of unpaid work. Initially, the key division in our data seems to be about age. Older, established, creative workers experienced a very different labour market and social safety net early in their career. Yet, underneath this headline division, we'll see how class matters as much as age.

Unpaid labour and the generational divide

We can see the experience of unpaid work for younger interviewees well captured by Molly, a twenty-something White, female artist, whose parents were senior managers. She offers a bleak vision of artistic work, having never been paid for her practice, and only having received money intermittently from the art world for invigilating exhibitions or gallery openings:

> I've never been paid to make or do anything … I would see anything that I've done within a gallery context, that's all been unpaid. Yes, I have a studio and I do exhibitions relatively frequently and I have done a residency and have worked for a couple of galleries but it's always been unpaid.

However, her story of the relentlessness of unpaid internships is common across our interviewees as a core means of establishing a career. Louisa, a White woman in her thirties who was working in publishing and was the daughter of a journalist, had a similar narrative to Molly:

> I joined publishing job agencies and they told me that there was no way in hell that I was getting a job in publishing without an unpaid internship.

These stories were extremely common across the interview dataset for younger people, albeit nuanced by occupation. Molly, an artist, experienced unpaid work as the inability to receive remuneration for her practice. A similar narrative came in design and performance. For those working in areas with stronger institutions, such as museums or publishing, the unpaid internship was the more common story.

These experiences directly contrast with older people's experience of working unpaid or for free. For older and more established creative workers, the story was one of underpay or choice and autonomy. We can use three short comments by way of illustration. Jo, a middle-class origin woman in her forties, was a freelancer working to support a variety of arts organisations when we interviewed her. She experienced *under*pay but she rejected the idea of working for free itself:

> Not for free. No. Not necessarily. I have done projects where the fee did not in any way relate to the amount of work that needed doing. I have never done something completely for free.

Gerald, a White, middle-class origin senior curator in his fifties, based in London, and Rose, a designer in her forties, offered a perspective more grounded in their autonomy and ability to choose, and to 'gift' free work, whether as part of formal occupations or as a volunteer:

> Well I have chosen to do bits and bobs for free, when I have been a consultant. I think partly that is a generational thing.

I'm a trustee and before that I was a volunteer, I always will try and do something which is consciously free.

These comments point to important differences between older and younger creative workers in their experiences of unpaid work. It develops the distinction set out by Percival and Hesmondhalgh.[18] It is not only attitudes, but also *experiences* of unpaid work that are differentiated by age and stage of career.

We understand this differentiation, in the context of social class, by turning to consider how our interviewees drew boundaries between work and non-work when thinking about pay.

It is obvious to state that those with more resources, more economic capital, are more able to afford unpaid work. We saw this intersect with age in our interview data. The older, established, middle-class origin cultural and creative workers were most able to blur life and work in a sustainable way. This was very different to our younger, working-class origin respondents.

The narrations of unpaid work attached to this division is crucial in explaining why unpaid work is seen as an inescapable part of cultural work. If everyone, regardless of demographic position, is working for free, then it becomes hard to mount direct forms of resistance to the practice. It is just, as one of our older interviewees suggested, that 'There's no way that you get paid to do the arts.'

The story of resignation, and the attendant ability to resist, is socially distributed. This is demonstrated by Anna, a White, middle-class origin woman in her thirties, working in publishing. Anna's story is of a blurred line between work and not-work, and of resistance to free or unpaid labour afforded to those who have been successful:

It's interesting to note what different people think of as work. When I started I didn't think of it as work and so if someone asked me to do a reading I wouldn't think oh they are not paying me, like I am doing something for free, it was more like they were doing me a favour ... Now I don't really do readings for free that often unless I really want to do it. Now I would say probably 70% of the things I get offered do have a fee attached, but it might not be a huge fee but, and I would be more bothered now because I see it as my career, and also I increasingly don't like doing things if I am not going to be paid for doing them.

We have deliberately chosen a voice from affluent social origins to illustrate the blurred boundaries of work and non-work, along with a sense of resistance. This narrative of the blurred boundaries between work and life or leisure, alongside the problem of drawing distinctions between underpay, volunteering, or gifting work, are common issues across our dataset. Yet we have presented a narrative of someone from an affluent class origin very deliberately, to highlight the importance of class and social origins.

Class, solidarity, and unpaid work

Our middle-class origin respondents who were earlier in their careers narrated a sense of autonomy and choice over engagements with unpaid work. Our working-class origin respondents offered more constrained and pessimistic visions of working life.

We turn now to three pairs of narratives to illustrate the classed difference in how unpaid work is stratified. Anna, in our previous section, spoke of unpaid work as a choice related to her developing career. That choice was underpinned by her resources, including home ownership in London, and the affordances associated with her social class. Georgie, a designer in her early thirties, was typical of the middle-class origin, younger respondents:

> I think it's always been a choice to work. I've done some place-ments which were unpaid and I've done some projects which were unpaid or very, very low paid but I never had to do them because I didn't have other work … I haven't personally felt like, 'If I didn't do unpaid work, I'd never be able to get a job.'

In contrast to Veronica, also in design and in her thirties, but from a working-class social origin:

> There were girls in my year, I think, in the summer were spending, I think it was, six months in London, in Shoreditch, being able to work for free, whereas I could only do it for three months and that was a struggle. So, it is something that you really should be doing as a fashion designer because it really does help you, but then if you don't have the money to do it, you don't really get a chance to grow, so it's not really fair.

Veronica's perception of the advantages of social class and the constraints of lack of resources, coupled with the impact on her career, shapes her sense of agency. She feels she had to work for free to compete with those for whom it is a choice. We can see agency and resistance demonstrated by Ellie, a theatre maker in her twenties, discussing her experience of low pay on her first job:

> I think it is good that I had such a precarious horrible experience straight out of [drama school] because it just meant that I just thought I am never going to be in that position. If I am going to not be paid a proper wage at least I am going to enjoy myself doing it, and you know if someone asks me to do something that

> I don't want to do and they are effectively not paying me to do it
> I am just going to say no.

In contrast, our working-class origin workers found their working lives to be much more of a struggle, with success defined by the ability to be paid, rather than creative freedom or autonomy, as told by Sean, an artist in his early thirties:

> Yes, it's hard to earn a full-time living. You have to do other jobs that you don't particularly want to do. You have to compete with lots of other people, but for very few opportunities, and it's very, very difficult … just getting a few opportunities would be success for me, and occasionally getting paid, perhaps.

And Christine, an illustrator at the same age, but an earlier career stage, having retrained from a routine manual job:

> I have done pieces for free to go on there but it has all been free at the moment. I have had a couple of people approach me with their ideas of projects but it seems like there is never really much of a budget, and people either expect you to do something for next to nothing or either for free for them so I don't really want to go down that road if I don't have to.

Christine offers a sense of hope of being able to avoid the trap of always working for free and thus ultimately being exploited. This sense of hope is different to the sense of control, choice, and autonomy narrated by our younger interviewees from affluent social origins.

We have a division in the stories and experiences of unpaid work. For some, unpaid work is bound up with resistance and the ability to refuse. For others there is inevitability and only a sense of hope that it will be something they can avoid or escape.

Our data suggests these differences serve to reinforce the sense of inevitability of unpaid work for those from less affluent social origins. This is particularly as the more affluent are able to blur the distinction between work and life.

We started the chapter discussing the joys of cultural work. We saw how, to quote Lauren again, '[having a] job that is also my hobby to some extent' was an important factor in cultural workers' attachment to their occupations. When we think about this comment in the context of experiences of unpaid labour it takes on a negative dimension. As John, a young man of working-class origin making his way in television and film, told us:

> This isn't actually a career. It's just a glorified hobby because everyone else is managing to do it for free or doing it for cheap.

It means unpaid labour, in a variety of forms, is more likely. It also obscures how unpaid labour is more likely to be exploitation for those from working-class origins. In contrast it may be a choice for those from middle-class origins.

The class distinction intersects with age. The blurring of work and life is a discourse that is also prevalent in older workers, regardless of social origin. However, for older workers, the work/life distinction associated with their occupation was enabled by various aspects of the social state.

Older workers told us of access to housing and (un)employment benefits. They also discussed support from the public state, rather than private familial affluence. This is an important factor in understanding our older interviewees' attitudes, and experiences, of unpaid work.

For a minority of our older respondents, when asked about having worked unpaid or for free they would simply say no, moving on to the next question in the schedule, but, tellingly, would point to some element of volunteering or gifts as a form of unpaid work. As with elite social origin younger respondents, the ability to choose was key.

Hazel, a White, working-class origin woman in her fifties, was working in publishing at the time of interview. She was blunt when asked about working for free:

No, and I never would. No, no, no, no, no. Never work for free as a writer. Sorry, I write poetry and I do that for free, and perform it in public for free, but no. I do that for fun.

While Graham, a White, working-class origin man in his sixties who was working as a film and television writer, give us a sense of his autonomy:

Only by choice … as a favour … it has been a pleasure to do it … it has never been onerous really.

They were all, reflexively, able to situate the ability to think of free or unpaid work as a choice. This choice was perceived to be the result of the social structure and social support they had earlier in their careers. Felicity, a theatre maker in her fifties from a middle-class background, is a good example:

I've been unbelievably fortunate, I really have. You know, I come from a generation where there were no university fees, you know? You could get … I've been unbelievably lucky.

The sense of being fortunate and coming from the 'right' generation here is crucial, as it shapes expectations of working life and cultural, creative or artistic practice. Moreover, the narratives of luck and creative freedom track the narratives offered by those from affluent class origins detailed in the previous section. We'll come back to the idea of 'luck' when we look at men running cultural occupations in Chapter 10.

For now, it is crucial we keep one point in mind. Even though narratives of older workers and younger, middle-class origin, workers seem similar, the generational difference matters. It matters for how we should understand the possible consequences of a shared sense that 'everyone' works for free.

We close with two comments to illustrate this point. The first is from Jenny, a middle-class origin woman in her fifties, who was working on marketing for cultural sector organisations. She focused on the funding opportunities coming from the state and associated London institutions, meaning she was always paid for her 'niche' cultural work:

> Nobody ever got paid much, but there was quite a lot of public subsidy swishing around at that point, particularly for the sort of work that I was working in; niche, diverse work. We all got paid. I mean, nobody got paid anything like everybody was earning in the City at that point, but we all knew that. I have to say, at that point, I don't think anybody really felt they were getting paid that badly. We were having so much fun.

Kerry, a working-class origin woman in her fifties working in publishing, had a similar narrative. It was a story of being paid, being supported by the social state, and (later on in the interview) being able to work unpaid on a variety of her own interests and projects:

> We went to Edinburgh in 1990 and we made money and paid ourselves like 500 quid and that was probably the last time that was possible actually. So stand up, impro, beginning to write but not get paid for it, and occasionally bits of acting work. A couple

of ads occasionally, which of course was loads of money. And
I think I probably, I lived on the Enterprise Allowance Scheme.
I got the Enterprise Allowance Scheme to become a stand up.

For our older interviewees there was a sense of a social state
supporting their understanding of unpaid work as a choice. For
younger people the lack of social support means individuals
only have their own resources in a labour market that expects
and demands unpaid work. Those who have the economic capital, from middle-class origins, are able to meet these demands.
They have some degree of choice or autonomy, whether or not
they resisted expectations. Those from working-class origins
had no such resources, whether individual or social.

Conclusion

Kerry and Jenny's stories point towards the importance of social
support from the state in sustaining early career creatives. At
the same time, they raise questions about making comparisons.
We must be cautious about the numbers enjoying such support,
particularly given the relative size of the creative industries, the
numbers accessing higher education, and the growth of events
such as the Edinburgh Fringe. We're going to examine these
sorts of historical comparisons in detail in the next chapter.

For now, we are going to conclude by restating the three key
messages from our analysis of the experience of unpaid work.
First is that, as we know from existing research, cultural workers
love their jobs. They are highly committed to cultural work and
see the downsides as a worthy trade-off for the vocation of being
a cultural worker that some felt they were compelled to do. It is
also worth it for avoiding a regular or 'normal' job.

As Angela McRobbie and others have noted, the avoidance of a 'normal' job and the veneration of occupations that can be insecure and uncertain can have terrible negative consequences. This is especially important as a lack of security in terms of holiday and sick pay, occupational pensions, as well as routine and secure working patterns, is rarely the subject of celebratory discourses of cultural and creative occupations.

The good economic news that started this chapter rarely engages with the problems of being a cultural worker. Unless we take seriously the trade-offs associated with cultural work then we are likely to see the continuation of the labour market inequalities we discussed in Chapter 3. This is in addition to the broader debates about middle-class professions in general becoming 'precarious'.

This connects directly to our second point. The downsides of cultural occupations, such as the inescapable demand for unpaid work, seem to be experienced by all creative workers. Certainly, our interviewees had not escaped working for free.

The prevalence of unpaid work creates a sense that low and no pay is how the system works. A sense that low and no pay is a *characteristic* of cultural occupations, rather than the *consequence* of decisions. These decisions may be by governments, in terms of funding levels and support. Decisions about pay are also made by private companies and institutions, in terms of where risks and profits are distributed.

The sense that unpaid work is how cultural occupations function not only obscures the uneven distribution of risks and profits. It also hides how differently unpaid work is experienced. This is our third point. The shared experience of unpaid work creates a false sense of social solidarity. The experience of working unpaid, as we have shown, is distinct according to age and class origin. It is, in fact, *not* a shared experience at all.

Age matters. Over thirty years ago, when many of our older interviewees were starting their cultural occupations, the support systems were very different for a much smaller set of entrants into a smaller cultural sector.

Class matters. Those with higher levels of economic, social, and cultural resources are better able to survive a hostile labour market and the cost of living close to cultural work opportunities. In this chapter we've seen that greater economic resources give access to much more rewarding forms of unpaid work, and they allow individuals to carry the economic costs of no pay in return for their creative labour.

The three issues we have discussed in this chapter can be related to broader economic and social changes. To give just one example, we could point to the impact of digital transformations on specific sectors, such as journalism and music, radically changing the expectations of pay and deepening the expectation that people work for nothing. We could also discuss potential oversupplies of entrants into creative labour markets, meaning those with higher levels of economic resources are better placed to compete with their peers.

Yet there is another story of social change. This is the move from social to individual responsibility for getting in and getting on in cultural occupations. This change, as we saw in the introduction to the book, is part of more general shifts in contemporary society.

In the case of working for free, the consequence is not only that those without economic resources, those from working-class origins, are less likely to get in and get on in cultural jobs. We saw these cultural labour force patterns in Chapter 3.

The consequence is also that the shared experience of working for free means the problem of unpaid work may go unrecognised. In particular, we've seen how even though the experiences of unpaid work differ by age and class, the story is still that 'everyone' works for free. How can we generate recognition that the burden of free work falls more heavily on younger working-class origin workers if our cultural occupations all think 'there's no way that you get paid to do the arts'?

7

Was there a golden age?

Introduction: Lisa's experience of social mobility

Well if you look at what's happened culturally, and you look at the
'50s and the '60s, and you look at the rise of somebody like Joe
Orton from a leafier upper working class estate … Then if you
go into the '70s and the early '80s, when culture was community-
driven, you look at all the political stuff that came out, not all of
them were posh kids. Quite a lot of them were working class kids
… it's because it was being run by working class people. In the
'50s and '40s it had been run by very upper-middle-class people,
and then suddenly there was this massive churn where culture
became radicalised … I was formed and made during that time,
and maybe if I was born now, or I was 20 now, I might look at
theatre as having huge thick glass walls …

What was happening there was, 15 years ago, I couldn't have
gone, but the government decided to open up university and pay
us to go. My fees were paid for, and then I was given a grant
each month, which was generous. We went to university, we had
an opinion, somebody listened to us. Whereas before, I think, in
the old fashioned working classes in the '50s and '60s, we were
told, 'Nobody wants to listen to you, you set your pipe, you put
your flat cap on and get your pipe lit and that's it.' We came out,
we were hopeful, we didn't have to live at home, we could live

independently, we were in London, and suddenly, 'Shit, there is nothing we can't do.' The upper middle class had been doing that for years, it never occurred to us, people who are now in their mid-fifties, that this was a possibility. That, I think, was a flourishing, because we also took over business, and we took over culture, and we took over music, and film-making. Suddenly there was this tsunami of working-class people who were just going, 'We've got a voice', and people listened to us.

Lisa was in her mid-fifties when we met her. A White, working-class origin woman, she had a long and successful career as a writer and theatre maker. In many ways she was a perfect illustration of social mobility into cultural occupations.

Lisa's recollections of the social and cultural changes during her career connect directly to the data we've just seen in Chapter 6. There we saw our older, established cultural workers talking about how the state was important in supporting their careers. Our older interviewees also discussed their sense of luck, having been born and entering careers at a time when things were perhaps easier compared to their younger colleagues now trying to get in and get on.

Lisa's story is about her perception of the success of working-class origin people in the cultural sector. This connects us back to Chapter 3's discussion of who, currently, works in cultural occupations. There is a stark contrast between Lisa's story and the current dominance of those from middle-class origins.

In Lisa's story there is a sense that the past was a more equal time, when people from working-class origins had more opportunities. There was access to education, access to work and professional progress, and access to culture.

The narratives exemplified by Lisa suggested there was a strength and critical mass in working-class origin creative workers that is not present today. This idea is very common in public discourse, for example in comments by several high-profile working-class origin actors, such as Julie Walters and Julie Hesmondhalgh.[1] They lament that if they were trying to enter the profession now they would not be able to do so.

This narrative also applies to discussions of cultural education. The debates we highlighted in Chapter 5 are echoed in public discourse. Here the same figures worrying about getting in and getting on in cultural professions worry about cultural education. Fees and loans are seen as a barrier that would have put them off entering higher education, as compared to the era of grants and other forms of state support.[2]

We are not mentioning this to comment on the accuracy of these statements. Rather we highlight the *perception* that social mobility has declined in cultural professions.

In this chapter we delve into data on this issue. We'll see that, in fact, things have *always* been difficult for working-class origin people trying to make it into cultural jobs.

This point is important when we are thinking about the relationship between culture and inequality. It seems that cultural jobs have, for a long time, been exclusive, irrespective of the vast social and cultural changes we've seen during most of our cultural workers' professional lives. As a result, we need to understand *why* this is the case.

The long-standing problem of social mobility into cultural occupations can't be understood without thinking about how class intersects with other characteristics. These include our key focus of gender and ethnicity, along with things like geography and the dominance of London. In doing so we think about the patterns of social mobility into creative occupations. As we understand the *patterns* we open the space for a discussion of the *experiences* of social mobility in Chapter 8.

Social class and social mobility

What are we talking about when we talk about class and social mobility? In Chapter 3 we saw that social class is a complicated and contested term. Social mobility is equally tricky.[3]

In this chapter we're looking at people's class origins, which are based on the occupation of the main wage earner in the household when a person was growing up. Usually this measure means finding out their parent or caregiver's job when the individual was aged fourteen.[4] These jobs are then analysed on the basis of the NS-SEC (also introduced in Chapter 3).[5]

This is not the only way to think about social mobility.[6] There's a major debate about whether incomes or occupations are the right measure to understand social mobility.[7] In keeping with the rest of the analysis in the book, we're going to focus on occupations.

Academics are interested in how questions of social mobility – people's class origins and destinations – play out across whole societies. They look at the chances, or probability, of moving or staying in a class or income band. This then lets researchers talk about whether societies are open and fluid, with lots of movement, or closed and static.[8]

The field captures how, for some people, there is no movement, and the class they are born into is the same class they end up in. For other people, there is mobility between classes, for example when those who grew up in households with working-class parents end up in middle-class occupations. This is upward mobility. Downward mobility describes when those who grew up in households with middle-class parents end up in working-class occupations.

We can obviously be critical of this approach. It is difficult to measure the class origin of some social groups, for example people who were raised in care. Some, through parental ill-health or other misfortune, experience much greater deprivation than their parents' occupation would suggest.

There are several critical questions about social mobility. These range from the extent to which social mobility is happening, and improvements or deteriorations in its rate; through whether specific interventions are effective at enhancing or encouraging social mobility; to the legitimacy of the term and the associated politics and ideologies.[9]

There is also sometimes seen to be a conflict between the social mobility agenda and social justice. Some argue that rather than worrying about the ability of individuals to 'escape' their social starting point, we should be concerned with improving the conditions of all people who lack socio-economic privilege.[10]

These ideas are not directly in conflict. Social mobility is only as important as the gap between classes. If society is more equal, then the *risk* of downward social mobility, or the *reward* of upward mobility, is less important. The greater the loss of privilege associated with downward social mobility, the more that the privileged might use their (economic, social, or cultural) resources to preserve the social position of their families.[11]

This means it will be harder for those not born into privilege to break into more advantaged positions, such as professional occupations. We saw a really clear illustration of this in Chapter 6's discussion of economic capital and unpaid work. Those from middle-class origins were much more able to survive the demand for unpaid work and thus make it into cultural jobs.

This is just one example of how social mobility research is vital to help us understand creative occupations. In particular, as we have shown in Chapter 3, focusing on class origins can reveal patterns of inequality in occupations that claim to be open and meritocratic.

Social mobility in the UK

Describing social mobility can be difficult. The two key terms here are *relative* and *absolute*. These two ways of describing social mobility are distinct, and the difference is important in what it tells us about society.

Relative mobility refers to the chances, the odds and probability, of an individual from one social class ending up in a different social class, adjusting for overall changes to the labour market. The *relative* rate of social mobility is usually what academics refer to when they talk about whether social mobility is going up or down. The rates of *relative* social mobility in the UK have been fairly stable for several decades, although there is debate about the exact numbers.

Absolute social mobility is not about chances, odds, and probability. *Absolute* social mobility is about numbers, the volume, of people moving between social classes. This has changed considerably over time. This sounds contradictory, but we can explain it by thinking about two trends in British society.

The sorts of occupations constituting the British economy have changed. There are now many more people in professional occupations, including accountants and marketing managers, than there were 100 years ago. There are also now far fewer people working routine manual occupations, such as coal miners or factory workers.[12]

This change means that the proportion of people working in more skilled, professional, or managerial occupations has increased. The proportion working in less skilled, routine, occupations has gone down. Because the fraction of middle-class occupations in British society has increased, so has the fraction of people who were brought up in middle-class households in the 1980s or 1990s. This is compared to the 1950s and 1960s when there were more people working in manufacturing and manual labour occupations.

Second, most social mobility has been in an upward direction. Those from working-class origins have been more likely to move 'up' the ladder and end up in professional occupations. This is compared to their middle-class peers moving 'down' into working-class occupations. The middle class have stayed middle class in part as a result of their dominance of the increasing proportion of middle-class jobs in the economy.

This is for a variety of reasons. Some of these relate to the economy and society. With an expansion in middle-class jobs there was more room for both working-class origin people to move 'up', and for middle-class people to maintain their position. In addition, as we encountered in Chapter 5, middle-class parents can invest more social, economic, and cultural resources in protecting their children and making sure they stay in the same social strata in which they start.

Sociologists tell a particular story about absolute and relative rates of social mobility in the UK.[13] After the Second World War there was an expansion of professional and managerial jobs. This 'long boom' in these occupations meant there was more 'room at the top'. Working-class origin men[14] entered these professions along with their middle-class peers. The absolute numbers of working-class origin men getting professional jobs went up. Yet changes in the overall structure of the economy means the relative chances of working-class men being socially mobile have been stable.

The long boom in social mobility was driven by the expansion of professional occupations, rather than by policy interventions aimed at improving social mobility. This is a very important point. It suggests structural changes to the type of jobs that are in the economy, rather than specific policies such as grammar schools, were the cause.[15]

Rates of relative social mobility may have been stable, with some evidence they were going upward, but they have still been relatively low. The chances of men born into NS-SEC I/II families (doctors, teachers) ending up in the same class (rather than in working-class jobs) are around six times greater than the chances of men born into working-class families ending up in NS-SEC I/II jobs (rather than staying in working-class[16] jobs).

The long boom started in the middle of the last century. More recent evidence seems to be that the expansion of the professional and managerial classes has slowed if not stagnated. This is where we see lots of debate over social mobility.

Narratives of a crisis in social mobility have motivated policy activity, for example the government's Social Mobility Commission.[17] This has done much to highlight more general inequalities associated with education and geography. But from the occupational approach we still see a much more complex landscape where many interventions have limited success in the face of structural changes in British economy and society.

Social mobility as a problem for cultural and creative industries

Alongside studies of social mobility between 'big' class groups sits research that looks at specific groups of occupations, known as 'microclass' mobility.[18] This uses a more detailed, granular level to look at movements into and out of specific occupational groups – such as doctors, lawyers, or teachers.

Microclass mobility is particularly relevant for thinking about cultural and creative workers. It provides a framework for analysing whether specific occupations tend to be more socially exclusive than others. For example, we can ask if the children of doctors become doctors.

The jobs with the strongest associations between generations tend to be those where credentials are essential, such as medicine, and the associations are most common between fathers and sons.[19] We can also connect this back to 'big-class' studies of social mobility. We do not only need to know why so many children of doctors become doctors. We also need to understand why so many of the remaining children of doctors go into other professional jobs, rather than becoming bus drivers.

There has been relatively little analysis of cultural and creative workers by academics focused on occupational or income social mobility. Cultural and media studies have been the main academic fields grappling with social mobility into cultural occupations. In this chapter we're going to bring these two areas together.

Our discussion of the 'long boom' and associated analysis of social mobility is the sociological side of the story. The other, cultural and media studies, has looked more directly at cultural production.

The cultural analyst Mark Banks[20] draws on the sociological work we've already discussed to argue that it is likely there was an expansion of *absolute* social mobility into creative occupations during the long boom from the end of the 1950s. However, he is cautious as to the *relative* rates of mobility.

Banks sounds the alarm at the prospect that rates of both absolute and relative social mobility may be declining in cultural occupations at the moment. We've shown in Chapter 3 that cultural occupations are *currently* highly unequal, with clear class inequalities. How has this situation developed over time?

In Chapter 3 we noted how most cultural and creative occupations are categorised as NS-SEC I and II, managerial and professional, jobs. They sit alongside doctors, lawyers, teachers, and nurses as well as business managers.

Some of these occupations have changed classification over time. This is because the relative socio-economic status of jobs change. Journalism, for example, has moved from a job that most people trained for through doing an apprenticeship, to one with the status of a profession, undertaken largely by graduates.

A particularly complex example is occupations relating to craft, which are retrospectively difficult to disentangle from skilled manufacturing. In the current SOC 2010 coding craft occupations are grouped together with skilled manufacturing, rather than with arts or cultural jobs. This is one of the reasons we haven't included crafts in the analysis presented in this chapter, as they would be too inconsistently coded.

It is also worth highlighting that we are only looking at creative occupations, not creative businesses. We noted in the introduction to the book that there is a crucial difference between creative occupations and creative industries. Not all jobs in creative industries are in creative occupations.

For example, in this chapter, box office staff in theatres are not included in the analysis, but a photographer employed by a manufacturing firm is. That is not at all a comment on the relative importance of box office staff to theatres! Rather it recognises the difference between customer service as a cluster of occupations in the economy, and photographers as a cluster of occupations.

In this chapter our 'core cultural' occupations are those settled in the academic literature as artists, musicians, and actors, and those working in publishing, media, libraries, museums, and galleries.

To do the analysis we are using the Office for National Statistics Longitudinal Study (ONS-LS).[21] This is the dataset we use for our analysis of mothers in Chapter 9. The ONS-LS is a dataset of individuals in England and Wales created from a 1% sample of Census returns, chosen using four (undisclosed) birthdays, linking records from each Census from 1971 to 2011.[22]

One of the reasons there has not been a detailed analysis of social mobility in creative and cultural jobs has been a problem of data quantity. These jobs are not a large part of the economy, when compared with working in heath, or financial and legal services. The ONS-LS means data quality is good, and the sample size is large.

It also contains details of other household members at each Census.[23] We therefore have access to the occupations of the study members' parents when they are children, which we use as the basis for determining class origin (using whichever parent has the more advantaged NS-SEC classification, if both work). This deals with the problem of adults (mis)remembering their parents' occupations, which could have been an issue in the LFS data we discussed in Chapter 3. Indeed, the ONS-LS tells a similar story to the LFS's picture of the social origins and demographics of creative workers.

We defined four cohorts, which are groups of people born 1953–62, 1963–72, 1973–82, and 1983–92. For each cohort, the members were aged between nine and eighteen in the first Census we use for our analysis, and therefore closest to age fourteen for recording parental occupations. They are aged between nineteen and twenty-eight at the second Census, either studying or early in their working lives. In the following censuses they are aged between 29–38, 39–48, and finally 49–58. For the oldest cohort we have four observations during adulthood (19–28, 29–38, 39–48, and in 2011 they were aged 49–58). For the youngest cohort, we only have one observation, as they were between nineteen and twenty-eight in 2011.

We are including analysis of the social origins of creative workers in their twenties, which is not usually the case in much social mobility research, as they are not considered to be occupationally mature.[24] However, including workers in their twenties reflects what we know about cultural occupations from the research literature, and it enables us to compare the social class origins of four different generations or cohorts. In addition, none of what we've uncovered *depends* on including people in their twenties, rather their data just confirms the trends we describe below.

At the same time, we will see in Chapter 9 that some individuals may come to creative work from other occupations, for example becoming artists or writers later in life. We haven't yet found particular class based patterns on this issue, but as Chapter 9 will show, gender discrimination is a powerful force behind women being much more likely to leave creative work in their thirties.

Social mobility and cultural occupations: evidence from the ONS-LS

As we mentioned, most creative occupations are classed as NS-SEC I or II. For working class or intermediate origin people (NS-SEC III–VII) working in a creative occupation represents upward social mobility.

Table 7.1 shows the number of people in each of our four cohorts that ever report working in a 'core cultural' occupation. The largest subgroup is those that ever work as artists, musicians, or performers, followed by those working in media or publishing, and the smallest group are those in museums and libraries.

The total for all core cultural is slightly less than the sum of each creative occupation, as some people report more than one core cultural occupation across their careers. For completeness, the table shows the number ever reporting any occupation, and ever reporting one that is classified in NS-SEC I.

Notice that Cohort 4 has had reduced opportunity to have worked in any job over the course of their career: the maximum age of cohort members is twenty-eight, but some are only nineteen. In addition, the total number of people in each cohort varies – the first cohort is part of the baby boom generation, a population bulge caused by an increased post-war birth rate.

The differences in the size of the cohorts, in the length of their working lives, and the size of different sections of the creative economy over time, makes analysis of this data complex. However, what we are most interested in is social origins of our core cultural workers. We would like to know how class origin shapes the proportion of those in each cohort that work in creative jobs.

Table 7.1 ONS-LS cohort sizes, by occupational group

	Cohort (birth years)			
	1	2	3	4
	1953–62	1963–72	1973–82	1983–92
Ever any occupation	69,862	76,711	57,271	44,516
Ever artist, musician, performer	751	821	414	278
Ever media	404	531	444	218
Ever museums/libraries	201	103	80	25
Ever publishing	398	448	377	160
Ever core cultural	1,643	1,778	1,295	681
Ever NS-SEC I	12,999	14,157	9,873	3,527

Source: ONS Longitudinal Study, authors' analysis.

In Figure 7.1 we compare the social class origin of those from each cohort that ever report working in core cultural occupations to other occupations. In this chart we are only looking at the most and least privileged origins. We'll discuss other social origins later in the chapter.

This shows us that there has been a dramatic change in the social class origins of core cultural workers. There has been almost a doubling of the proportion of cultural workers from higher managerial and professional families, and almost a halving of the proportion from working-class (routine and semi-routine) families.

We can see that this has been accompanied by a similarly dramatic change in the social class origins of *all* cohort members who are working. The middle class has expanded, and the working class is now a smaller proportion of all jobs overall.

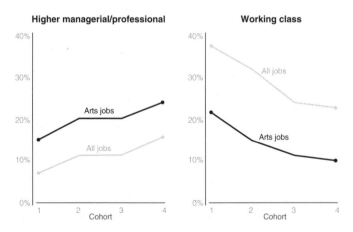

Figure 7.1 Percentage of LS members in core cultural vs any job, by parental NS-SEC.

This analysis reflects academic research about social mobility. The cohorts we are analysing, no matter what their occupation, have experienced the 'long boom'. This is the expansion of professional jobs that Goldthorpe and others have identified, and that Banks discussed in relation to creative work. Each cohort is more likely than the previous one to have had parents in professional and managerial work, and less likely to have had parents working in working-class jobs.

This has important implications for how we understand social mobility in cultural jobs. It also helps to contextualise the interventions of high-profile working-class origin creative workers who are worried about social mobility.

Members of Cohort 1 were in their late forties or in their fifties at the time of the 2011 Census. They are right to see the younger generation of creative workers as having much more privileged class origins than theirs and their peers. For Cohort 1 – our Gary Oldmans and Imelda Stauntons, our Grayson Perrys and Sarah Lucases – working-class origins are in fact *more common* than higher managerial and professional origins.

What their perspective is missing is that this is true of *all* working people. The patterns we see for younger core creative workers are also representative of younger cohorts in all jobs. So, for Cohort 4 – our Riz Ahmeds and Phoebe Waller-Bridges, our Ed Sheerans and Lily Allens – this situation has reversed. More privileged class origins, coming from a professional or managerial class origin, are now *twice as likely* for this group.

What this means is that there has been a clear decline in *absolute* social mobility into our core creative occupations. In 2011 there are fewer working-class origin people in our younger cohort who are working in cultural occupations, as compared with working-class origin people from the oldest cohort.

What are the odds of working-class people making it?

Let's think back to the distinction we introduced earlier in the chapter, between absolute and relative social mobility. Figure 7.1 seems to tell us something interesting, and counter-intuitive, about social mobility into cultural jobs. What is not clear from Figure 7.1 is whether the *chances* of a person from working-class social origins accessing creative work have changed. While absolute mobility has changed, what about relative chances of mobility into a cultural occupation?

Figure 7.1 also shows us how the overall class origin profile of all jobs has changed. The all jobs line shows the rise of middle-class origin people in society, as society has more of these occupations overall. It shows the corresponding decline of working-class jobs, and the associated decline of working-class origin individuals. We can obviously debate the way in which occupations are categorised and how we think of class. At this point, the easiest way to understand these social changes is that Britain has fewer coal miners, fewer factory workers, and more office workers than in the 1950s and 1960s when members of Cohort 1 were born.

Figure 7.1 sets up a discussion of the rate of *relative* social mobility into cultural occupations. To explore this we use statistical modelling of this data. This allows us to look simultaneously at the chances of someone accessing creative work according to their social class origins, their ethnic group, their gender, and their region of upbringing. This analysis also allows for changes over time in the underlying social structure, the proportion of parents in each social class category.

This means that we can test if the changes in the proportion of creative workers from each social class are simply in line with underlying trends. We can also test if those from working-class backgrounds have worse (or better) chances of accessing creative work. The analysis allows us to look at the change in this probability that is associated with each factor – social class origin, gender, ethnic group, region, and education – separately from the overall probability, which will vary according to the size of the sector at a given point.

Finally, we also take into account that there are substantial differences within each group. These differences change over time. For example women are less likely than men to be in paid work, but this difference changes over the decades.

In Figure 7.2 we show the odds ratio, or change in odds, that is associated with each of our factors. All of the data is taken from people's Census responses – including whether or not they

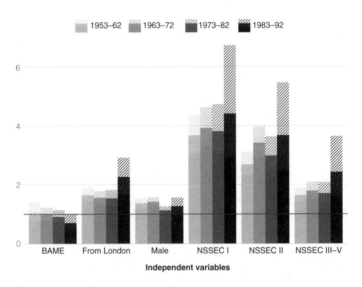

Figure 7.2 Odds ratios, probability of ever having a core cultural job 1981–2011.

were living in London during the Census that took place when they were between nine and eighteen.

Each of the bars shows the change in odds of creative work based on a particular characteristic, for example being from London or being a man. There are four bars for each category, one for each of our cohorts.

The confidence intervals for each of these bars – shown as the hashed areas above and below the tops of the bars – is a measure of uncertainty of the odds ratios. While we're not sure of the exact differences between these groups, as some of these groups are relatively small even with the large sample from the ONS, we're reasonably sure the differences are within these confidence intervals.

In the case of social class origin, the reference category is having parents in routine and semi-routine (working-class) work. People with higher managerial and professional social origins have about four times the odds of at some point having a cultural job, as compared with working-class origin people. For lower managerial and professional origins it is about three times the odds, and intermediate occupations just under twice the odds.

So far this analysis tells a very similar story to what we had seen previously. What we can now see is that, in terms of class, *there is no big difference in the relationship between social class origin and the probability of a cultural job between the cohorts.* The bars are of a similar height, and differences between them are smaller than the confidence intervals.

The story of relative mobility, the chances, of getting a cultural job for a working-class person have been consistent over time. *The sector was exclusive in the early 1980s when Cohort 1 entered cultural occupations; it is exclusive now.*

According to this analysis, social class origin is a key factor in access to cultural jobs. Men have slightly higher odds of having a cultural job, while being from London is also advantageous (and it seems that this is possibly increasing). Belonging to an ethnic minority does not seem to be strongly associated with the probability of having a core creative job, having controlled for class, but we need to treat this data with caution.[25]

There are many reasons for the central role social class plays in keeping cultural occupations exclusive. These can be related to practical problems, such as pay. We saw this in Chapter 6's discussion of how class interacts with unpaid labour. There is also the influence of taste and cultural capital, along with social networks and 'who you know', as we saw in Chapters 3, 4, and 5. We're going to see how class operates, and may be even more crucial than practical issues of pay, when we discuss experiences of social mobility in Chapter 8.

The role of education

Our analysis shows a strong class gradient in the probability of ever having a core cultural job. At the same time, many organisations report that they can only employ qualified candidates. This could mean the inequalities in access to higher education (including vocational arts training) is the cause of a lack of diversity of candidates for cultural jobs. We'll encounter this narrative in Chapter 10, and we saw indications of this idea in the data on meritocracy in Chapter 3.

Education is also critical in the social construction of cultural tastes, and an important means to accumulate cultural capital. This was one of the key points of Chapters 4 and 5.

This is another reason why it is important to think about the role education plays in influencing our understanding of social mobility.

In particular, higher education has a complex relationship with social origin in mediating class destinations. Higher education is critical in accessing more privileged occupations, and higher education is also more likely to be accessed by those from more privileged social origins.

There has been significant, uneven, growth in the proportion of the population gaining a degree, which has varied according to class origin, gender, and ethnicity. We've therefore repeated the analysis shown in Figure 7.2, separating people who reported having at least an undergraduate degree (or equivalent), and those that didn't, shown in Figure 7.3.

This analysis echoes our previous findings. It demonstrates that a lack of qualified candidates is not *alone* responsible for the exclusions from creative work. The left-hand panel shows that, even for those with a degree, class origin has a very strong association with the probability of having a cultural job. A graduate with parents in higher managerial and professional occupations still has about twice the odds of a graduate from a working-class family. This may relate in part to the prestige of the institution attended. Class also shapes access to the most prestigious institutions.

Figure 7.3 also shows that male graduates have a better chance of creative work than female graduates, and graduates from London have a substantially increased probability of creative work compared to those from elsewhere.

The strongest difference compared to the previous analysis is for ethnic minority graduates. They have significantly lower probability of reporting creative work than their White

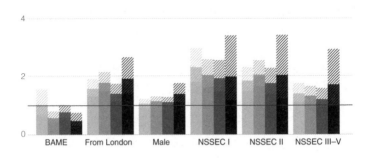

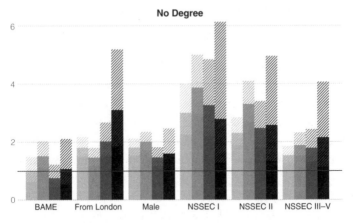

Figure 7.3 Odd ratios, ever having a core cultural job by education.

counterparts. This is consistent with the experiences reported by people of colour who attempt to access creative occupations. We're going to see how it plays out in Chapter 8. It is also in line with the figures from the LFS we used in Chapter 3.

The importance of class and gender is even stronger for those who are not graduates. Partially this reflects some of the non-graduate routes into cultural occupations. It also reflects that those who are not graduates, but who are privileged, can still use social networks and other types of familial resources. Think about Isabel, who we met at the end of Chapter 5. Her story of family connections and child stardom could have meant she did not need a degree, although her subsequent work for organisations was dependent on having credentials.

Conclusion: getting in and staying in

The absence of working-class origin people from cultural occupations is not a new phenomenon. According to our data and analysis, it has been an issue for at least forty years. The absence of working-class origin people is matched by a long-standing dominance of those from professional and managerial backgrounds. It is therefore likely that there was no golden age for social mobility in the cultural sector.

Our analysis has established that the substantial changes in the social origins of those working in core cultural jobs are driven by changes in the underlying social structure. The odds of those from working-class origins entering cultural occupations, as compared to their middle-class counterparts, have been consistently low over time.

This finding raises important questions about the *causes* of the lack of representation of working-class people in core cultural occupations. Recent discussions have tended to focus on policies such as the introduction of university tuition fees. No doubt these have caused difficulties. However, it's clear that there were mechanisms which excluded working-class people from creative work well before the introduction of these policies.

We can round off the chapter with an important point about the way the labour market works for cultural jobs. Throughout the book we've kept noting how tough it is to sustain a career as a cultural worker. Our analysis in this chapter reflects that fact.

More detailed analysis[26] finds that the class origins of core creatives in each cohort don't change much between censuses: Cohort 1 has a consistently higher proportion of working-class creatives than the other cohorts, and that's true in 1981, 1991, 2001, and 2011.

There is substantial turnover in the specific individuals involved. They have a similar social class profile, but they are not all the same people. Of members of Cohorts 1–3 who were in core cultural work in one Census and observed again at a subsequent Census, only one-third (33.5%) are in the same occupation – 8.7% are in a different cultural occupation, but 51.9% are in a non-creative job and 6% are no longer employed, on average.

This throws the reality of sustaining a cultural job into sharp relief. If only around one-third of each cohort are able to make it in the same cultural occupation over a decade, then it should be unsurprising that those who survive are those with the best resources.

Of course, these resources include hard work and talent. Yet we can theorise a more critical take that brings in the sort of cultural, social, and economic resources, or capitals, held by those from privileged origins. This reinforces what we saw in the previous chapter, about unpaid work.

In order to understand more about this process, we are going to focus on the experiences of those who are socially mobile into cultural occupations. Let's go back to Lisa, who we met at the start of the chapter. She told us of her worries about being out of place, and feeling not good enough, as a result of her class origins:

> Every day now in theatre when I'm dealing with what is now an Oxbridge chum, there is always a little voice in the back of your head going, 'You're not quite good enough. Get back in your box. You've got nothing interesting to say to them.' You have to override the voice, but it will be with me for the rest of my life. Of that, I have no doubt at all, and as a working-class girl in this field, it will always be there: 'Shut up, you've got nothing to say.' Whereas actually, I have 27 years' experience in lots of different areas, and I think I've got quite a lot to say.

It is already difficult to sustain a career in the harshly competitive cultural labour market. This additional psychological burden gives clues as to why so many do not make it, irrespective of issues of pay, working patterns, and location. It is this sense of not fitting, and feeling out of place, which we unpack in Chapter 8. In doing so we explore another side of social mobility research, to foreground the qualitative analysis of interview data as a partner to the quantitative analysis of the ONS-LS we've presented in this chapter.

8

How is inequality experienced?

Introduction: Sam feels out of place

> You know that feeling where you feel like someone is going to tap you on the shoulder and say, 'Wait a minute, you are not supposed to be here. You are not posh, you are not supposed to be here.'

Chapter 7 closed with Lisa's reflections on her experiences of being out of place in many professional situations. Despite Lisa's long career working in theatre, these experiences were a crucial part of her career and working life.

Sam, a non-binary arts practitioner in their fifties, further develops this sense of being out of place. Not only is there the worry that, in their case, the visual art world is not for them and they do not 'fit'. There is also their fear that somehow this will be discovered, and they will have to leave.

This sort of testimony opens up a broader discussion about cultural occupations. This discussion is about whether these occupations are, or are not, welcoming spaces for particular social groups. This question is the subject of this chapter.

As we will show, cultural occupations can be unwelcoming and, in some cases, hostile. This is another element in the explanation of the overall inequalities we have demonstrated in cultural production and consumption in Chapters 3 and 4. To explore this, we're going to look at a subset of our interviewees, those who are socially mobile from working-class origins into cultural and creative jobs.

We use three ideas to frame our analysis. First, we'll extend Chapter 7's discussion of social mobility. Rather than explaining the concept again, we're going to think about various criticisms of the idea. In doing so, we introduce a second theoretical insight, the idea of a 'somatic norm' in cultural and creative occupations. Here we draw on work by the sociologist Nirmal Puwar.[1]

We link this idea to research that has been critical of social mobility as a policy agenda, and as an unquestioned social good. It is through this connection that we show how social mobility into creative occupations carries important emotional costs.

At the same time, connecting social mobility and the somatic norm allows us to analyse those taking decisions in creative occupations. We say more about this in Chapter 10.

In this chapter, through the experiences of the socially mobile, we show that the assumptions of those hiring, commissioning, and taking decisions in creative occupations are heavily shaped by a somatic norm of White, male, middle-classness. These two intersecting issues provide a powerful set of barriers in addition to previous chapters' discussions.

Being the somatic norm for the creative industries is an important resource for the individuals who possess those characteristics.[2] Attempts to change inequalities in cultural occupations are often based on suggesting that people should try to be more like that 'norm'. These approaches are offered instead of changing occupations, or changing society.

More comprehensive changes would mean the somatic norm in the creative industries would no longer have the same status and same value. It would no longer be the standard against which people are measured.

This is the point where we bring in a third theoretical idea. This is about the resources people have, and how these give them advantages in the labour market. We've already encountered resources, or capitals, earlier in the book. We'll look at them in more detail here. Resources can be economic, for example people's wealth allowing them to work unpaid. They can be social, for example the contacts they might have who could commission them or offer them work. Most importantly for this discussion, they can be cultural.[3] This is the idea of cultural capital we discussed in Chapter 5.

In this chapter we focus on the way cultural capital can be associated with people's demographic characteristics, such as their race, class, and gender. Cultural capital can be, as we show, *embodied*. One example is how decision-makers have assumptions about the social position and social worth of accents.

Critical writing on social mobility, the 'somatic norm' in cultural occupations, and the idea of cultural capital, all help to explain inequalities in creative jobs. They show how people do, or do not, get in and get on. This is not purely a consequence of talent or hard work. It is also due to their class, race, and gender.

These characteristics should not be taken in isolation from each other. We think about how exclusions associated with the core demographic categories we are using – class, race, and gender – intersect with each other.[4] Chapter 3 demonstrated that it is at the intersection of these categories that individuals are most likely to be missing from our picture of culture in the UK. Specifically, women of colour from working-class backgrounds face some of the most difficult barriers to success.

As a result, several of our key case study interviewees are long-range socially mobile people of colour. These individuals are the least likely to 'make it' into cultural jobs and are most under-represented. We are not at all arguing that race, class, and gender are interchangeable. Nor are we saying that the experiences of adverse treatment or discrimination are the same, or of the same kind, for women, people of colour, and those from working-class origins. Neither are we setting these exclusions in competition with one another, to discover which is the 'worst' problem.

The risk of an intersectional approach may be to flatten or reduce these distinctive issues. By highlighting the intersections of class and race, and class, race, and gender, we draw attention to some of the mechanisms of exclusion in cultural occupations, rather than suggesting these mechanisms operate in the same way for all.

Social mobility and the 'somatic norm' of the creative industries

Chapter 7 noted how social mobility has been the subject of extensive critical academic literature. Media and popular commentary have also questioned its appropriateness as a frame for policy interventions.[5]

There are several objections. The language of social mobility and the idea of 'escaping' working-class origins; the emotional costs and negative impacts of social mobility; the lack of radical social change associated with social mobility policies; and the specific problem of social mobility into creative jobs. This last point focuses on the low pay and poor job security in creative work, which is different to more secure professions and jobs.[6]

In the following discussion we are going to move away from the sociologically-informed understanding of social mobility that we looked at in Chapter 7. There we analysed the probability of people growing up in families with parents working in one social class ending up in occupations with a substantively different socio-economic position. In what follows here we are going to focus on how social mobility is understood and deconstructed within public, media, and policy discussions.

As we mentioned in the previous chapter, the focus on social mobility can be accused of distracting from the need for better working conditions across the British economy; it penalises those who are *not* socially mobile from their working-class origins; and it aims to only to take a small number from working-class origins into middle-class professions, rather than benefiting all in society.

This latter point has been expanded to a critique that rejects social mobility in favour of a focus on social justice. Rather than looking to 'rescue' gifted children from their working-class starting points, governments should aim to improve education and living standards for all.[7]

We can take this a step further. The most critical line of thought suggests social mobility is seen as a means of erasing or correcting any traces of working-class culture and origins to fit middle-class destinations. The implication here is that working-class origins are something needing to be 'fixed' or 'cured'.[8]

These ideas are reflected in much of the academic critiques of social mobility and the broader idea of meritocracy.[9] This questions social mobility as an appropriate ideology for tackling social issues. In particular, this research has drawn attention to the impact of the language of social mobility.

First is the way that social mobility is overly focused on moving *upward* with no interest or concern with the need for analysis or policy concern with *downward* mobility. Here social mobility discourse claims everyone can be a winner, thus obliterating concern and analysis with structural barriers causing disadvantage.[10]

At best social mobility discourse takes focus away from challenging entrenched inequalities, for example, class, gender, or racial discrimination. At worst it insists we start by denying the existence of these issues altogether. The focus is on the individual, and their ability to escape, rather than being limited by the social situation shaping their careers and lives.[11]

The focus on the individual leads to moral judgements associated with social mobility. In terms of moral judgements, the risk with social mobility is that middle-class positions are seen as deserving of social status and rewards. By contrast the working class who are not mobile are seen to get what they deserve, because they have failed to 'overcome' their social origins.

This critique is closely linked to moral judgements about the desirability of being middle class, beyond just professional occupational destinations. Middle-class status is given a superior position to being working class and of staying in working-class social origins. Social mobility discourses may see the rewards of specific occupational destinations conflated with moral judgements about working-class origin people.[12]

Social mobility and the 'somatic norm'

The idea that social mobility encompasses a hierarchy of social positions is important to understand who, and who is not, given value in these settings. Those who are not from middle-class professional starting points potentially face judgements or negative stigma.

There has been considerable debate on this subject, reflecting different methods of research. While large-scale survey data suggests the socially mobile show no negative impacts on their self-reported well-being,[13] qualitative approaches suggest a more complex picture.

Sam Friedman,[14] based on interviews with socially mobile individuals, noted a sense of 'unease, anxiety and dislocation', along with anxiety about background and social origin when moving into professions that have middle-class cultures. These emotional effects sit alongside alienation or distance from working-class family and friends.

We noted in Chapter 7 how the academic study of patterns of social mobility was initially grounded in the analysis of social class, supplemented by gender and race as the field developed. Gender and race are vital categories when thinking about the individual, psychological, experience of social mobility.

This is demonstrated in the extensive academic work on how class and mobility intersect with gender and race. When taken together, these categories underpin the broader sense of social mobility as a synonym, in public policy, for a sense of fairness or equal opportunity. In the academic setting, this broader understanding of social mobility as fairness draws attention to gender pay gaps in professional occupations, or the absence of ethnic minority leadership.

Work by Nicola Rollock and her colleagues provides a good example.[15] They detail how the Black British middle class who have been socially mobile face issues associated with racism *and* the transition from working-class origins to professional middle-class destinations.

The socially mobile Black British middle class have to develop strategies to navigate double discriminations.[16] They face potential alienation from their White middle-class peers and their Black working-class starting points. Indeed, the category of 'middle class' is itself 'heavily saturated by whiteness'. This points us back to the idea of a default individual, a 'norm', which we mentioned earlier.

Similar issues are highlighted by research on gender and mobility. Much of the discussion of social mobility has been dependent on the figure of a working-class 'boy done good'.[17] This embeds into policy a specific set of assumptions as to *who* the socially mobile individual is.

Women's experience is markedly different,[18] with middle-class occupational destinations marked by significant sexism. Here we are reminded of things like gender pay gaps and the unequal impact of parenting on careers.

For working-class origin men, the boy done good, there may be a relatively smooth path into the middle-class destination. For women and people of colour, who are further from the ideal type, this path is more difficult.

We have already mentioned the importance of Nirmal Puwar's research on the British civil service.[19] She sought to understand why the senior civil service was dominated by White individuals, while people of colour were absent or even excluded. In the civil service, the somatic norm was embodied by the middle-aged, middle-class, White man. This was inseparable from the idea of what a rational, objective, and neutral civil servant was supposed to be. To fit this role was to be one of these people. To be a civil servant was to be a middle-aged, middle-class, White man.

For those without these embodied characteristics, those who were not the somatic norm, the professions were a less hospitable place. For women and people of colour there was the experience of being invisible in professional settings. Invisibility was coupled with their own senses of disorientation and the dissonance between themselves and their colleagues and occupations.

The demand from the profession, in this case the senior civil service, was to copy or mimic the middle-aged, middle-class, White man, rather than being and expressing themselves. Otherwise the experience of being out of place – of being a 'space invader' to quote the title of Puwar's book – has a heavy price.

The somatic norm and inequality in creative occupations

We have introduced the idea of the somatic norm to do two things. First, to expand some of the criticisms of social mobility to connect more closely with the issues of getting in and getting on in creative occupations. Second, to provide a way of organising our data, as we're going to be thinking about how the somatic norm relates to embodied forms of cultural capital.

First, we will take some time to think about how the somatic norm works in creative occupations, and how it structures particular individuals' chances of success. A simple and straightforward example comes from the world of acting.[20] Getting work in acting is tough. It is highly competitive and decisions are often based on intangible qualities, rather than formal credentials. It is also highly precarious, with very uncertain patterns of employment, even for the relatively successful. Finally, it has a range of structural inequalities, with many more parts in mainstream productions available to men, particularly men with specific characteristics.

Here we can see the somatic norm in operation. The roles individuals are encouraged to audition for, and get, follow a set social 'type'. The type reflects demographic characteristics of age, gender, ethnicity, region, disability, sexuality, and class. In some ways this is benign, as there are parts available for a range of actors depending on their type.

Yet the fit between actor and part operates in a highly unequal way. A White, male actor, with a received pronunciation accent, is assumed to be the default. He is capable of playing any role. This is the somatic norm for actors. Those without these characteristics face a more limited set of opportunities. They are assumed to only be able to play their type. This type is determined by casting directors, writers, and producers.

This somatic norm is then coupled with broader structures of inequality in the profession. There are fewer parts for women, and for people of colour. Moreover, the parts offered to those not fitting the somatic norm can present a dilemma. Often parts are crude caricatures of the lives of the working class, of women, or of people of colour. These parts are commissioned by those with sometimes little or no experience of what is being represented on stage or screen.

There is a burden of representation that is not demanded of the men that are the somatic norm. For the White, middle-class origin man there are frustrations, for sure. They may be confined to play leading men, key parts in Shakespeare, or only rarely offered the chance to do challenging or ground-breaking roles.

For women, working-class origin individuals, and people of colour the frustrations are different. They will be offered unrepresentative and offensive roles: one-dimensional love interests, benefits cheats, drug dealers, or terrorists. They are not afforded the same, highly privileged, constraints associated with the somatic norm. In turn, these negative representations have real-world consequences for how particular communities are viewed.

The operation of the somatic norm in acting reflects the dominance of the middle class in hiring and commissioning decisions. It also reflects the more general forms of middle-class norms that dominate and discriminate in creative jobs. It was one of Catherine's worries that we highlighted in the conclusion to Chapter 2.

Existing research shows that in creative jobs the socially mobile are disadvantaged by not having the 'right' networks and the 'right' set of cultural references. This is alongside not having the knowledge of the 'right' way to present themselves. These are almost all unwritten rules.

These rules reflect changing middle-class norms, for example the type of cultural interests and modes of consumption we discussed in Chapters 4 and 5. The unwritten rules do not reflect objective criteria for success. Existing research is especially powerful when it analyses the intersection of race, gender, and social origins, showing how unwritten rules interact with the expectation that the ideal type cultural worker, our somatic norm, is a White, middle-class origin, man.

Not getting in and not getting on in creative occupations

The somatic norm helps us to think about more subtle barriers to success, and to think about social mobility in a different way. We can connect critical scholarship on policy discourses about social mobility to research explaining how people are marginalised and uncomfortable in particular organisational settings.

It is not a lack of individual hard work or talent, rather there are powerful structural barriers in operation in cultural occupations. Some barriers confront all cultural workers. These include pay, social connections, and insecure working patterns, even if (as we have seen in Chapter 6) their effect is felt more strongly by some than by others.

It is the socially mobile, particularly socially mobile women and people of colour, who encounter the highest barriers. In some cases, as we show, there is outright resistance to their presence. More usually, and as the idea of the somatic norm indicates, the barriers are much more subtle, and thus are harder to challenge and change.

Can you afford to work in the creative industries?

People have access to different sorts of resources, or capital, as they struggle for success. The way these capitals interact is key. If we think about economic capital first, we can see its operation usefully distilled by Chris.

Chris is a working-class origin mixed race man in his thirties, working as a museum curator in a city outside London. We're going to hear from him, and his story of long-range social mobility into museums, several times in this chapter.

Chris' understanding of the role of money, of economic capital, captures much of what we've been discussing in the book. The routes in to cultural occupations are so dependent on economic resources that the playing field is totally uneven:

> Basically, you need a certain level of financial backing or financial stability to get a look in when it comes to jobs within the

heritage and museum sector. I was in a relatively lucky position, as I was living at home, and wasn't having to pay any board, I had a relatively small amount of money to raise to be able to do the MA. I was able to do the 11 months voluntary work at a local museum because I was living at home. I certainly wouldn't have had the financial capability to go to another city and live there whilst volunteering. My volunteering was very based around an institution I could do whilst living at home.

You could plot your financial status against opportunity, and you would see a direct correlation. Then on the other side you get individuals who haven't got employment, haven't got the backing of parents, who are really struggling financially. Their opportunities are drastically reduced, because they can't possibly volunteer. They need to be dedicating most of their working hours to earning money. They're not going to be able to raise £3,000 to £4,000 to do an MA. How do they compete in the job market, with people with MAs, when they've got an undergrad? On the other side you've got individuals who are London based, and living at home with parents, able to volunteer at huge national institutes like the British Museum, the V&A, places like that. Places that look really, really good on a CV. Albeit volunteering work, it still looks very, very good. If you could shadow [a curator] at the V&A for twelve months, you're able to do that because you don't need to work, your parents live in Central London, that's going to sit you in very, very good stead to getting a job. So I think, as far as diversity in the heritage and museum sector, there's a real correlation between somebody's financial situation and the opportunities they get.

Chris is well aware of the role of economic resources, of economic capital, in explaining why cultural occupations are unequal. He also shows the need to link economic capital to social and cultural resources.

Kirsty, a British East Asian woman from a working-class origin, was in her early thirties and attempting to break into

202

acting when we interviewed her. For her there were the same financial constraints identified by Chris.

Like Catherine in Chapter 2, Kirsty points out the consequences of the over-representation of those from affluent backgrounds in the workforce. She tells us how gatekeepers – whether writers, directors, casting, or commissioning – become a 'closed shop':

> I think in the arts it certainly counts because I think, definitely, it's so expensive to go train as an actor or anything artistic, and the chances of you making that money back are quite slim or difficult. And, so, by logic and practicality it ends up being that people who are already fairly quite affluent are going to be able to take the risk of going into a career in drama or acting or whatever. So I think that does make a difference and I think these people then become, maybe, eventually, the gatekeeper so you – people work with what they know and so if you're already working in something that's quite a rich upper class arena, then they tend to not realise the working class people out there as well. And, so, sometimes it becomes a bit of a closed shop.

Who do you know?

The idea of a 'closed shop' is particularly useful when we consider the second set of resources, social capital. As with economic capital, we're highlighting this here in a more expansive sense than just having access to social networks. We are also thinking about how individuals might *not* create and sustain social connections and social networks. This might be as a result of being or feeling out of place in cultural professional destinations.

This is the opposite of Lydia's comment in Chapter 5, in both her assumptions and her doubts about everyone having access to art classes. It is also the converse of Isabel's story. In Chapter 5 we saw how she felt totally at home in the cultural world, as the child of two creative parents and as a successful young star.

In contrast, we can turn to Catherine. We met her at the end of Chapter 2. She was in her thirties and working in theatre and as a writer at the time of the interview. She outlines how economic and social capitals interact. She had access to economic capital in emergencies, but didn't come from a background that offered much social capital when she was starting out:

> It can be frustrating to see other people particularly in a way that you know that you could achieve, but with that additional support I guess. It's not only financially. I think sometimes it's the links. If I was in a position where, I don't know, I needed a wall building or my car fixed, I'm pretty sure that my parents would come up with the goods. They don't have any contacts with the cultural sector.

Our interviewees were well aware of the types of problems identified by academics writing about cultural occupations. For the socially mobile the awareness of inequalities played out as a sense of frustration, just as Catherine's comment shows. The sense of frustration raised the prospect of how the socially mobile might challenge or resist the expectations of decision-makers, and the somatic norm, in cultural destinations.

Catherine's frustration echoes Kirsty's perception of a closed shop for cultural production. There are consequences in terms of social capital. The limited nature of who produces culture (Catherine is here focused on theatre) is self-fulfilling. It leads those from outside that limited social group to feel excluded and unwelcome:

There's an imbalance in the people who are writing, creating, performing in the theatre that we provide, which then means that people growing up, their perception of theatre is … It's a much bigger step to then say, 'Oh yes, so this is all the theatre that I've seen, but what I want to create is a theatre that tells a story about me.' It's much easier to go, 'This is all the theatre I've seen. I don't belong in that world because it doesn't say anything about me.' I guess it's a much bigger challenge to be creating that theatre that makes people from other backgrounds feel that that is a part of a world that they can access.

There are, of course, smaller scale issues of networks and connections that play out in terms of access to the profession. They create knock-on effects in terms of confidence and common frames of reference. The latter two issues are difficult to entirely separate out from the next section's focus on cultural capital. For now, it is with looking at the idea of confidence when linked to networking and knowing the right people.

Claire and Carys are both White women working as artists, and their comments captured so much of what we heard from our socially mobile interviewees about the role of confidence.

Carys, who we met in Chapter 5, told us 'It doesn't matter how good your work is if you can't network and can't make those connections apart from being in amongst people or with people that are already in that world, you don't have a chance. It's just not going to happen.'

Claire, a White woman in her fifties from a working-class background, gave a comparison that was a common story:

I think the trouble with the arts industry is that it's so based on networking and the sort of social skills, how you behave at openings, how ready you are to chat with people … I have a colleague who is an artist … from a middle-class background and he's a bloke and I was just left stunned by his ability to just introduce himself and start talking to people and networking in the middle of this seminar. I just don't do that. I just find it really, really hard … it's something that is so culturally ingrained I think and it's that sense that you can be at ease with people.

Confidence is particularly problematic when we connect it to the idea of a somatic norm. The ability to network, to seem to be at ease and be in the right place, is clearly related to having social capital. Yet it is often seen as an individual personality trait, being or having 'confidence'.

The focus on the need for individuals to have confidence, on their character, obscures broader structures of inequality. This focus echoes many of the criticisms we noted about social mobility earlier in the chapter. The broader structures mean those entering cultural occupations from working-class origins start without the same social resources. This then makes 'networking' and creating contacts more difficult.

The problem of focusing too much on individuals and confidence is thrown into sharp relief when we think about the relationship between race and social resources. Here it is important to keep in mind the absence of people of colour from key parts of the cultural workforce. This is especially important in occupations in museums and galleries and theatres which are often public, or publicly funded, institutions.[21]

The 'who do you know?' question is associated with social capital. It becomes a question of 'am I the only one?' when thinking about race and ethnicity.

We first met Meg in Chapter 3, were we heard her story about getting into theatre. Here we're highlighting Meg's story again, because she captured what we heard over and over again from our interviewees:

> My whole time at [two London theatres] I was the only non-White person. There was the security guard, but in terms of in an artistic team, I'm the only person who hadn't been to university. And these are two progressive theatres.

The sense of being out of place, of not fitting in, is perfectly captured in the phrase 'I was the only'. In the case of race and ethnicity, along with gender in fields such as design and film and television, the absences may be more immediately striking than for the more subtle cues associated with class.

'I was the only' shows how it is easy to think in *individual* terms about problems of absences and under-representations in cultural occupations. By contrast, by thinking about the intersections of race, class, and gender, along with the intersections of economic, social, and cultural capitals, we can focus on the structures that are sometimes hidden in individual narratives.

We noted earlier that our socially mobile interviewees were *reflexive* and acutely aware of the problems of inequality in creative occupations. We return to Chris, who tells the intersectional story of having social capital through his occupation, but still being an outsider to occupational networks. Part of this is geographic, as he is not based in London. Part of this is class, as he notes education and parental background:

> Whenever I need to go down south for work, because I've got friends and colleagues at the [London museums] that have collections that I need to engage with, they will have come from quite a different background to me. They won't be anything like me in education, or in our parents' background, or things like that. Again, I don't like to think that class affects any decisions I make, or has any influence, but that's not to say that I'm not still aware of the differences between me and a lot of the people I meet within my sector.

And part of this is about his ethnicity:

> There's always the sense that I suppose I could walk into a room
> and think, 'Yes, I'm the only non-White person in this room.' And
> definitely within the sector there are very few other mixed race
> individuals I've come across. But that doesn't have any bearing on
> how I interact or how I feel other people interact with me.

Chris stresses how these structures don't shape his interactions.
He is, however, aware of them and as a result offers a clear picture of the operation of social capital and the somatic norm.

Chris' stress on his own agency is a good reminder of what
we are *not* arguing. We are not arguing that it is impossible
for those from outside the somatic norm, women, people of
colour, and those from working-class origins, to access cultural
occupations.

Rather, we are pointing to the way that what might be a
stressful and demanding experience for every cultural worker
is an especially difficult task for those who start without the
same levels of resources. This is acute when we think about the
absence of people of colour from the cultural workforce and
the embodied nature of a lack of social and cultural capital.

Accents, tastes, and bodies

Our expanded understanding of social resources is hard to separate from cultural capital. Chris' experience of being the only
person of colour in cultural spaces is a good example of the
blurred boundaries between social capital and the somatic, or
embodied, elements of cultural capital.

Our interviewees pointed directly to how it wasn't just their
knowledge of the arts or their educational backgrounds that

presented barriers. There were also instances of assumptions, and outright discrimination, based on characteristics such as accent.

Interviewees told of assumptions such as 'you're Scottish, you're working class' through to experiences of discrimination, 'in London, people think I'm going to rob their bag'. The assumptions made about class and accent remind us again about the somatic norm of the creative industries, and how this is maintained in relation to those without these characteristics. It is also a reminder of how hidden and subtle barriers to success can be.

We met John, a film and television worker in his twenties, of working-class Latin American origins, earlier in the book. We're now going to concentrate on his story to show how embodied cultural capital functions. His experience of social mobility and the role of cultural capital, whether embodied or expressed in tastes and interests, captures what many of the interviewees told us. Reactions to his accent and mode of speech created an experience of difference and alienation for him in his educational and work environments:

> I know in myself that I don't speak 'posh' because I've been in environments where people do and I stick out like a sore thumb.

Accent was part of his embodied experience of being out of place in work, adding to the stress of trying to make it and present a particular persona:

> In these production companies it's literally just lily white everywhere. It gets to the point where every day I go to work I just have to go to the toilet, have a 10-second prepare and just enunciate my words, like a performance, just because I didn't want people thinking any less of me if I say one thing wrong or something else.

There is extensive research showing how social groups from outside the White middle class are expected to conform to the codes and practices of the White, middle-class working environments they enter. Puwar's work on the somatic norm was all about this problem. There is extensive evidence of similar problems in cultural spaces such as newsrooms, television commissioning meetings, and advertising agencies.[22]

The somatic norm for cultural workers is found in the open, liberal, meritocratic, and omnivorous cultural consumer.[23] We set up these characteristic in Chapter 3 and 4's discussion of values, attitudes, and tastes. We'll see more of this in Chapter 10, because it has been embodied in the White, middle-class origin, man.

There is a cruel irony in the meritocratic omnivore contributing to an environment that is hostile to difference and diversity. We asked John who succeeds in film and television. His answer sets out the role of the cultural occupations' somatic norm, along with cultural capital in creative industries:

Middle-class White people because they know how to talk to the people who can commission their ideas. It's difficult to break into because there were times – this happens to me all the time, where I'm talking to someone at work, this is not even a professional setting, so let's say a pub having lunch. And they don't know what I'm saying because they say my slang is too advanced. Even for the context of this interview, I'm putting on my TV voice, just because I think you need to be able to understand what I'm saying. And I just think it's like a vicious circle that's very difficult to break out of. And I don't even think it's a race thing. It's much more to do with a class thing because I've seen TV production companies who hire people of colour, mainly because they're from the same class background, keeping it real. They can have a little banter about which French Alps are the best to ski down.

'What's your favourite fondue?' 'This muesli tastes so much better with blueberries.'

Accent, slang, race, and class all run together in the idea of a shared repertoire of classed 'banter'. This is exactly the world that Daniel Laurison and Sam Friedman[24] describe in their work on television commissioning. It is hard to challenge as this shared culture seems open and meritocratic, without hierarchy. Yet it is a new sort of closure at the top of cultural occupations.

Industry lore, somatic norms, and gaps in the market

These experiences indicate the existence of powerful structures preventing success. These are in addition to the issues of low pay, insecure work, and highly competitive labour markets faced by all cultural workers.

We are going to connect our discussion of economic, social, and cultural resources to the somatic norm by discussing Rachel's experiences. Rachel shows the structures we're uncovering and how they operate.

Rachel was in her fifties when we interviewed her, a working-class origin woman of mixed ethnic heritage running a company in the music industry. She had a whole range of creative jobs throughout her career, combining creative practice with a variety of cultural business activities. By any measure, she was highly successful, and an example of long-range social mobility into cultural occupations.

In Rachel's story we can see the connection between production and consumption we discussed in Chapters 3 and 4. We can see how the assumptions, the 'industry lore', of commissioners and decision-makers shape what gets made. What gets made then shapes who gets to make culture and who is successful in the cultural and creative industries.

The story here is partially about financial success and having a stable, long career. It is also about cultural legitimacy in mainstream outlets such as television, West End theatre, pop music, publicly funded museums, and mass market publishing. It is also true in more esoteric, but equally culturally significant, avant-garde artforms. The somatic norm in creative occupations shapes the assumptions of who is the ideal type creative worker. This influences what those creative workers think *should* be made. It underpins their judgements of quality, value, and worth.

For those outside the somatic norm there are constraints on their freedom to make culture. They are seen as a greater risk. Their ability to generate audiences or revenue is questioned. The aesthetic and cultural value of their ideas is also seen as a problem, in comparison to what commissioners and decision-makers already know as being 'hits', or of being 'important'.

This system creates a difficult bargain for working-class origin people, people of colour, and, in specific industries such as film and television, for women. They are offered opportunities, albeit in numbers that are more limited than their White, male, middle-class origin colleagues. They are allowed, as the academic Anamik Saha[25] suggests, only to fill specific 'gaps in the market'. They are not afforded the same creative freedoms associated with the somatic norm of the ideal type creative worker.

How does this work, and how can we substantiate these ideas? Rachel is clear about the operation of race and its role in limiting her opportunities. Not only is this another example of being 'the only', but it is also a good introduction to the trade-off between opportunities and creative freedom:

When I go to industry events, I am still the only Black person in the room and that, for me, is shocking. It's also very isolating. Then people feel embarrassed about talking about race, it's really weird. If I go to some event and there's a question over race or something like that then suddenly I have to be the authority on it because I am, I'm Black. That's the only time that they'll come to me to discuss something to do with my race, not to ask me about the things that are my expertise. It's very, very frustrating.

She is included in industry events, and is given status, but only in the limited circumstances where the questions are about race. Her success as an entrepreneur, business manager, and creative practitioner are, in the spaces of her industry, secondary to the colour of her skin.

As government and organisational policy has shifted to focusing on addressing inequalities in cultural and creative organisations,[26] similarly constrained opportunities have been offered to her:

Any time there's a bit of funding to do with diversity, then suddenly we're flavour of the month. We don't hear from these people year on year and suddenly there's a funding deadline coming up and guess what, they need to show some kind of diversity and so will get a very short cultivation, as in, 'Oh yes, come and see us. Let's go for a drink', or something. Then the next bit of communication is, 'Do you think we could have a letter of support.' It's not even a pretence at real partnership.

In Rachel's case her ethnicity, and the focus of her organisation, becomes akin to the capitals associated with the somatic norm. We encountered similar narratives around class and gender. Fundamentally these opportunities are not equal. Nor does this sort of alternative or outsider capital have the same status. It carries with it questions that undermine her talent and ability, despite her track record:

> I still feel like we're on an uneven playing field, I do. We're still having to almost justify our very existence. We've been up against a number of people and organisations who've felt that you're only getting the funding because you're Black. That's absolutely not the case. At what point do people start thinking, 'Well they might actually be good at what they do?' It feels like a continuing battle to be acknowledged for the quality of the work that we do.

This is in the context of the wider racism still structuring contemporary British society:[27]

> When I was looking for a school for my daughter, we'd go to the local school. Obviously we come from a musical background so of course we're interested in what's the music provision here. Interestingly, the first thing they'd say to us, 'We've got a lovely steel pan group.' It is like, 'Why do you assume I want my daughter to play steel pan?' The question was, 'Yes, but what about the brass instruments or the stringed instruments?' I think they try very much to fob off our kids. I think they're selling kids short. There's this assumption that all working-class kids and all Black kids will like hip hop, grime, what they call urban music and all of that.

There has been detailed research on the experience of explicit racism, along with racialised assumptions, for people of colour and their families entering the middle class and entering the education system.[28] The double action of class and race discrimination serves to place a heavy burden on individuals.

We have seen earlier on in the book that placing responsibility for structural problems onto individuals is one way that inequality is maintained and reproduced. We've seen this in this chapter in Claire's individualised account of lacking confidence, or Meg's experience of being the only woman of colour in an all-White environment. Even Rachel, with all her experience and her success, was still struggling with the effects of these structures:

> When you're up against people who've got ten degrees and MAs and everything else and they've been head of major corporations and stuff, then I think there's bound to be a bit of insecurity. I actually think, and I have to keep reminding myself, I've been doing this work a long time, I have a lot of experience and my opinion on it is as valid as anybody else's.

The psychological effects, in the context of an already highly competitive labour market, indicate the need for a greatly improved response from the cultural sector.

Challenging the somatic norm

Currently we can see a whole range of schemes designed to support and develop those who don't have the same levels of resources, access to the same cultural, social, and economic capital, as those currently over-represented across the cultural workforce. At the heart of many of these schemes is not a demand for institutional or organisational change. Rather, many are hopeful of remedying lack of representation by offering substitute forms of capital.

In essence, current career development schemes and many diversity policies do nothing to challenge the somatic norm.[29] At worst, they simply focus on changing and adapting under-represented groups to be more like that norm. This is similar to the critique of the focus on social mobility – that it is about lifting individuals out of their underprivileged state, rather than challenging how privilege is constructed and misrecognised as legitimacy.

This critique has been at the core of much recent scholarship critiquing diversity schemes.[30] For the media scholars Sarita Malik and Clive Nwonka such diversity schemes risk contributing to the maintenance of inequality. Rachel's comments about funding for diversity, along with the assumptions about the quality of her work and her organisation's, are clear examples.

There is a trade-off between filling a gap in the market for under-represented groups and being creatively constrained by the assumptions held by decision-makers. For our interviewees this trade-off was often placed into an unstated bargain between organisation and individual. Individuals were allowed access to the resources that major organisations would offer, in ways that would set up their careers. The price was to be marginalised by those very same organisations, have their creative freedoms constrained, and face psychological costs as part of that marginalisation.

Several of our socially mobile interviewees, our interviewees of colour, and our female cultural workers told us this exact story. They had a couple of years or a single contract at a key organisation followed by an escape to much riskier, but much less psychologically exhausting, self-employed status.

It is probably no coincidence that many of our most successful interviewees of colour, especially women, had set up their own organisations. Outside of a large organisation the daily burden of representing a community, in the face of the assumptions of those often very ignorant of the reality of that community, is alleviated. It is never, as Rachel's comments about her treatment by other creative organisations shows, removed.

Organisations and institutions move on to the next individual hire, unchanged, albeit awaiting the next round of puzzling questions as to where, exactly, the missing women, people of colour, and working-class origin individuals are in their workforce. Special attention, and special policy interventions, are given to this problem in management and later career positions and stages. Yet still the structural problems of this diversity bargain are not addressed.

To bring this together, we are going to close with a long excerpt from Meg. As she opened our discussion about the inequalities in the workforce in Chapter 3, it is fitting that she shows us why change is slow, if it is happening at all.

Meg gives a clear sense of the bargain she has been offered by the creative sector. The sector wants to use her working-class origin and her race, and offers opportunities in exchange. These opportunities marginalised her skill and talent, reducing her to her class and race for organisational needs. This shaped her sense of self and security in her work, in a way that is an additional form of pressure in a sometimes highly unforgiving cultural labour market:

> I've definitely felt like I've been put on a pedestal because of my background, and that people have tried to use me because of it. I found out that I've had jobs because of the colour of my skin. And I've had people come up to me and say things like, 'You're from the ghetto', and stuff like that, which is just proper weird. In terms of opportunities, I feel like I've had more opportunities because of my background. I've got a really good friend who is White. We basically had a really big chat, and she said that sometimes she felt frustrated with me, and how lucky I had been with

my opportunity, because she's struggled so much. She feels like because she comes from just a normal background, she's not rich, she's not poor, she hasn't got an amazing degree, she's just like middle of the road, she just felt like when applying for opportunities she always has to think of the [Megs] of the world, that are going to come and take them. I was sort of like, 'Okay, well, you've obviously got some insecurities going on there', but I do kind of get that. Because there's such an emphasis on diversity at the moment. I know through positive discrimination if I can hit a job description I will get an interview. I was really uncomfortable with that for a while, and I got really upset, and I had massive issues about identity and stuff, and just thinking, 'Who am I? Am I the working class girl or am I not?' … I challenged my old boss and said, 'Did you hire me because I was Black?' She was like, 'Yes'. I didn't expect her to say that. Then I said, 'Why?' She was like, 'Well, we want to engage the next generation of theatre makers, and when I look at you that's what I see, and so I figured you would be able to engage them.'

Even when organisations want to change, have the best intentions, and attempt to be supportive, the burden still falls onto individuals. It is a heavy, additional price to pay for success in cultural occupations for those who are not the somatic norm.

Conclusion

How can cultural and creative occupations, with their risks, precariousness and rewards, be reformed to equally benefit all of their current and prospective workers? We saw in Chapter 3 that our cultural and creative occupations have a class problem. Chapter 7 showed that this problem is a long-term one.

For sure there are *aspirations* to see more people from demographic groups that are currently under-represented in cultural and creative jobs. We saw this with the end of Meg's comments.

Yet these aspirations will do little to change the working conditions that are part of the reason for under-representation in the first place. Under-represented individuals are less likely to rise to the very top of professions, less likely to be in decision-making roles, and less likely to be visible role models.

The structural barriers and the 'somatic norm' we've outlined mean that a focus on individual access to cultural and creative careers may do little to address the problems that limit social mobility into cultural occupations.

Our analysis has shown how social mobility asks a great deal from the individual in terms of risk-taking and personal transformation, and little or nothing from their destinations. As a result, the social mobility agenda may leave questions of inequality in production, representation, and consumption unchanged and unchallenged. Although we're writing about cultural and creative occupations, there is much here of relevance to studies of social mobility across the rest of the professions and 'top jobs' of the UK and elsewhere.

Meg is important because she is deeply reflexive about how cultural occupations function. She knows full well what is going on, how her race and class are commodified, and the bargain she is being offered. One reading of this story is that the 'pedestal', the being 'used', *is how the system of cultural production functions*.

Meg is clearly talented and good at her job. Later on in her comments, she recounted how her boss had assured her that 'If you were rubbish you would have been out of the door.'

Yet she bears a burden that her White, middle-class origin, male colleagues never encounter. She is offered positions in exchange for organisations to use her race and class, but always with a sense that there is no real organisational commitment or organisational change. We suspect Meg will experience a career path that is similar to Rachel. Perhaps, if culture and inequality is taken seriously she will experience more stability, as Chris has. Sadly, as we will see in Chapter 10, reflexivity is not an entirely positive thing. More awareness of the problems may actually contribute to stability, stasis, and the continued dominance of those groups who benefit from the status quo.

9

Why don't women run culture?

Introduction: Katie's worries about starting a family

Not being able to have a steady income is hugely challenging for anything from, you know, planning a future, paying a mortgage. I think, particularly for women, having children, that's a really difficult one at my age. I'm 30, so you start thinking about, you know, where money would come from, for having a family, and, you know, temporary contracts don't lend themselves to that. My main frustration is, the kind of jobs that I'm applying for now … they're all temporary. Everything is a temporary contract. So it's impossible to have a child, you know, to have maternity pay, if you're on a temporary contract.

Katie was thirty when we interviewed her. A middle-class origin White woman, she was working in the visual arts and reflected on how her career had gone and what the future might hold. She offered a detailed understanding of how temporary contracts, which are a key structure of the labour market for many cultural workers, were shaping decisions about her life. Entering her thirties was a time when she was thinking about future motherhood. Yet there was a clear tension between her work and her future family life.

In this chapter we are going to highlight a key moment when women seem to be dropping out of cultural occupations. We saw in Chapter 3 that across creative occupations there are gender imbalances. Film and television have a striking absence of women; museums and galleries have fewer men. There are numerous reasons for these differences. In this chapter we're going to look at the impact of having children.

It is important to stress that the academic literature not only focused on motherhood, but has also problematised this focus as the sole explanation for gender inequality in creative jobs.[1] Women are absent from film and television, and from the highest profile and highest level positions in theatre, publishing, the arts and in museums, whether they have children or not. Motherhood is not the whole story.

We've tried to strike a balance when writing about parenting and creative work. We'll demonstrate that starting a family is a crucial moment where women leave cultural occupations. Yet we should not let a focus on motherhood obscure the wider sexism present in many parts of the creative economy.

A charge of sexism may seem like a bold or excessive statement. However, we can support this in several ways. We've just seen, in Chapter 8, how specific individuals are given value in cultural occupations, based on their race, class origin, and gender. The White, male, middle-class creative worker is afforded the status of the 'norm', facing the fewest barriers to success. We'll see examples of sexism from our interview data later on in this chapter. Finally, there is the existing research on women in cultural and creative industries.

Gender and creative jobs

Gender in creative industries is now an established area for academic research.[2] There are numerous books, papers, and research projects all detailing the significant issues encountered by women in these supposedly open and meritocratic occupations.

Film and television, as part of media industries more broadly, has seen detailed interrogation. Key writers concur that we need to understand a whole range of individual behaviours and structural conditions. These all cohere to explain women's absence from senior roles (despite being the majority in some junior roles in specific cultural occupations), and to account for women's experience in work and careers.[3]

Many of the behaviours have entered public consciousness in the aftermath of sexual harassment scandals in media industries and the #MeToo movement.[4] However, many such behaviours are not of the same magnitude (and illegality) as sexual harassment. Time and again academic research demonstrates how women are given lower status than men, and the positions of director, producer, writer, and other senior roles are seen to be men's work (even if this is only rarely made explicit).[5]

Women are stereotyped in various ways that afford them less prominent roles, doing the emotional labour in organisations and denied creative expression. Women are left out of, or uncredited, in the creative process, even where they have been leading projects.[6] They are treated as 'risky', both in terms of the possibility of needing time away if they chose to start a family, and in terms of industry assumptions about women.[7] These include the beliefs that the absence of successful women in, say, directing roles, means women will not 'sell' films; that women-led stories will not attract audiences, for example in Hollywood blockbusters; and that the pressures of hiring and commissioning mean that men are seen as a safer bet.

These individual biases point towards the structural problems facing women. They exist beyond film and television, in most other parts of the cultural sector. Long and unpredictable hours, the need for constant socialising and network building, and informal hiring practices are all core elements of creative work.[8] These confront all workers, irrespective of gender. The result, however, is that these labour market conditions connect with sexist assumptions to mean women face heavier barriers to success than men.

The research literature suggests many creative organisations end up with an informal segregation based on gender. Women are over-represented in support roles, but under-represented in creative areas such as artistic director, writer, or producer.[9]

Biases and structures are difficult to separate and tend to reinforce each other. Motherhood is a crucial example of this. There may be an individual hiring bias that sees a woman as a 'risky' investment because she requests flexible working hours. This goes hand-in-hand with the way freelance work does not offer paid maternity leave in the same way as more secure contracts of employment.

Obviously, these issues are hard to separate from the way society is organised. Barriers to success that are associated with parenting, for example childcare costs, reflect the decisions by government and society not to offer sufficient social support to the labour of social reproduction.[10] This social basis for the barriers to women's success is sadly another potential excuse for cultural occupations to explain women's absence from the labour force beyond their twenties and early thirties.

This point has been central to much of the research on motherhood and cultural occupations. While motherhood is a key factor, we must not let this obscure the individual biases and structural sexisms that mean that, even where women do not have children, they are still not getting the highest profile roles. While some of this is changing, with recent high-profile appointments in theatre and the visual arts and prominent successes in film, the most likely decision-maker in a position of power is still an affluent origin White man.

Recent research on gender and creative labour has stressed the need to focus on structural issues. Much of this uses interview data on women's experience of motherhood. Women are very well aware of the penalties they face in cultural occupations. However, at present they often see these as barriers to overcome, or see exit from higher profile creative roles as a decision for which they themselves are responsible.

Women internalising the responsibility for structural unfairness is not unique to creative industries, and reflects post-feminist ideas about equality in the workplace.[11] What has been especially valuable in academic research on creative work has been the stress on the continued existence of sexism and the need for feminist consciousness.[12]

This is most striking in comparisons between fathers and mothers. For men, balancing fatherhood and the demands of creative labour markets is challenging, of course. The challenge is of a different magnitude for women. For fathers there was not the same fear of the impact or penalty on creative careers. In some of our data fathers told us they were celebrated for being parents in the creative industries.

For women, not only is there a set of harsh questions about their career and life choices, but they can be stripped of their identity as creative workers and positioned solely as mothers. In turn, they are presented with a set of narrow expectations that they will abandon creative work in favour of caregiving. There is a double bind of potential struggle or failure as a mother and as a creative.

We see this over and over again from our interviewees, as they bear the burden of cultural occupations' failure to support them as mothers. At the same time, as we will see in this and the next chapter, *awareness* of the problem will not be enough to address gender inequality.

Where are women in the creative economy?

Before we look at discussion of parenting in our interviews, it is useful to look at data on women's and men's path in creative jobs. We're returning to Census data for this, the same data source we used in Chapters 3 and 7.

We have divided people in the ONS-LS into cohorts according to when they were born: 1953–62 (our first cohort), 1963–72 (second cohort) and 1973–82 (third cohort).[13] Each cohort is ten years older at each Census. We can look at who was working in one of the core cultural occupations, and see whether they kept that job or moved on to something else. For the first cohort we see their working lives from their twenties through to their fifties.

Figure 9.1 shows the proportion of men and women in each cohort who were in the same core cultural occupation ten years later. Regardless of whether people are with the same employers, the important question is whether they are still in a cultural occupation. Are they still artists, actors, directors, or writers?

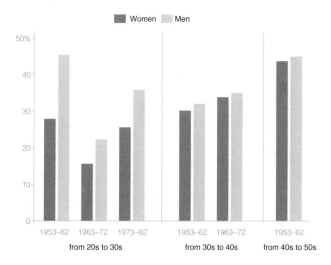

Figure 9.1 People in the same core creative occupation ten years on (percentages).

We have organised this first chart according to how old they were at each transition. We can only show the transition from forties to fifties for Cohort 1, as the others aren't old enough yet. We can immediately see that women are consistently less likely than men to be still working in the same creative job ten years on. The difference is greatest going from twenties to thirties, and becomes smaller at each later stage, but it does not disappear.

It is worth noting that for everybody, at every age, the most probable outcome ten years on is that they are not in a cultural occupation. As we've seen in Chapters 3, 6, and 7, getting in and staying in is very difficult within precarious and competitive cultural labour markets.

Figures 9.1 and 9.2 help to us understand this further. They show, for the same cohorts, the proportion who had left a core

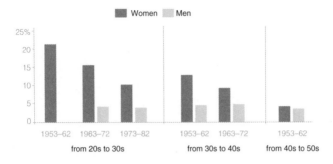

Figure 9.2 People not in work ten years on (percentages).

creative occupation and were no longer in work. This could be because they are studying full-time, caring for others, ill, retired, or unemployed long-term. Again, there is a consistent difference between women and men, this time with women in core creative jobs being much more likely to be out of work, compared to men, ten years later.

The differences between men and women are greater in younger people, and become smaller later in life. Given that the largest exit from work, and the largest difference between men and women, is centred on women in their thirties, it is likely that they relate to parental responsibilities rather than other explanations. For example, some people may return to study, or leave work due to ill health, but we would not expect this to explain such a large difference between men and women.

The differences between the cohorts also show the increased pressures in the labour market for cultural occupations. In our first cohort, just over 45% of men in cultural occupations were still in the same cultural occupation in their thirties as in their twenties. By the third cohort, those born between 1973 and 1982, we can see this is only 34%. A small proportion are working in different core creative jobs: men and women are equally likely to be doing this.[14]

There are important historical reasons for this. It is crucial we do not make sweeping statements about cultural occupations without considering the changing nature of the economy and particular historic circumstances, for example whether the economy is growing or if there is a recession.

What we can do with this data is use it to think about 'getting on' in cultural careers. Not working in a core creative occupation, having been recorded as working in one in a previous Census, is a likely outcome for men and women and at all ages. Cultural occupations are difficult to sustain over a long period of time. This is the case even as governments have devoted more attention to the creative industries and have argued that these occupations are playing an increased role in the British economy.

Data from the ONS-LS demonstrates that for women the transition from their twenties to their thirties is a crucial time for leaving cultural occupations. This reinforces what is already well known from many other research projects. In particular it highlights this moment in both the life-course and the career as one that needs particular attention. We can do this by looking at our interview data.

Parenting and cultural occupations

The fieldwork questions we used focused on childhood, career development, and working life, as well as some attitudinal questions. The overall project was not focused on parenting or caregiving, partially because there is already a rich academic literature on that topic.[15] It was also because we wanted to keep some questions open, to see what interviewees would highlight.

As a result, we collected a range of experiences across a very diverse cohort of participants, where some topics came up more frequently than others.

However, we were struck by the way certain issues, ideas, and experiences were repeated across the interviewees. We've shown this in Chapter 6's discussion of unpaid work, which was a specific topic in the interview. Childhood experiences of culture also had questions, but were a less specific part of the discussion compared to unpaid work.

Parenting was an issue that appeared unprompted, in response to a general set of questions about career and work experiences. It was clearly an important topic for a subset of our interviewees.

A useful way of starting is with the discussions of parenting by those who did not have children at the time of the interview.[16] This allows us to connect parenting's relationship with social inequality, and to the inequalities which are specific to cultural occupations.

These issues did not only affect women who had children, which is the main focus of the chapter, but they also impacted many women in terms of how they thought about and planned their future creative careers. Of the fifty-nine women aged from their early twenties to early forties who were not parents, fifteen women spontaneously discussed the difficulty of combining parenting with a creative career. Notably, women were bringing this up from their early twenties, although the youngest interviewee who was a parent was thirty. Clearly the anticipation of the problems of combining parenting and creative industries casts a long, anticipatory shadow for young women entering cultural occupations. Notably, no men discussed parenting in realtion to creative careers unless they were already parents.

Stephanie, a working-class origin White woman in her thirties working in a museum, is a good example of many of the sentiments of these interviewees. She was very well aware of the gender inequalities in her creative occupation, the stratification of leadership and senior management that skewed in favour of men, and the moment of women's 'disappearance' from the workforce:

> I think it's quite notable here and I think it's replicated across a lot of big museums. Most of the senior management are men, most of the junior curators are women. Obviously we're disappearing somewhere and there is – It's funny because on the one hand, museums are very, very good at offering flexible working and long maternity leave and things like that and that makes a lot of people go 'they're wonderful working environments for women then aren't they?' To me it begs the question, hang on, why is it only women requesting flexible working? There seems to be this assumption that museum work, particularly at the lower levels is very feminised and you'll come in in your mid- to late twenties, you'll go off and have a baby in your early thirties and then you'll come back part-time or something. It's as if you're not quite taken as seriously after that. I don't personally, I don't have any children, I'm not particularly hankering to have any, but that's part of the reason why. I feel like there's this sense that a lot of women in museums they're just sort of hung out middle class dabblers and they're not really serious about pursuing their career in the long run.

Stephanie highlights how even in an occupational sector seen to be 'very, very good' at supporting women, that of museums, there is a particular culture, which underpins the sorting of women *out* of leadership and senior roles and *into* less prestigious parts of the sector.

231

Stephanie also indicates a theme that will be crucial in the rest of our discussion. She is keenly aware of the structures and cultures of museums that are hindering women's advancement into senior roles. She speaks of having adapted her decisions about having a family in response to these structures. We are reminded how the burden of facing structural inequalities falls to individuals, who have varying levels of resources to address these inequalities.

In some ways Stephanie is acting rationally in the face of how creative occupations incentivise some decisions and penalise others. We see this dilemma repeatedly expressed in the experiences of women with children. It is part of the explanation for why gender inequalities associated with parenting are so long-standing and influential in cultural occupations, as well as in society more generally. It is also something that much of the academic research on this subject has sought to challenge, to place responsibility onto the occupations and not the individuals. This challenge is a direct reversal of how many in cultural occupations think and talk about motherhood and parenting.

Raising culture

What, then, are the experiences of mothers in cultural occupations? Before we move to the personal stories of these women, it is worth looking at the extent to which motherhood was discussed by our interviewees.

The women that mentioned having children at all were fairly well distributed by social class origin – 56% were middle class, 29% intermediate, and 15% working class. However, there were stark differences in how much they mentioned their children in relation to their career. They worked in all areas of the creative industries, including performing, media, publishing, and museums.

Nearly half of the most privileged mothers did not mention any impact of motherhood on their creative careers, only that their children existed, whereas this only applied to 7% of intermediate and 10% of working-class women. For our interviewees, there is a clear social gradient in the impact of parenting on sustaining a creative career.

We can see this in Hazel's comment about the positives of a cultural occupation as a parent. Hazel, who we first met in Chapter 6, was working as a successful writer at the time of interview, as well as having links to work in higher education. She was working-class origin and White. She highlighted a narrative often seen from policy and in some public discussions. This is the idea that cultural careers provide a more flexible way of working compared to the traditional office job:

> Flexibility. The reason I got into it is because it's flexible for a mother of very young children, and it wasn't terrible pay for a job that you could do at home. I used to drop them off at school, for example, or at nursery, depending on their age, work for six hours and go and pick them up, and I could fit that in with spending time with them, in a way that I couldn't have in a conventional office job.

We have started with Hazel's comment in order not to lose sight of the *potential* of cultural work, as well as the contrast to the 'conventional' office job. We're also using it as a way of showing how even the positive potential presented by cultural occupations contains problems.

Ruth, a mixed race woman in her fifties, from a middle-class origin, was working in publishing and journalism at the time of interview. She was candid about the constraints that came with the potential in the freelance based parts of the cultural economy:

> Freelancing suited me because it was ad hoc, part-time; you can say yes, you can say no. But on the other hand, if you didn't say yes all the time, people would very quickly scratch you off the list of available freelancers. So it can work for you and against you.

We can develop this idea of potential and constraint with another example, this time focused on creative practice. The impact of parenting on working life can give rise to new perspectives on creative practice. Charlotte adapted her practice to the time pressures of raising children in the context of moving from London to afford suitable accommodation:

> Because I had small children I was working quite quickly and I didn't want to get bogged down in things that took forever to make. I was at a real crisis of confidence. I had lost a lot of confidence in moving away from London, in having two children and in losing my work. But I put some framed work into a local gallery who were doing an open exhibition and they were keen to hold onto it in the gallery and sold four pieces for me and I thought, 'Right, I'll do some more.'

Charlotte, a White woman in her forties, from a traditional professional origin, shows the tensions within positive narratives of the impact of family on creative work. As an artist she had been dislocated from the networks of the London art world, losing work and confidence. It is not a story of choice from a position of empowerment. Rather, Charlotte's story is of making the best of the compromises of raising children.

Charlotte indicates that underneath positive stories are struggles for parents in cultural occupations. Charlotte went on to be candid about the tension between the demands of creative careers and parenting:

> Everything is on a weekend because you're part of people's relaxation, you're either a workshop that they want to book into when they're not at work or you're at an art event that's going to run on the weekend, so I then can't work every weekend because our family life would go up the spout. I don't know how you'd get around that, but it does mean that I can't – if I didn't have kids, my life would be very different. I'd probably still work more in the industry side of things and maybe not work for myself doing the art I do, but I can see that as my children grow up and leave home, I will have far more time available to have a creative job, which seems to take up more hours than your average job because you never switch off, so you're sort of always on the go with it. You have to put a stopper in the creative bottle when you've got kids because their needs need to come first.

The reality that 'you never switch off' in a creative job, along with recognition that the flexibility of working hours translates into demands for evening and weekend working, with the associated impacts on family life, was a dominant story for the subset of interviewees that we are considering here.

'You've got a baby, and you can't do this'

Even where interviewees had positive stories, they were ambivalent. The majority of the women with children were candid about the negative career experiences that had followed parenting. We're going to explore these by using extensive quotes from two women. Jessica and Nicole provided striking narratives of the cost of combining (or trying to combine) parenting with a career in performing arts. They were both from working-class origins.

One managed, after some knock-backs, to sustain a successful career. This was thanks, in part, to a supportive employer and well-paid husband. This career still took enormous effort. The other, a single parent, also struggled enormously and was not able to support herself through her performing work. The opportunities she won in the form of agents and bursaries did not accommodate her parental responsibilities.

We have chosen them for several reasons. They capture so much of what we heard across the interviews with mothers. Crucially, they were both in theatre. There has been a great deal of public and policy discussion about theatre, so it is important to add to key projects researching the industry. At the same time, there is space for more research as theatre has not seen the same extremely detailed and extensive analysis as film and television and other media industries.[17]

While the industries are different, the dominant narratives are the same. Cultural occupations are hostile to parenting and associated caring responsibilities; there are significant career penalties associated with parenting, even where these occupations insist they are supportive and open to all; the attitudes of key senior individuals can often be unhelpful, if not outright sexist; these occupations reflect an ideal type of worker, the 'somatic norm' we demonstrated in Chapter 8.

Jessica was working backstage in theatre at the time of the interview, a working-class origin woman in her early forties. Her initial experience of pregnancy was a blunt rejection by her then employer:

> I got married and then I got pregnant … they said to me, 'Do you
> want to come back?' I said, 'Yes, I don't think I can do the hours
> that I've been doing.' … So when I had a baby it was like 'I can't
> possibly do these hours.' At that time it was like, 'Well then, you
> can't come back.' … Then, I, basically thought, 'Well, as I'm off
> now I might as well just have children.' So I had a second child,
> stayed at home.

We can see how the withdrawal from the labour market to raise
children operates here. For sure, there is a rational choice in
response to her employer's actions. There is also no question
that the long hours associated with theatre-making presented
no options for her. In essence her choice for a second child represents a forced exit from a cultural occupation.

 She returned to theatre three years later, at a major London
institution:

> It was just, like, full on. I was the only person; I didn't really have
> any staff. It was just manic and I was back to working those hours
> that I was working before but just with small children and the
> having put in place this variety of child minders and babysitters
> and neighbours and my husband. We juggled it because I really
> wanted to go back into it. I didn't feel at the time that it is a kind
> of thing that you could ask your employer – having been knocked
> back [previously] – I didn't think it was fair going into [the theatre]
> to say, 'Look I've got these small children and I can't do 70-hour
> weeks.' It just felt like, 'Why am I even applying to them if I can't
> do it.' This is the job. The job is this many hours … So I would say
> for the first two or three years, I was working the most unbeliev-
> able, crazy hours … Then, I suddenly like, I was just very, very
> tired and I really hadn't seen my children for a couple of years.

The labour of raising children, even with a supportive partner
and some financial resources, did not fit with the demands of a

job in theatre. This is not a story of the need for flexible working across the week; rather the expectation of a hugely demanding level of working hours, far beyond what is reasonable, as a basic part of the job. This is not compatible with family life. In fact, we might question whether this sort of working pattern should be compatible with anyone's life.

We can also see how Jessica's analysis of the situation further explains the gendered absences we've identified in cultural jobs. Many academics have critiqued post-feminist discourses that suggest women have been empowered in the workplace and key battles have been won. The media theorist Sarah Banet-Weiser,[18] for example, explores how many women internalise the inequality and unfairness of modern workplaces.

In the case of Jessica we can see how her response to poor working conditions was to assume that she wasn't capable of doing the job, despite a successful career. She did not become resentful of the industry, but rather questioned herself. This is not to criticise Jessica. Instead we make this point to show how it explains the slow pace of change.

Jessica highlights the levels of support needed to sustain these working hours. The situation improved for two reasons: because of a supportive boss; and because of major theatre organisations slowly starting to take seriously the issues associated with parenting,[19] and the consequences for both organisation and artform:

> I started to take a bit more control over my working life and the work–life balance. My boss agreed for me to work like the other end of the day, to come in really early – starting at 7:30 am, finishing at 4:00 pm – doing the school run. That was hard work, I mean I don't know how they did it because it was exhausting but I managed to then see my children at least in the evening. It

was like 'Okay, now I'm at least getting the evenings' ... That was just a given that I would do all of those, and not for anything that needs me. I wanted to do those hours. I wasn't being bullied or anything. I wanted to do them, I wanted to have that control over everything. So, I did that, that was great and I did that for about a year, a year/two years. Then, gradually started moving away from the seven o'clock start, moving back towards the nine/ten o'clock start.

Jessica leads us to ask two questions. First, why should she, as a parent, be stopped from doing a job she is both good at and is clearly committed to? What is so special about theatre (and cultural occupations) that the industry can say 'this is the job' and thus exclude those with caring responsibilities? We return to this question in the conclusion to the chapter. Second, what happens if there is not practical or financial support from a partner, or an understanding boss in an organisation committed to change?

The answer to that second question can be seen in Nicole's story. Nicole, a working-class origin White woman, was also in her thirties at the time of interview, working in a variety of routine jobs to support her acting career. Acting is an especially demanding and difficult part of the theatre world, and very few individuals sustain careers over the long term.

Nicole shows us how even in the context of a hugely competitive labour market, things are stacked against parents as a result of attitudes embedded throughout the sector:

I got pregnant. I think it was about a year and a half into my [acting] course. I remember continuing the course pregnant ... Then, after I'd had my daughter, I think I had to stop my course, because obviously I was looking after a child ... I went off to London to do [a theatre] course when my daughter was four months old. [My daughter] stayed with my mum for three weeks

> … I remember going into college with my baby, into the theatre.
> One of my tutors … I remember him stopping me going into the
> theatre and saying, 'You can't go in there, you've got a baby, and
> you can't do this'. And I remember him being quite firm about
> that. 'You can't do this.' I remember a lot of people at the time
> saying, 'Well that's it now, you're not going to be an actress. It's
> never going to happen, that's not going to happen for you now.
> You've made your bed, lie in it. You're a single mum.'

After this experience of lack of support, the issues continued
as she entered the second part of her drama education. What
is notable from both the first part of her career, and what followed, is the overwhelming sense that hostility to parents is just
how the theatre world works.

Similar experiences have been comprehensively demonstrated in film and television, where media studies scholars
Natalie Wreyford,[20] Anne O'Brien,[21] Susan Berridge,[22] and
Tamsyn Dent[23] have all shown how parenting is both considered incompatible with film and television work, as well as a
'risk' for companies. In Nicole's story, we see this hostility and
the way the hostility is internalised:

> The schedule was really gruelling. I was dropping her off with
> a child minder at 7:00am in the morning and getting home at
> 7:30pm at night. I will never forget being in a rehearsal room
> with a female tutor … I remember saying to this lady, 'I've got to
> go because I'm going to miss the train.' And she said, 'Nobody's
> going anywhere, I'm not finished with you all.' And I said, 'Look,
> I'm going to miss the train, I need to get back to my daughter.'
> And she said, 'Why did you come to drama school if you can't
> do it? Blah blah blah.' And I just remember tears rolling down
> my face and I was thinking, 'I really want to do it, I really want to
> do it. It's just that I have somebody that's relying on me and that
> needs their mum to pick them up.'

I kind of started toying with the fact, 'Can I be an actor? Can I have my daughter? How much am I going to have to give up as a single mum? How much am I going to have to sacrifice for my career?' How can you weigh that up? How can you find a balance in that? Accompanied by having no money, it's not really a great combination for becoming an actor, because how do I get to London to auditions? When I graduated drama school I had a chat with an agent ... And I can remember him sitting there and saying, 'I'd be interested in you but I want you in London.'

I kind of made the decision, 'Right okay, so that's not an option'. So I did bits and bobs around [the Midlands] ... It's not really the kind of work I would have wanted to do ... And then just drifted back into work and ended up working jobs that I just hated and being like a really frustrated creative person.

We could say that the oversupply of labour in the market for actors means that we should expect harsh competition. That does not excuse the sorts of discrimination we can see from Nicole's story.

Ultimately, she left acting, and at the time of interview was returning to theatremaking via another degree and a more devised and community-focused form of practice. But her exit was not based on a lack of talent or hard work. It was based on a system of education, agents, and a theatre world, all hostile to those with parenting responsibilities.

Nothing in Nicole or Jessica's stories should be surprising given the existing academic research on the subject. The juxtaposition of the two shows the importance of support, in Jessica's case from a partner and organisation, in sustaining women's careers when they have families. Nicole shows the harsher reality for women who do not have these structures to support them.

The practical issues of losing networks and contacts that provide job opportunities are hugely important. This loss of networks means some women leave; others carry on but face much worse conditions. They are in the same occupation but starting again, sometimes from the bottom of the career ladder, and with vastly worse working conditions.

Mel, a White woman in her fifties whose parents had worked in creative industries, worked in a range of roles in the television industry, after she had been working as an actor. Her work outside of acting came as a result of what happened when she had children:

> I did bits and pieces … I did do some television, I did an episode of [TV serial] … And I did a film and [a pilot episode]. All these were proper jobs paid for. Then I had children and it kind of like, disappeared. And then when I came back to being an actor, which was ten years ago, I knew that I had to, what I call, start at the plankton level again. And I was quite happy to do that … Managed to get a different agent … They would put me up for all sorts of jobs that were paid or some low paid, commercials, television. Never really got very much with them at all, but then started to do – did some other fringe unpaid, did lots of play readings, rehearsed readings that were unpaid. Did some student films unpaid. Did a couple of corporates or students that were very low pay. And then it wasn't until about two years ago that I started to be properly paid for stuff again … I have had some good – early on I had some good, decent paid work. In the last ten years that's been much harder to come by.

Ruth, who we met earlier in the chapter, told us about the long-term impact of stepping away from full-time work on her career:

> I absolutely love [what I do] it but I wish there was more of it … I do it part-time, but I could do it full-time now because my kids are leaving home, but I can never build up enough work … I'm

in my mid-fifties and all the stats show that middle-aged women have some of the worst outcomes in terms of poverty and trying to get on in the merry world of careers. After their children have left home their chances of succeeding or even getting a job are very, very small so they take jobs that are much below their educational attainment because the odds are stacked against them.

These comments show how even staying within the same cultural occupation can mask the penalties women face to their career. When mothers manage to maintain a creative career, it is with lower professional status, and less income. This persists decades after the period of pregnancy and babyhood, with financial implications that reach into their retirement.

We have also drawn out Mel because of something she mentions just in passing. She was happy to 'start at the plankton level again'. She didn't highlight the failure of the industry to support her and her family. Rather she suggested that this was what happened when women became mothers in the acting industry. Sadly, this was a very common theme in the discussions.

The *individual* mother in creative occupations

Our discussion of Mel's, as well as Jessica's and Nicole's, experiences touched on the distance between the structures of cultural occupations that are, at best, unsupportive of parenting, and the individuals pursuing careers. Placing the responsibility for these structural conditions onto individuals is at the heart of understanding why there are so many inequalities in creative work. It's a theme we've seen throughout this book.

We are now going to look at the sense of identity that is, or is not, fostered as creative workers become parents. In particular, we're going to show how motherhood shapes what is seen as

possible in creative careers and how women's sense of themselves as creative workers is affected. It is important to stress
that while these are individual narratives, they align with the
quantitative data we've presented, and point us towards structural problems.

Jane was a musician from a working-class origin in her early
forties, due to give birth shortly after the time of interview. Her
narrative was striking because it focused on her own choices, in
the face of a hostile music industry:

> I am leaving it really late at forty-three and I have had so much
> guilt about I should have done it ages ago because of all the risks.
> But everybody, like, female singer-songwriters and female artists
> would say, 'Try and put it off as long as possible because once you
> have a baby you can't do it anymore. There's no support there
> and you don't have the energy and it'll be the end of you as an
> artist.' So I don't know what the future holds. Maybe I will have
> to get an arts administration job or something, you know. I don't
> know. I mean obviously I will keep making because that is what
> I do but whether I will be able to carry on making a living to be
> able to support my child as well, I don't know. I chose the path,
> I have to take responsibility for it.

The career advice from others in her position was candid that
'it'll be the end of you as an artist'. This understanding of the
hostility of the music industry to pregnancy and parenting
meant Jane was already thinking about leaving her occupation.
We can see the idea of vertical and horizontal occupational
sorting[24] here, as Jane was already sorting herself out of music
and into another job. She was realistic about the demands that
would come with parenting and being a professional musician.

Music is a competitive labour market, with lots of demands
on everyone, not just mothers. However, the distance between

the idea of hard work and talent, and the reality that 'there's no support there' is clear.

What is perhaps depressing is that Jane is making what seems to be a choice, to plan to leave to carry on making a living elsewhere. The structures that are hostile to parenting and to women remain, reproduced in these choices, and the advice of her colleagues.

We saw this change of position over and over in our interviewees' career stories. Women stayed within the creative economy, but left either senior roles or performing work. Deb, a White, working-class origin woman in her fifties who we met in Chapter 6, reflected on her career as a disabled woman in theatre, giving a similar narrative of career choices to Jane:

> My daughter toured as a prop in the show, which was great, but it's a bit hard when they start to walk. I realised at that point that what I enjoyed was the setting up and the running of stuff far more than the acting at which I was always aware that I was just a little bit mediocre. I wasn't quite good enough ... I could get by as a playwright, but I wasn't ever going to set the world alight. So I spent a while just finding what I could do really well and what I can do really well is make stuff happen, so that's how I kind of fell into producing, although I didn't really call it that ... I think the biggest barriers have been in my own head ... 'Oh, well I've got kids now, that means I can only do this.' 'Oh, this has happened, that means I can only do this.' So I think quite often the barriers are there, I think they're real to start with but they become barriers in your own head so you don't even try and push through them.

Notice again how she recognises barriers, but foregrounds her own role in not trying to 'push through them'. This individualised story has somewhat of a happy ending, as Deb was a very successful theatre maker with a long career. However, her story reinforces the critical points made repeatedly in the academic research we discussed at the start of this chapter.

Conclusion

We opened the chapter with Katie, who gave a clear illustration of how pay and conditions interact with gender, and how this interaction was shaping her decisions. Aged twenty-nine at the time of interview, she was at the age our analysis of the ONS-LS suggests women leave cultural occupations. From our analysis we can speculate as to how her career will be constrained if she chooses to start a family.

Research has repeatedly demonstrated the need for structural changes, as have various public campaigns in industries including film, television, and theatre. Yet, the subjective experience of our interviewees was still of individual choices and individual decisions. This is emotionally draining, as we saw with Jessica, Nicole, Mel, and Deb accepting the responsibility for industry and occupational failings to support them as mothers. It also explains some of the slow pace of change.

The failure of cultural occupations to create an atmosphere of support for parenting, and in particular for mothers, has a whole range of consequences beyond just the impact on the demographics of the sector, especially in senior and leadership positions. It means that crucial narratives and experiences are excluded from cultural representations. It underpins other forms of exploitative conditions that normalise a hostile environment for other individuals and communities who do not fit particular ideal type workers.

The failure to support motherhood is not just a question of workforce demographics. Rather, it reflects a set of expectations about *who* is a creative worker. The ideal type version of a creative worker is not only about being fit and able-bodied, being able to work long hours at short notice and be part of close-knit cultural networks; it is also attached to a specific gendered body. Jane reminds us of the somatic norm in the context of parenthood:

> We went to Brazil, me and all the female members of the cast and the crew we are all childless and single. Everyone, all the males that were out there all have kids, you know, because they have partners who can do that while they continue to work in what is a lifestyle that doesn't really suit the stability that a child might need. But the partners can do that so yes. Then, you know, sometimes when you are having a clash of egos in a creative sense. Like a male artist might actually use that to shoot you down a wee bit. You don't have children … I do. You make a better artist but I have got children and you are lacking in that. I have had that in the past, you know.

In the introduction to the book we noted that many of the patterns we would be describing, whether in terms of cultural consumption or cultural production, were not only depictions of inequality. They also reflected struggles over worth and value.

Jane illustrates these struggles over value and worth perfectly. She is made to feel illegitimate whatever her maternal choices. This is because the music industry is structured to reward men and their particular parenting arrangements. We saw this several times with our respondents who were fathers, all referencing how difficult parenting was, but never suggesting it would cost them their careers. Indeed, the sense that they were rewarded and validated, rather than problematised and punished, was clear.

In recent work on computing and IT, the historian Mar Hicks has charted the changing gender basis of these industries following the end of the Second World War.[25] Our data from the LFS in Chapter 3 suggested IT occupations are overwhelmingly male. This was not always the case. Hicks' research tells us that there is no inevitability about gender-based exclusions from specific occupations.

Exclusions come as a result of decisions. Some of these are small, for example how advertising for particular positions changes. Some are everyday acts of sexism, for example refusal to hire or promote women as the status of occupations in computing changed in business and the public sector. Some of these are grand, structural changes.

As computing gained status it became equated with men and as a male set of occupations. This was because men were seen as what a high-status individual within an organisation *is*. The fact that women were in strategic IT roles did not fit this 'somatic norm' of men as managers and women as low level secretarial workers.

Hicks' work shows how what seems inevitable or a settled status quo in a profession develops over time, and how things can be challenged. Yet the seeming inevitability of inequality also *benefits* some groups. Jane's story in the conclusion to this chapter hints at this process. To learn more, we're going to hear from senior men in our next chapter.

10

What about the men?[1]

Introduction: Howard recognises racism in the TV industry

The arts is one of those strange democratic organisations, parts of Britain where you can actually break out of your class system if you want to call it that, being a working-class person to break out and be the top of your profession, and therefore in that way I think the performing arts and the arts are classless once you've got into them, and it is the getting, giving the opportunities to the people is the hardest thing … it depends totally on the people, the quality, and the artistic quality of the people that are trying to become, break into the arts if that makes sense to you … I certainly think, I certainly think the race issue is quite considerable. I think it is much harder if you are of African, West Indian, Black origin I think it is much harder. I don't know why it is but it seems to me to be … I think, I mean not that I had much experience, but from looking I think that for a Black male it is much harder. Their input is not seen, is not seen sadly.

Howard was in his early seventies when we interviewed him. We heard from him in Chapter 2. There he told us about the power of culture to influence people and to change the world.

A White, clerical origin, man, he told us about his long, and seemingly successful, career in the television industry. He was modest, reflecting on his frustrations and missed opportunities. He told that the idea he has been successful 'is what people tell me anyway'.

Part of Howard's ambivalence and modesty about his career was the sense that he wanted more people to engage in the arts. He felt television 'opened doors and opened windows to the possibilities of new things' in the arts. Television could be a force for bringing in new, and more, audiences to visual and performing arts. However, Howard saw this, and in some ways his own, potential unfulfilled.

Howard echoes themes from Chapter 2. For Howard, culture is a good thing. Working in culture rewards talent and artistic quality, irrespective of class origins. We can see Howard's take on who is successful connecting us to the views on meritocracy that we saw in Chapter 3. Yet this is not the whole story he is telling us.

He recognised many of the inequalities we've been discussing in this book. As we can see in the quote that opens this chapter, even though Howard was committed to meritocracy in the arts, he was still aware of barriers to success. In general, 'the getting, giving the opportunities to the people is the hardest thing'. More specifically, Howard was aware of the struggles that his Black colleagues have faced, that 'their input is not seen'.

Howard was a senior leader in a key cultural occupation, taking decisions that shape what gets made. His type of position, the leadership and decision-making roles in cultural and creative occupations, has traditionally been the least diverse.[2] These roles have been the most likely to be occupied by those fitting the dominant 'somatic norm'[3] of White, middle-class origin, masculinity that we discussed in Chapter 8.

Even though Howard was committed to the good culture can do, he was frustrated by the problems within cultural occupations. Yet he was in a position to, potentially, challenge and change some of the inequalities he recognised (and which we've discussed in this book). Indeed, part of Howard's career was making space for new talent and new voices. In spite of that, structural inequalities persist.

We are going to see how Howard's understanding of inequality is quite typical of our senior decision-makers in cultural occupations. By doing so, we'll help explain why change seems so slow in cultural and creative occupations. *Recognising* inequality is not enough to ensure social change.

Crucially, the recognition of inequality may be, in itself, part of the problem. At worst, it is a potential strategy for ensuring the continued dominance of already powerful social groups.[4] We'll see this in analysis of senior men's stories of their career biographies, and explanations for their position and success. The analysis demonstrates a considerable distance between their rhetoric and how occupations need to change.

This 'inequality talk' is an important part of understanding how the current settlement, excluding women, ethnic minorities, and those from working-class origins, persists. This is despite the public proclamations and sincere intentions of senior men.

The focus on 'inequality talk' also offers us a depressing irony about our focus on structural problems. It cautions us to the potential limitations of our critique of inequality in cultural occupations.

As we will see, our senior men are well aware of the structural problems. Even with the best intentions of individuals, structural inequalities are replicated and reproduced. As a result, we need to better theorise the relationship between culture and inequality, and think about how to go beyond just raising awareness of the structures underpinning inequality in cultural occupations.

Unspeakable inequalities in cultural and creative industries

Throughout this book we have been highlighting key theorists and researchers who have analysed cultural occupations. They all suggest working in cultural and creative industries has lots of problems.

We have, of course, added to this existing work with our own analysis. Most importantly, we've shown there are a range of structural barriers[5] raised against those who do not fit the 'somatic norm' of the White, middle-class origin, man.

This latter point is important, as it frames the discussion in this chapter. There has not been as much focus on those running the cultural and creative industries, in contrast to those who are excluded. Those who *are* the somatic norm can sometimes be absent from research on cultural occupations.

This is for very good reasons. It is obviously important to show the existence of inequalities in the workforce. It is also obviously important to attempt to explain these inequalities by showing the sorts of subtle barriers affecting those furthest from the 'somatic norm' of White, male, middle classness that dominates senior decision-making positions.

In the previous chapter we focused on the challenges faced by mothers in cultural occupations. In doing so we highlighted existing research which rejects industry and policy's focus on motherhood as the only explanation for the absence of women from the cultural workforce.

In this chapter we would like to mirror and extend this analysis by placing the focus on the men who make it to the top. This is so we can look at their perceptions of the problems and issues in the cultural sector. We would also like to show the sorts of actions they may, or may not, take in response.

Throughout the book we have highlighted how almost all of our interviewees were very clear about issues of inequality. In the previous chapters many interviewees offered detailed, almost sociological, accounts of the inequalities in the sector, and how they experienced them.

Our senior men were, almost, no different. They too seemed to be well aware of the inequalities highlighted by academic research. This was the case even if they had no personal experience of, for example, the issues we highlighted in Chapters 8 and 9. The understanding of inequalities shared by almost all interviewees played out differently, with different consequences, in the case of senior men.

This point starts off the line of thought that will eventually form a core conclusion to the book. There is now a very pressing question as to how cultural occupations change in response to the inequalities that research, in particular academic research, on gender, class, and race has revealed. One of the things we are seeking to highlight in this chapter is the complex impact of discussions of inequality on those who are most able to make change happen by commissioning, curating, and hiring.

Before we turn to the 'senior' men in our dataset, it is worth pausing to consider some of the existing work on inequalities of gender and race in creative occupations. This is especially useful as it lays the ground for a new, troubling, understanding, of inequality in these industries.

Howard's comments that opened this chapter suggest senior figures in the cultural sector know of the problem of inequality and are determined to address it. This would *seem* to contradict what we know from the existing academic research.

Three authors are especially important at this point. Angela McRobbie,[6] Rosalind Gill,[7] and Sarita Malik[8] have all, in differing and distinct ways, shaped both the theoretical and empirical setting for understanding inequality in cultural occupations. Gill and Malik have focused on how inequalities are marginalised in policy and practitioners' language and activities. McRobbie's theorisation connects this creative industries-specific research to broader social struggles in employment, education, and consumer culture.

In Malik's work the focus is on the way in which recognition of racial discrimination has been made difficult, if not outright impossible. This is caused by the displacement of antiracist campaigning in favour of the framework of diversity and the idea of creativity in cultural production.

'Creative diversity' as the dominant frame for discussing inequalities associated with race and ethnicity 'signifies a post-multiculturalist, falsely post-racial understanding'.[9] This understanding seeks to suggest struggles for equality are now settled and past. We can see parallels with post-feminism, as discussed in our previous chapter. This also adds to Chapter 8's analysis, as it means the negative experiences of our socially mobile people of colour are less likely to be recognised.

Post-racial understandings of cultural production, particularly those in broadcast policy, mean discrimination and exclusion are made 'unspeakable'. This is a central insight from Ros Gill's work on sexism and misogyny in media organisations.

Gill and McRobbie have analogous perspectives on the issue of gender inequalities. The former has focused specifically on creative industries, and the latter on the more general social position of post-feminist discourses. They were both intervening against popular and media discourses that suggested sexism was, increasingly, no longer an issue in workplaces. Apparently, the struggle for equality was being won, and all that was required was for women to be more assertive. A good example of this is the career advice literature exemplified by *Lean In*[10] by Sheryl Sandberg of Facebook.

This 'post-feminist' set of discourses tends to point away from structural understandings of inequality caused by sexism and misogyny. Both Gill and McRobbie reject these claims, demonstrating the existence of a new set of demands on women to be 'top girls' in the labour market, in education, and in consumer society.

These new sets of demands are also part of rendering sexism 'unspeakable' in creative and media occupations, such as in the radio industry. We saw this play out for mothers in creative occupations in Chapter 9.

Gill's work is particularly important in this context. She identifies how the post-feminist moment in creative industries obscures the 'subtle yet virulent forms of sexism'[11] that are entrenched in creative workplaces.

The result is that workers adopt the language of openness, and faith in talent and creativity, to explain their and others' success. This is a powerful 'myth of inclusivity' that not only leaves structural inequalities unchallenged, but also reinforces and replicates them. Inequalities are thus 'unspeakable' for creative workers in the post-feminist and post-racial workforce.

These three perspectives are in keeping with the discussion of meritocracy in Chapter 3. The best paid were likely to be committed to talent and hard work as the explanation for success. This fits with inequality being 'unspeakable'. More generally, our respondents' attachment to meritocractic explanations for how people get in and get on in creative careers points to the marginalisation of issues of inequality.

We are therefore confronted with a puzzle. Men like Howard, along with most of the other senior men in our interview sample, all seem to recognise structural inequalities. Inclusivity and diversity, both in terms of workforce and audience, was at the centre of the comments. Inequality seems very 'speakable'.

In some ways we could be celebrating that senior men recognise inequality. Key theorists' critiques may have been taken on board. Behaviour at the top may be changing. Sadly, as we will show, this may not the case.

In fact, the issues identified by Malik, Gill, and McRobbie have not gone away. What has happened is that the language addressing inequality has evolved. Within the recognition of structural inequalities lies the absolution of responsibility for change.

Inequalities may now be 'speakable' but they are still persistent, as previous chapters have demonstrated. There is a real danger that speaking about inequalities is a new way to marginalise and ignore them. This operates in the same way that meritocratic language and beliefs were used to deny the existence of systemic exclusions based on race and gender.

Unspeakable inequalities or inequality talk?

What does this inequality talk sound like? Denying the existence of inequalities, and asserting the idea that talent and hard work would prevail, was rare from the senior men we interviewed. *Recognition* of inequality and structural barriers was much, much more common.

However, it is worth noting where the minority rendered inequalities unspeakable and the sorts of ways they did so. Here we can see David, a White, middle-class origin designer in his forties, questioning the existence of inequalities:

> I don't think there is an issue at all of class. I don't think there is an issue at all with background. I don't think there is an issue with any kind of social strata. I think the [design] world is incredibly open and actually, there's a pretty low entry-level which allows many different people to access it … Gender lines, I think it's actually now more female than male … it's at least 50/50.

The position that creative occupations were open, irrespective of class or gender, was unusual from our interviewees. What dominated the data was a more complex version of 'inequality talk'.

In contrast to David, recognising and discussing inequality was a dominant mode of discourse for our interviewees. This manifested in three ways.

First, as an analysis of problems in the interviewee's industry. Adam, an editor in his twenties, from a middle-class origin, discussed the inequalities marking the publishing industry (and his frustration and disappointment about that fact):

> I find one of the huge negatives across this as an industry, as a sector, is the lack of diversity in terms of ethnic diversity across

the industry, across all levels. Everybody in publishing is White. I mean, well, not everybody, but ridiculous proportions ... More than that, there are gender inequalities at the higher levels ... the majority of people are women, but not in the boardroom ... historically the successful people were White men, there's probably a class element to that too.

Adam's sense of frustration at inequality in publishing was echoed by Lawrence, a White, middle-class origin journalist and editor in his forties.

Lawrence provides the second mode of discussing inequality. He was more explicit in feeling the need to try to challenge and change the inequalities he saw in both the television and publishing industries:

I'm conscious of the space I take up I think and try not to. I try to champion new items through the new screenwriters, new actors who haven't come from the conventional background that most actors and writers have ... I think in terms of TV there's still a lack of representation. It's improving, but I think possibly worse than on screen is behind the scenes. If the commissioners are all White and middle class, then their tastes are going to a point reflect that, and even their attempts at diversification are still coming from that perspective. So, they will commission something that they think is diverse or is catering to or reflecting a certain part of the audience perhaps, but it's still their idea of what it is.

Even when inequality was recognised and foregrounded in discussions of working in cultural and creative professions, talent and hard work were still seen as vital to success. Our third example comes from Richard, a White film and television director from working-class origins, in his forties at the time of interview. In his comments we see echoes of David's insistence that his industry was open with low barriers to entry.

Richard, even in recognising the clear gender disparity in the film industry, still held on to the importance of talent as a key part of success. He suggests class barriers might be rendered irrelevant by talent. However, he is still clear that gender is still a source of discrimination in film:

> I just think talent doesn't see class in that anyone can be born talented … Sex, I think does, I think from my experience, I have a lot of female friends, I would say that opportunities are still fewer for women, particularly, if you will, behind the camera. If you go on a film set there's still probably only 10% of women in the crew and writers and directors as well … So that does still have an effect.

The lucky gentlemen producing culture

If the majority of our senior cultural and creative men were aware of, and keen to challenge and change, inequalities in their occupations, surely this is grounds for good news and celebration? It might suggest that inequalities are no longer 'unspeakable'. It may also be a sound basis for change, especially given that recognition seemed to go hand-in-hand with frustration. We saw this clearly from Adam and Lawrence.

We might *expect* this recognition of inequality. This is perhaps in response to the way inequalities in cultural occupations have been highlighted by media and academic discourses in recent years. Not only have media and academics highlighted the issues, but high-profile campaigns and policy interventions have attempted to address inequalities.

We should be cautious. The comments from Richard remind us that belief in the role of talent is still a powerful force in the creative sector. In some ways this is rightly so. Talent and hard work matter and it would be strange to see them totally marginalised in a discussion of who succeeds.

Notwithstanding this point, recognition of inequality eventually reinforces Rosalind Gill's analysis of the marginalisation of the realities of sexism in creative work. This works in two ways.

Faith in talent is coupled with a powerful sense that cultural and creative work are 'good' occupations, important to social change and ahead of other professions in terms of diversity and equality. We saw this sense that culture is good for you earlier in the book. It is an important discourse in policy as well as practitioner understandings of culture and cultural work.

For our senior men, the sense that arts and culture are 'good' occupations was coupled with the failure to recognise the role of inequality in their *own* career success. They understood that inequality marked creative occupations. Inequality, by contrast, did not mark their careers.

Here our senior men echo a broader discussion of class and inequality that has a long-standing history in research on this subject. People can see that society is unequal, and that there are social divisions. They can offer explanations that point to social structures underpinning those inequalities. They do not, however, *foreground* structural explanations for their lives. Rather they tell individual, biographical, stories.

The individual 'middling' biographical narrative is common even with those at the very top of the social scale. People seek to be ordinary, in the face of the current, unequal, social settlement.[12]

For our interviewees there is also an important gendered dimension to consider. Recent work by sociologists Andrew Miles and Mike Savage[13] explored how men working in professions discuss their sense of success in their careers, as part of a broader tradition of research seeking to understand experiences of social mobility.[14]

For men in the professions, there is a specific 'gentlemanly motif' within their stories. This is marked by modesty about one's own success, the importance of luck in explaining professional careers, and the unstatedness, or downplaying, of individual agency 'in the dice game which is held to determine one's prospects in life'.[15]

We could say that some of our men are reflecting a broader trend of people generally claiming to be ordinary and in the middle of the social structure. This even as they recognise inequality.

Beyond this trend, there are specifics that Miles and Savage make us attentive to. The gentlemanly mode of discourse is especially important. It allows our interviewees to at once recognise the problems of inequality in their cultural and creative occupations, but still leave those issues as unspeakable thanks to the 'luck' that explains their success.

There was a distance between our interviewees' 'inequality talk' about cultural occupations, and their understandings of their own lives and careers. It is a striking dissonance, particularly as our interviewees were in positions to effect change in the sector. The dissonance between inequality talk and narratives of lucky gentlemen is crucial to understanding how issues of inequality continue in creative industries.

There were, of course, variations in the narratives of luck and the self-effacing mode of delivery. The gentlemanly narrative of success, and the contrast with an awareness of inequality, is distilled by Adam.

In the previous section we noted Adam's analysis of the inequalities in publishing and his frustrations about working in such an unequal industry. When asked about his own career Adam moved away from structural narratives, such as his own White, male, middle classness, and focused instead on a core gentlemanly trope, that of luck:

> I'm now in a position that is very enviable and relatively senior. Almost entirely through luck, of having been able to rise quite quickly through the ranks … possibly other people have had a very hard time of it because they've gone straight to a company where they want to work and found it very difficult to rise through that company … I was at a fairly uncompetitive, big company where I was able to rise through the ranks quite quickly and then just say 'Look, I've got this experience, I'll land myself a good job here.' I think that's as much through luck as many other factors.

The contrast to Adam's inequality talk is stark, although, as we have noted, not entirely unexpected. Awareness of structural issues is often in contrast to biographical narrative, whether in terms of positioning oneself within a broader social hierarchy or in accounts of career success.

In some ways Adam is reiterating the individualised narratives of inequality that we saw from mothers in Chapter 9. However, when he does so it means that the role of unequal structures in his *success* is played down, just as our mothers marginalised the role of unequal structures in their career *struggles*.

Recognising inequality, but playing down the role of the structures underpinning it, is a perfect fit for gentlemanly narratives of career success. This frame plays down the role of hard work and talent, as well as marginalising structural advantages.

This part of the gentlemanly narrative is distinct from luck as a driver for things like job appointments, but foregrounds the sense of gentlemanly, amateur, approaches to work. For example, we can turn to Graham, a man in his sixties from a working-class background, working in film and television. He drew a contrast between himself and his peers in the television industry:

> You know it's, I think of myself as having not had a great deal of focus. I recognise that there are other people that have been extremely focused from very early on and focused on succeeding whatever it takes and you know that is their way of doing it, and it is kind of, I would say it has not been mine.

The sense of self-effacement was present for Gerald, a White, middle-class origin senior curator in his fifties who we have met several times in this book. His story culminated in a narrative of effortless success and the luck of being in the right place at the right time or era, even when background or social origins were part of the explanation for success:

> I was very lucky because both background and confidence wise and because of the state support in place, and I suppose because I was good enough to get the state support, I was able to do all that. I think I was very lucky. I would never get my job if they advertised it now … I had no career plan. I mean I had that lovely optimism you have in your twenties that … you just can go anywhere.
>
> I have only really ever got three jobs and they … were willing to take a punt on me, and certainly in my first two jobs … people explicitly have said to me we are taking a piece of a risk employing you.
>
> I suppose in both cases I wasn't qualified to do the job, but … I find when you see things like that, when I see job ads I have lots of ideas and I suppose they were interested in my ideas but they also had a sense I could probably do it. I was probably practically

minded enough that I could implement at least some of what my ideas were.

This narrative of luck, and the gentlemanly fashion of self-effacement, is distinctly gendered. Writing on women developing careers as a classical musicians, Christina Scharff[16] has also highlighted luck in career narratives.

For Scharff's interviewees 'luck' played an important part of accounting for privileged positions. However, it was luck in terms of parental affluence and support. Reducing or equating class inequality to luck is a means of deflecting discussions about the role of social origins in career success.

We can see important similarities from our senior men. The rhetorical effect of 'luck' can refer to the luck of being born male in a middle-class, well-connected household, as much as it can to the luck of being in the right place at the right time. This connects us back to Chapter 6. There we saw our older workers talk about the luck of being in the right era for cultural success. We saw it from Lisa at the start of Chapter 7.

Emphasising luck in one's life and career may not be a total disavowal of one's privilege. At the very least it can be understood as a euphemistic account of it. This is especially important at the intersection of gender and class within our senior men's narratives.

For example, discourses of luck may seem entirely at odds with 'inequality talk'. Participants' accounts of their trajectories almost entirely disregarded the structures in which they found themselves. Thus, luck for our interviewees, for example Adam and Graham, is also suffused with a specifically gendered, gentlemanly flavour. This is in contrast to their understanding of inequality in cultural occupations.

This discourse intersected with a particular insistence on the importance and difference of creative and cultural occupations. Here self-effacement and distancing from structural explanations for success gave rise to the belief that doing a creative occupation was 'lucky', and that these occupations could be differentiated from other professions.

This is distinct from luck as an *explanation* for career success and opens up the discussion of creative occupations as good occupations that are doing 'better' than other professions and industries. Ben and Jack can illustrate this. Ben was one of the youngest in our sample, in his twenties, but was already an established and successful theatre director.

Ben offered a sense of privilege at being able to work solely on his artistic interests, rather than being constrained, a situation in which social structures easing the careers of White middle-class men in theatre were absent:

> I have been really lucky that I have been able to make a career out of something that I have always been interested in and always wanted to do. I have been really hugely lucky to get quite a lot of the opportunities … quite quickly. I have had … opportunities to make pieces of work that I definitely wanted to make and that felt driven by my artistic impulse and nothing else.

The opportunities to make work, and to be driven by artistic impulse, render the imbalances of gender and race in theatre, particularly in writing, absent or irrelevant. These are exactly the 'unspeakable inequalities' identified by Gill.

Moreover, cultural and creative industries are marked out as different from other professions. They are different in terms of doing 'better' on equality and diversity, and in terms of the importance of the social function of cultural production. An

excerpt from Jack, a White, working-class origin museum director in his thirties working at an institution in an English city,
shows both of these themes:

> I've now been there for ten years, I've started seeing some longi-
> tudinal big wins with individuals that we've worked with when
> they were very young people that have now gone on to do fan-
> tastic things. I get to see that first-hand and see the impact that
> the work that we do has had on people's lives. That, for me, is the
> fundamental reason why I work in the arts – because I believe
> in its ability to change people's lives forever, because I've seen
> it in myself and I can see the opportunity for others ... I think
> [inequality matters] less so in our industry because, hopefully, as
> organisations, we're open to all.

Throughout this book we have been keen to show how even
things that are shared perspectives or experiences need nuanced and differentiated understandings. Unpaid work is a
clear example. We saw how there were important class and age
differences. Jack's comments remind us that even where our
interviewees shared a dedication to the idea that 'culture is good
for you', as we saw in Chapter 2, there are crucial differences
when we analyse this commitment.

In Jack's case the faith in the power of culture, that it can
'change people's lives forever' allows him to play down inequalities. We see, again, an evolution from the idea that culture is a
meritocracy, to the idea that the impact of culture marks key
occupations and industries out as different from other jobs.

The risk with a discourse of culture is good for you, in Jack's
case, is that it allows cultural occupations to ignore inequality.
In the context of our senior men who *recognise* inequalities, the
importance and impact of culture can be a powerful justification for being slow to change.

The lucky gents who can't change inequality in cultural and creative jobs

We can bring the themes of this chapter together in a detailed engagement with data from one interviewee. Thomas was from a White, middle-class, professional household and had attended a fee-paying school followed by an undergraduate degree at one of England's most prestigious universities. He then worked in performing arts, eventually combining his creative work with a role as an arts manager. At the time of interview he was in his forties, and occupied a senior role in his organisation.

His narrative of his career trajectory was suffused with gentlemanly modesty. His original move into arts management was prompted by being asked to apply for a new post at a company that he had an existing connection with:

> If I remember correctly, I was the only person they saw, but I had something like a three-hour interview, with proper tasks, and, you know, all of that stuff. So, it wasn't like they just let me walk in and sit at a desk.

Discussing his later application to work at his current organisation, he talked up his lack of knowledge of the artform, playing down the significant professional expertise he had gathered from previous work as an arts manager. While some of this was exaggeration for effect, it is important in terms of the gentlemanly narrative:

> I knew almost nothing about [the artform], but I thought I would apply for that job and use my ignorance of it as the, sort of, central plank of my application. You know, if I can, through a position of ignorance, talk about [the artform] effectively, then perhaps we can persuade other people who are ignorant about it to understand it. Somehow, that worked.

In keeping with the idea of a gentlemanly motif, we see Thomas' modesty and distance from expertise or experience. His is a story of chancing his arm and 'somehow, that worked'. Would someone who did not fit the somatic norm have been the only person interviewed for the earlier job? Would the strategy of foregrounding his ignorance of the artform have been successful for someone not of his background?

The gentlemanly narrative is important in framing his understanding of inequality. He did not dismiss or play down the structural inequalities in his part of the cultural sector. In fact, he showed an acute and detailed understanding of the problems facing creative workers, albeit tempered by the puzzle of how best to address them:

> I feel like that question of diversity is a really important one, that I would happily grapple with for a long time, but I feel frustrated that I don't have any answers for it. [At an event] a lot of the room was White, female, middle-aged, and of a certain class. It felt like everyone's hearts were in the right places, and yet, we still didn't know quite what to do about any of it. I want us to do something meaningful, and yet I don't know what the thing might be.

Even where, in the interview, there might have been moments of post-feminist or post-racial discourse to render inequalities unspeakable, Thomas was still keen to show that he understood the issues:

> Let's start with gender, because that's easy: almost everyone who works in [my artform] is a woman, anyway. So, at least we don't discriminate too badly against women generally, although, having said that, there is still, I think, a disproportionate … All the big famous [leaders] are boys, and women do all the real

work, and the men do the showy bits on the top … I suspect we are not the worst offender of any industry in the world, as far as that goes.

This mixture of recognition of inequalities, and faith that the cultural sector, or at least the areas Thomas was working and practising in, were doing better than other areas of economy and society is important.

This reminds us of Jack's comment earlier in the chapter, as well as pointing us back to Chapter 2. Thomas' insistence that 'hearts were in the right places' sat alongside the belief that 'we are not the worst offender of any industry', with cultural jobs being better at addressing inequality than other professions.

These two points were the context for Thomas' frustration at the lack of change in the cultural occupations. Thomas focused directly on his capacity to effect that change, suggesting he was limited and constrained. This was even where he had specific power and responsibility for hiring staff and shaping programming:

You put out an advert for a junior job at an arts organisation … and you'll be deluged with responses. There are hundreds of them. So, what are you going to do? You're going to pick the one with the best education, for the most part. You know, we can talk about diversity all we like, and we can mean it until our hearts are breaking, but in the end, when you've got one post to fill, you really don't want to fuck it up.

His lack of agency in the face of a structural issue of oversupply in the labour market was, in turn, related to much broader social and economic divisions shaping contemporary Britain:

> We are forced, and I say this with some caution, we are pretty
> much forced into maintaining the un-diverse status quo, because
> the damage has been done before we get to the point at which we
> could inflict any damage. I dare say, we do our fair share of it.

Thomas' comments extend Jack's defence of cultural occupations. Thomas also returns us to the broader theme of recognition of inequalities. Thomas seems to be recognising his
role in replicating inequality. He is not offering a meritocratic
story that talent and hard work will ensure success in cultural
jobs. He suggests a structural explanation, even as he describes
how in hiring he is 'forced into maintaining the un-diverse
status quo'.

Conclusion

There is a distinct irony when Thomas highlights social structures to explain inequality in cultural occupations. He is the
direct beneficiary of our unequal society. He points to these
more general social inequalities to account for how he replicates
and reproduces inequality in cultural jobs.

We are concluding with this to make two points. The first
is to draw together some of the themes we've seen across the
book. The other is to think about the limits of our analysis.

By not wanting to 'fuck it up' when hiring, Thomas suggests
it may be a risk to appoint specific people. This follows directly
from Chapter 8's discussion of the somatic norm in cultural
occupations.

For Thomas, the focus is on education. It is unlikely he, or
any of our other interviewees, would focus on specific demographic characteristics such as race, gender, or class origin. Yet
education, in our unequal society, is related to the categories of

race, gender, or class origin that we have discussed throughout this book.

By framing certain appointments as 'risky', we can see how Thomas' hiring practices result in the sorts of unequal labour force we saw in Chapter 3. We can also see the importance of things like education and cultural capital, which we highlighted in Chapter 5. Finally, we can see how *recognition* of inequality is not enough. It is a particular problem when recognition draws on structural explanations to justify decisions that reproduce and replicate inequality in cultural occupations.

This is our second concluding point and brings us towards the overarching conclusion in the book. The key theorists we've discussed in this chapter who were writing on inequality in cultural occupations worried about discourses of meritocracy upholding inequality. We also saw these concerns when we discussed social mobility in Chapter 8.

Meritocracy suggests hard work and talent are enough for success because cultural occupations are open to all. These stories, as we saw from David's understanding of gender in design occupations, play down the way economic, social, and cultural resources are crucial to success. This was clear from Chapter 6's analysis of unpaid work, in addition to our more general discussion of inequality throughout the book.

Our analysis in this chapter suggests 'inequality talk' is a new discourse for those making decisions in cultural occupations. It may sit alongside meritocracy, or may even be replacing it as the key discourse for senior decision-makers.

The recognition of inequality as a structural problem does not extend to how our senior men understand their own careers and success. This is a reverse of the individual narrative we problematised in Chapter 9. There we saw that mothers

271

recognised inequalities in the creative sector, but often took personal responsibility for the compromises and damage to their career that result.

Conversely, individual narratives of luck serve senior men well, even as they understand the problems of the industries in which they work. They recognise, and regret, the inequalities in and exclusions from their industries. At the same time, they fail to recognise the processes that contribute to these inequalities as they play out in their own careers.

If our analysis is correct, it suggests new strategies are needed to challenge inequality. Moreover, we need to more fully theorise the relationship between culture and inequality.

The risk is that the strategies we choose, and use, to address inequality end up as a means of supporting the status quo. This chapter suggests recognising inequality as a structural issue in cultural occupations might end up justifying slow or no change. We must think carefully about strategies that will be successful. To do so we need to understand how culture relates to inequality and how inequality relates to culture. We hope this book has contributed to that understanding.

11

Conclusion

We started the book with a comment from Henna. She was talking about her experiences in the film industry. We're thinking about Henna again as we close the book.

We are going to focus on film and TV to bring together the four themes we've discussed in the book. Film and TV also show why looking at occupations is a useful way of understanding inequality in cultural and creative industries.

In the late 1960s the BBC broadcast two episodes of its *Man Alive* documentary series. These episodes looked at the changing patterns and perceptions of social class in Britain.[1]

We will start with the later episode. 'Top Class People' was first shown in 1967 and explored the lives of working-class origin creative workers. It interviewed the pop stars Sandie Shaw and Twiggy, and the television script writer Johnny Speight. They were all presented as emblematic of changing class relations. In this episode a working-class background was presented as an advantage in the emerging 'top class' jobs of design, television, and music. The successful creative workers profiled were 'helping the rest of us believe we really are becoming a classless society'. The voiceover suggested that, perhaps, these working-class creatives are to be envied by those 'suffering the disadvantages' of middle- and upper-class backgrounds.

Much of what we have discussed in the book is present here. There is a sense of the importance of cultural occupations as part of a changing Britain. This is alongside the classlessness of talent and hard work for successful cultural workers.

These are not the only elements of note in the programme. We're highlighting these as they tell us that cultural jobs, along with cultural 'products' like music and television shows, have long been central to our society. In turn, they have long been central to social inequality.

We see inequality in the interview with the artist and designer Alan Aldridge. He tells a story of social and cultural capital, a story we have seen earlier in this book. Aldridge is open about feeling 'self-conscious' as the art director for Penguin Books. He tries to be less cockney and more highbrow in his working day. His accent comes back when he meets his friends and family. Aldridge is a confident and successful man. Yet he still talks about inhabiting two worlds. These are the world of work for the publishing industry, and life with his family and friends.

The 1966 broadcast[2] is even more interesting. It wasn't about creative workers. It explored the rise of a comparatively new social science, that of market research. The film discusses some now classic tropes of popular class analysis. It comments on how people dress, and the use of words and language. It also introduces a market research mode of classification, the social grade running A to E.

The film reflects a popular perception of the 1960s as a time when class was being challenged and subject to scrutiny. That scrutiny comes from the 'hard sell' of market research and social science. The film's interviews with a range of people from different occupations are keen to discover the impact of this scrutiny on 'the old snobberies'.

The film is most fascinating because of the choice of occupation placed at the top of this 'new', social scientific and market research, class hierarchy. It is not the doctor, lawyer, or captain of industry. It is working in film and television that is used to represent the apex of Britain's class structure.

Mr Duffel was a filmmaker when he was interviewed by the BBC. He and his wife were recorded in 'the most with-it house, in the most with-it road, in London's most with-it borough'. The episode offers a fascinating insight into class as a category in the mind of what we would now call a creative worker.

The Duffels are explicitly against snobbery. They are defined by eclectic tastes, yet they also stress their ordinary interests. They 'don't really think about class' as part of their identity. Mrs Duffel refuses class as a category entirely, and they are keen for their children to be educated in a similarly anti-snobbish, open, and meritocratic way. This is even if they have to pay for a progressive school. Trevor Philpott's reporting gets to the heart of what we have been thinking through in this book, that 'inside the little lettered boxes of the new class system everything changes; everything is the same'.

Making inequality visible

Mr Duffel's values and his occupation as a filmmaker are, we argue, hard to separate. This is not an especially controversial statement. Many occupations have particular sets of values and attitudes attached to them. In Chapter 2 we showed the variety of ways in which our interviewees were committed to the power and value of culture. As we saw in Chapter 3, our creative occupations are characterised by liberal, left-wing values.

We have mentioned the Duffels to illustrate how the inequalities we've been discussing are not *new*. This was crucial to Chapter 7's focus on historical patterns of inequality in creative work. There our data began just over a decade after the BBC broadcast *Man Alive*. The data in Chapter 3 and in Chapter 7 might even include the Duffels' children! This is speculation, of course, although we think it is an interesting question.

We speculate because the book has demonstrated the long-standing dominance of elites entering cultural occupations. This dominance is coupled with Chapter 5's analysis of parents in cultural jobs helping their children to know the 'rules of the game'.

The long-standing nature of inequality in cultural occupations presents a pessimistic vision. It is especially pessimistic for those wanting to create a broader social basis for cultural production and consumption.

We want this book to be part of creating this broader social basis for culture. We hope it contributes in the struggle to challenge inequality in cultural occupations. In doing so, we hope to see change in the creative industries as a whole. As a result, the book contributes to the vast range of existing research on inequality by cultural and media studies scholars. Our earlier examples from film and television reflect how these industries have seen detailed study, particularly by research on gender inequalities.

This work has been an important inspiration for our book. Much of this work has been about making inequality *visible*.[3] Research has revealed sexist attitudes in the workplace and unequal access to finance and distribution. It has also interrogated the moments in careers where barriers are higher for women than men.

Recent analysis of sexism in the film industry by Irish academic Anne O'Brien[4] perfectly captures our aims of making inequality *visible*. It is worth quoting from her at length:

> In order to bring about change women need to name and understand the exact ways in which they experience gender inequality in media work. Women need to be clear about defining the problem and knowing what precisely needs to be addressed. They need to be clear about how much of the industry needs to change, and how radical the change needs to be, if screen production is to genuinely include women. We need to know that women do not lack confidence, they experience exclusion. We need also to understand how women have survived for so long in an industry that fails utterly to value them. We need to honour their agency and resilience and document how they inhabit their biased and discriminatory working worlds and even manage to derive great joy from their work. And finally, we need to be clear about what women value in media work and how we can nurture those aspects of screen production that can create a better industry, one that women are willing to engage with, one where they are, simply, equal. We need to start a fully researched and evidence-based conversation about gender inequality in media work, how women survive it and how the sector can be reinvented to better meet women's needs and better honour their contributions.

This project is not only one for the film and television industries. The same work needs to be done throughout cultural occupations. Indeed, we can say that there is much still to do throughout society.

Making inequality *visible* carries risks. Part of this is because of the current social context. Publicly funded culture is under pressure as budgets are cut, and many governments are *seemingly* hostile to the work of cultural institutions.

In the commercial world, the transformations of business models across film, television, music, and publishing, are at the roots of struggles over job security and pay. In addition, in the UK at least, cuts to local amenities have presented challenges for amateur and voluntary 'everyday' cultural forms, with fewer places and spaces for activity.

Discussions of inequality are difficult in the context of uncertainties about business models, sustainable funding, and access to cultural subjects in schools. This is in addition to uncertainties about the survival of cultural occupations against a backdrop of more general global environmental crises.[5]

We can thus be sympathetic about the challenge of confronting inequality. We can also recognise, as many of our cultural workers do, the social problems that are beyond the control of cultural occupations.

Recognition of social inequality cannot excuse inequality *within* cultural occupations. This is especially the case when we consider the problem of low and no pay, or forms of discrimination based on gender, class, and race. There can be no justification for refusing to engage with these issues.

Even then, there are still challenges. As we saw in Chapter 10, recognition of inequality is not enough to actually drive change. There are still embedded, structural issues to confront.

Some of these structural issues are as a result of cultural workers' seemingly shared experiences. These are the shared experiences of uneven and unequal cultural labour markets, or shared cultural interests and tastes. They might be shared experiences of marginalisation because of gender. They may also be shared experiences of a very different social situation for getting in and getting on in cultural occupations. By showing how shared experiences are stratified we hope to make inequality visible in a way that clarifies how issues might be addressed. This aim is also present in the theme of how individuals have to carry the costs of inequality in cultural occupations.

Our analysis of the impact of the role of social, economic, and cultural resources or capitals demonstrates the uneven playing field for cultural workers. Cultural occupations are starting to acknowledge that hard work and talent are not the only factors accounting for success. Yet, as Chapters 8 and 9 indicate, it is still the responsibility of individual cultural workers to respond to these problems.

Strong and weak theories of culture and inequality

The task of making inequality visible goes beyond just describing the problems. We also need to think about how best to theorise the connection between culture and inequality. In doing so we will be able to move beyond our data and make a contribution that will have longer-term relevance. It may also have relevance to other nations.

Theorising the relationship between culture and inequality may prove useful to fields looking at the demographic categories for which we have no expertise, such as disability and sexuality, or other humanities and social science disciplines. There may also be value for studies of other professions, as well as other social issues.

Throughout *Culture is bad for you* we've referenced two ways of thinking about culture and inequality. The first, which has been the core subject of the book, is about the inequalities within audiences and within workforces. We can see this subject most clearly in Chapters 3 and 4, and in our discussion of social mobility in Chapter 7.

The second is about the relationship between culture and broader social inequalities. We've seen this in Chapter 5's discussion of inequalities in the education system. It was there in Chapter 6's discussion of pay.

This relationship is also present in Chapter 9's discussion of unfair working conditions. The focus here goes beyond what happens in museums, theatres, and on film sets. Unfair working conditions reflect that costs and burdens of raising children are not fully recognised by society.

We can think about the relationship *between* social inequality and culture as a consequence of inequalities *within* the cultural sector. At the same time, it is impossible to separate inequalities *within* the cultural sector from the context of our unequal society. Culture reflects inequality; inequality reflects culture.

This is the point to conclude by thinking about *weak* and *strong* theories of culture and inequality.

There may well be changes in the demographics of the cultural workforce in the next few years. This may come as the result of targeted schemes or policies. Campaigning and audience demand will also be crucial.

In turn, this may lead to more staff being aware of issues of under-representation. This awareness may accelerate change. This awareness will sit alongside commercial pressure to find new audiences and new markets. This too may drive commissioning and staffing decisions.

None of this suggests inequality will be solved by itself. Rather, by making inequality visible in cultural occupations we will arm campaigners with the information necessary to make the case. We will also show decision-makers and policy-makers the limits of current approaches.

On the other hand, we can take a more structural, socio-logical, view. This is reflected in almost all of the chapters in this book. This suggests the failure to change the structures of cultural occupations by many inclusion, diversity, and career development policies. Individuals may benefit, while the problems remain.

We saw this really clearly as our interviewees reflected on their careers. The structures underpinning their exclusion are unlikely to be changed by the goodwill of senior staff, as we saw in Chapter 10. The sorts of policy intervention organisations and governments are currently willing to try are also likely to have limited success, as we saw in Chapters 7, 8, and 9.

Yet we should not be too conclusive in these assessments. We might think of our first assessment as a *weak* theory of culture and inequality.

This suggests there is only a weak relationship between social inequalities and the inequalities we have shown in the cultural sector. This weak relationship holds in the other direction, whereby there is only a weak relationship between inequalities in the cultural sector and our unequal contemporary society.

If the weak relationship holds true then much of the work for change, particularly at policy level, will have results. Results will happen even if they are slow in coming.

Naming this pessimistic but still hopeful take on culture and inequality a 'weak' theory might sound dismissive. That is not at all our intention.

Just as academic work on gender and media has inspired *Culture is bad for you*, campaigns for change are an important part of the ideas underpinning this book. Our original partnership with

Create London and our subsequent work with Arts Emergency have been crucial to shaping our sense that campaigning and interventions will make a difference for individuals.

The real problem comes if we take the second assessment seriously. Here we're thinking about a *strong* theory of culture and inequality.

In the mirror image of its weak counterpart, this would suggest a close relationship between social and cultural sector inequalities. This approach means much more radical change is needed. Social justice for our unequal societies may be the only way to achieve a more equal cultural sector.

The corollary to the strong theory is that much more radical change will be necessary within the cultural sector. New digital businesses models for content creation and delivery will have to bypass current modes of cultural production. They will have to be driven and controlled by the marginalised themselves. Audiences will have to make affirmative and radical demands of institutions. States will have to take responsibility for regulating labour markets, even where no and low pay seems intractable.

Ultimately, we will need a new theory of value, both of the value of culture, and of the value of persons. These, and many more, changes will be needed to sever the long-standing link between elite dominance of cultural production and consumption and social inequality.

If we take seriously a strong theory of culture and inequality, then commercial and state-funded cultural sectors are confronted with a challenge. To what extent do they really, truly, want that social justice and social change?

The 'right' theory, weak or strong, should be the subject of a new empirical research agenda. It should rise to the challenge set by the media theorist David Hesmondhalgh. He calls for work to properly understand the relationship between cultural production, cultural representation, and cultural consumption.[6] We are hopeful that *Culture is bad for you* has contributed to, albeit not completed, that challenge.

Ultimately, as Victoria Cann has argued, 'Taste cultures may appear trivial and inconsequential, but … they are not innocuous; regulating and limiting the parameters of who and what young people can be.'[7] Cann was focused on gender, but we can expand this point to race and to class.

Culture matters as it does so much to shape who we are, and what our world can and might be. Currently, in our analysis, that world is an unequal one, whether we are discussing the cultural sector or we are discussing society itself.

This offers a challenge in two senses. To live up to the positive potential for culture, inequality must be confronted in production and consumption.

If cultural production and consumption really can confront the inequalities we have shown, then perhaps the sector really does have a central role to play in making the world a more equal place. It is then that we will be able to say, to everybody, culture is good for you.

Appendix 1
Interviewee profiles

This section gives some more information about the interviewees that we have quoted in the book. We've tried to use their own self descriptions as much as possible, as well as giving information about their class origins.

- Adam is a White twenty-eight-year-old working in publishing, living in Yorkshire. He holds a postgraduate qualification from a Russell Group university, and his parents worked in professional jobs.
- Alex is a White twenty-seven-year-old journalist from a Southern European background, living in London. She holds an undergraduate degree from a specialist institution, and her parents worked in professional jobs.
- Anna is a White thirty-three-year-old author also undertaking a PhD, living in London. Her parents both worked in professional jobs.
- Becca is a White forty-three-year-old consultant living in Yorkshire. She holds an undergraduate degree from a Russell Group university, and one of her parents worked in a managerial job.

Appendix 1: Interviewee profiles

- Ben is a White twenty-eight-year-old theatre director living in London. He holds a postgraduate degree from a specialist institution, and his parents worked in professional jobs.
- Camille is a White thirty-year-old working in communications in the music industry, and living in London. She holds an undergraduate degree from Oxbridge, and her parents both worked in professional jobs.
- Carys is a fifty-seven-year-old White artist living in London. She holds a degree from a specialist institution, and both her parents worked in craft occupations.
- Catherine is a White thirty-one-year-old dramaturg living in London. She holds a postgraduate qualification from a Russell Group university, and her parents worked in intermediate occupations.
- Charlotte is a White forty-two-year-old visual artist living in the East Midlands. She holds a degree from a plate glass university, and her parents worked in professional jobs.
- Chloe is a White twenty-four-year-old consultant living in Wales. She holds a degree from a Russell Group university, and both her parents worked in traditionally middle class jobs.
- Chris is a mixed race thirty-year-old curator living in the North East. He holds a postgraduate degree from a Russell Group university, and his parents both worked in traditional working-class jobs.
- Christine is a White twenty-nine-year-old illustrator living in the North West. She holds a degree from a specialist institution, and her parents worked in working-class jobs.
- Claire is a White fifty-six-year-old visual artist living in the East of England. She holds a PhD from a Russell Group institution, and her parents worked in working-class occupations.

- David is a White forty-six-year-old graphic designer living in the Home Counties. He left school at sixteen, and his father worked in a professional job.
- Deb is a White fifty-two-year-old producer living in Yorkshire. She holds a degree from a new university, and her father worked in a working-class role.
- Ellie is a White twenty-seven-year-old designer living in the South East. She holds a postgraduate qualification from a specialist institution, and her parents worked in managerial jobs.
- Emily is a White thirty-three-year-old project manager living in London. She holds an undergraduate degree from a specialist institution, and her parent worked in a professional job.
- Emma is a twenty-three-year-old researcher in the creative industries living in Northern Ireland. She holds a postgraduate degree from a Russell Group university, and both her parents were self-employed.
- Erica is an African American twenty-four-year-old working in a senior role in the creative industries in Scotland. She holds a postgraduate qualification from a Russell Group university, and her parents worked in senior professional jobs.
- Farida is a twenty-four-year-old arts fundraiser from a South Asian background living in the West Midlands. She holds an undergraduate degree from a plate glass university, and her parents worked in working-class jobs.
- Felicity is a White fifty-five-year-old producer living in the Home Counties. She holds a postgraduate qualification from a specialist institution, and her father worked in a professional job.

- Finn is a White twenty-four-year-old producer living in Yorkshire. He holds a degree from a new university, and his parents worked in professional jobs.
- Gavin is a White thirty-four-year-old director living in Scotland. He holds a degree from a new university, and his mother worked in customer service.
- Georgie is a White thirty-four-year-old graphic designer living in London. She holds a degree from Oxbridge, and her parents worked in professional jobs.
- Gerald is a White Jewish fifty-five-year-old curator living in the Home Counties, with a PhD from a specialist institution. His parents were both professionals.
- Graham is a White sixty-one-year-old creative director and writer, living in London. He holds a degree from Oxbridge, and his parents worked in working-class jobs.
- Hazel is a White fifty-three-year-old author living in the West Midlands. She holds a degree from a Russell Group university, and her parents worked in routine or intermediate jobs.
- Henna is a thirty-two-year-old film and TV producer from a South Asian background living in London, with a graduate degree from an elite university outside the UK. Both her parents worked in senior professional jobs.
- Holly is a White thirty-five-year-old arts officer living in Northern Ireland. She holds a degree from a new university, and her parents both held creative jobs.
- Howard is a White seventy-one-year-old film/television producer living on the South Coast. He left school at sixteen, and his parents held clerical jobs.
- Isabel is a mixed race twenty-five-year-old programmes coordinator living in London. She holds a degree from a

Russell Group university, and her parents worked in the creative industries.

- Jack is a White thirty-seven-year-old museum manager from the East Midlands. He holds an undergraduate degree from a new university, and his parents worked in working-class roles.
- Jane is a White forty-six-year-old working in the music industry in Scotland. She left school at sixteen, and her parents worked in working-class jobs.
- Jenny is a White fifty-four-year-old communications director living on the South Coast. She holds a degree from a new university, and her father worked in insurance.
- Jessica is a White forty-year-old living in the Home Counties and working backstage in theatre. She holds an undergraduate degree from a new university, and her father worked in a working-class role.
- Jo is a White forty-one-year-old consultant living in the North West. She holds a postgraduate qualification from a Russell Group institution, and her father worked in a professional job.
- John is a twenty-two-year-old Latin American working in film and television. He holds a degree from a specialist institution, and his parents worked in working-class jobs.
- Katie is a White thirty-year-old working in the visual arts in London. She has a PhD from a university outside the UK, and both her parents worked in professional jobs.
- Kerry is a White fifty-four-year-old writer and theatre-maker living in London, from a working-class background. She grew up outside the UK, and holds a degree from the country where she grew up.
- Kirsty is a thirty-two-year-old actor from a Chinese background living in London. She holds a qualification in acting

from a specialist institution, and her father worked in a traditionally working-class role.

- Lauren is a twenty-seven-year-old museums professional living in Yorkshire. She holds a postgraduate qualification from a Russell Group university, and both her parents worked in professional jobs.
- Lawrence is a White forty-two-year-old journalist living in London. He holds a postgraduate qualification from a new university, and his parents worked in professional jobs.
- Lisa is a White fifty-five-year-old woman, working across publishing and theatre. She holds a degree from a new university and her parents worked in routine and manual occupations.
- Louisa is a White thirty-five-year-old woman working in publishing, living in the Home Counties. She holds a postgraduate qualification from a Russell Group university, and her father worked in a professional job.
- Lydia is a White twenty-four-year-old artist living in Northern Ireland. She holds a degree from a new university, and her parents worked in senior professional jobs.
- Matt is a Black forty-three-year-old playwright living in the West Midlands. He holds an undergraduate degree from a Russell Group university, and his parents both worked in professional jobs.
- Maura is a White forty-seven-year-old CEO of a venue, living in the West Midlands. She holds a postgraduate qualification from a new university, and her parents worked in working-class jobs.
- Meena is a forty-one-year-old consultant from a South Asian background, living in the Midlands. She attended a Russell Group university, and her father worked in a professional role.

- Meg is a mixed race twenty-five-year-old producer living in London. She undertook an apprenticeship after leaving school, and her mother was a cleaner.
- Mel is a White fifty-two-year-old actor living in London. She holds an acting diploma from a specialist institution, and her parents also worked in theatre.
- Michaela is a Black thirty-eight-year-old curator living in London, from a working class background, with a PhD from a new university.
- Michelle is a White twenty-seven-year-old book distributor living in London. She holds a postgraduate degree from a plate glass university, and both her parents worked in professional jobs.
- Molly is a White twenty-six-year-old artist living in London. She holds a degree from a new university, and her parents worked in the creative industries.
- Nicole is a White thirty-six-year-old actor living in the West Midlands. She holds a postgraduate qualification from a Russell Group university, and her parents were in working-class jobs.
- Rachel is a mixed race fifty-two-year-old producer living in London. She holds a diploma, and her father worked in a working-class job.
- Richard is a White forty-four-year-old director living in London. He holds a degree from Oxbridge, and his parents worked in working-class jobs.
- Rose is a White forty-two-year-old designer living in the South West. She holds a degree from a specialist institution, and her father worked in a technical occupation.
- Ruth is a mixed race fifty-three-year-old journalist, living in the South East. She holds a postgraduate qualification from

a new university, and her father worked in a managerial job while her mother worked in a professional job.

- Sam is a White fifty-four-year-old curator living in Yorkshire. They hold a postgraduate qualification from a new university, and their parents worked in professional jobs.
- Sasha is a thirty-eight-year-old director from a South Asian background living in Bristol, with a degree from a Russell Group university. Both her parents worked in professional roles.
- Sean is a White thirty-year-old artist, living in London. He holds a postgraduate qualification from a specialist institution, and his parents worked in working-class jobs.
- Stefano is a White thirty-five-year-old director living in London. He holds a postgraduate degree from a small institution, and his father was unemployed when he was growing up.
- Stephanie is a White thirty-year-old curator living in London, with a PhD from a Russell Group university. Her parents worked in working-class jobs.
- Tasha is a White forty-three-year-old curator from a Southern European background living in London. She holds a PhD from a specialist institution, and her parents worked in craft occupations.
- Thomas is a White forty-six-year-old working in publishing and living in a northern city, whose father worked in a traditional professional background. He attended Oxbridge.
- Veronica is a thirty-five-year-old fashion designer from North America, living in North West England. She attended a Russell Group university, and her parents worked in working-class jobs.

Appendix 2

Further reading

Throughout the book we have made reference to other work that we have done, both as a group of authors and in collaboration with our other colleagues. In this work we describe and explain the data we have used, and the methods we have adopted, in more detail. The following academic papers should be useful resources for anyone who wants to know more about our approach, and more about culture and inequality.

Brook, O., O'Brien, D., and Taylor, M. (2018) 'There was no golden age: social mobility into cultural and creative occupations'. Available from https://osf.io/preprints/socarxiv/7njy3

Brook, O., O'Brien, D., and Taylor, M. (2019) 'Inequality talk: how discourses by senior men reinforce exclusions from creative occupations', *European Journal of Cultural Studies*. Available from https://doi.org/10.1177/1367549419886020.

Brook, O., O'Brien, D., and Taylor, M. (2020) '"There's no way you get paid to do the arts": unpaid labour across the cultural and creative life course', *Sociological Research Online*. Available from https://journals.sagepub.com/doi/full/10.1177/1360780419895291.

Campbell, P., O'Brien, D., and Taylor, M. (2019) 'Cultural engagement and the economic performance of the cultural and creative industries: an occupational critique', *Sociology*, 53 (2): 347–67.

Carey, H., Florisson, R., Lee, N. and O'Brien, D. (2020) *Getting in and getting on: class, participation and job quality in the UK creative industries.* London: AHRC PEC.

Friedman, S. and O'Brien, D. (2017) 'Resistance and resignation: responses to typecasting in British acting', *Cultural Sociology*, 11 (3): 359–76.

Friedman, S., O'Brien, D., and Laurison, D. (2017) '"Like skydiving without a parachute": how class origin shapes occupational trajectories in British acting', *Sociology*, 51 (5): 992–1010.

Hanquinet, L., O'Brien, D., and Taylor, M. (2019) 'The coming crisis of cultural engagement? Measurement, methods, and the nuances of niche activities', *Cultural Trends*, 28 (2–3): 198–219.

McAndrew, S., O'Brien, D. and Taylor, M. (2020) 'The values of culture? Social closure in the political identities, policy preferences, and social attitudes of cultural and creative workers', *The Sociological Review*, 68 (1): 33–54.

Oakley, K., Laurison, D., O'Brien, D., and Friedman, S. (2017) 'Cultural capital: arts graduates, spatial inequality, and London's impact on cultural labor markets', *American Behavioral Scientist*, 61 (12): 1510–31.

O'Brien, D., Laurison, D., Miles, A., and Friedman, S. (2016) 'Are the creative industries meritocratic? An analysis of the 2014 British Labour Force Survey', *Cultural Trends*, 25 (2): 116–31.

Taylor, M. (2016) 'Nonparticipation or different styles of participation? Alternative interpretations from Taking Part', *Cultural Trends*, 25 (3): 169–81.

Taylor, M. and O'Brien, D. (2017) 'Culture is a meritocracy: why creative workers' attitudes may reinforce social inequality', *Sociological Research Online*, 22 (4): 27–47.

Notes

1 Introduction

1　House of Commons Digital, Culture, Media and Sport Select Committee (2019) *Changing Lives: The Social Impact of Participation in Culture and Sport*, Eleventh report of Session 2017–19, 14 May 2019, HC 734, available from https://publications.parliament.uk/pa/cm201719/cmselect/cmcumeds/734/734.pdf (accessed 20/01/2020).

2　A. Reeves and R. de Vries (2019) 'Can cultural consumption increase future earnings? Exploring the economic returns to cultural capital', *British Journal of Sociology*, 70 (1): 214–40.

3　B. Garcia and T. Cox (2013) *European Capitals of Culture: Success Strategies and Long-Term Effects*, available from www.europarl.europa.eu/RegData/etudes/etudes/join/2013/513985/IPOL-CULT_ET(2013)513985_EN.pdf (accessed 13/12/2019).

4　DCMS (2016) *The Culture White Paper*, available from https://assets.publishing.service.gov.uk/government/uploads/system/uploads/attachment_data/file/510798/DCMS_The_Culture_White_Paper__3_.pdf (accessed 20/01/2020).

5　What Next? (2019) *What Next? Briefing Pack*, available from www.whatnextculture.co.uk/wp-content/uploads/2019/11/What-Next-General-Election-Briefing-2019–4.pdf (accessed 13/12/2019); Creative Industries Council (2019) *Arts and Culture: Why the UK?* available from www.thecreativeindustries.co.uk/industries/arts-culture/arts-culture-why-the-uk (accessed 13/12/2019).

6　G. Crossick and P. Kaszynska (2016) *Understanding the Value of Arts & Culture: The AHRC Cultural Value Project*, available from www.ahrc.ac.uk/documents/publications/cultural-value-project-final-report (accessed 20/01/2020); A. Miles and A. Sullivan (2012) 'Understanding participation in culture and sport: mixing methods, reordering knowledges', *Cultural Trends*, 21 (4): 311–24; A. Miles and L. Gibson (eds) (2016) 'Everyday participation and cultural value: part 1' *Cultural Trends*, 25 (3) (Special Issue); A. Miles and L. Gibson (eds) (2017) 'Everyday participation and cultural value: part 2', *Cultural Trends*, 26 (1) (Special Issue).

7 D. O'Brien, D. Laurison, A. Miles, and S. Friedman (2016) 'Are the creative industries meritocratic? An analysis of the 2014 British Labour Force Survey', *Cultural Trends*, 25 (2): 116–31.

8 A. Atkinson (2015) *Inequality: What Can be Done?* Cambridge, MA: Harvard University Press; L. Platt (2019) *Understanding Inequalities*. Cambridge: Polity Press.

9 The literature on this subject is vast, but three illustrative starting points are: P. Bourdieu (1984/2010) *Distinction: A Social Critique of the Judgment of Taste*. London: Routledge; T. Bennett, M. Savage, E. B. Silva, A. Warde, M. Gayo-Cal, and D. Wright (2009) *Culture, Class, Distinction*. London: Routledge; and J. Lena, *Entitled: Discriminating Tastes and the Expansion of the Arts*. Princeton: Princeton University Press.

10 M. Taylor (2016) 'Nonparticipation or different styles of participation? Alternative interpretations from Taking Part', *Cultural Trends*, 25 (3): 169–81.

11 E. Belfiore and L. Gibson (eds) (2020) *Histories of Cultural Participation, Values and Governance*. London: Palgrave; Lena, *Entitled*.

12 C. Bunting, A. Gilmore, and A. Miles (2020) 'Calling participation to account: Taking Part in the politics of method', in E. Belfiore and L. Gibson (eds), *Histories of Cultural Participation, Values and Governance*. London: Palgrave.

13 Lena, *Entitled*.

14 P.-M. Menger (2014) *The Economics of Creativity: Art and Achievement under Uncertainty*. Cambridge, MA: Harvard University Press; C. Bilton (1999) 'Risky business', *International Journal of Cultural Policy*, 6 (1): 17–39; M. Banks, A. Lovatt, J. O'Connor, and C. Raffo (2000) 'Risk and trust in the cultural industries', *Geoforum*, 31: 453–64.

15 A. O'Brien (2019) *Women, Inequality, and Media Work*. London: Palgrave.

16 BEIS (2018) *Industrial Strategy: Creative Industries Sector Deal*. London: HMSO.

17 We're discussing various research agendas throughout the book, but key examples include B. Conor, R. Gill, and S. Taylor (2015) *Gender and Creative Labour*. London: Wiley-Blackwell; B. Conor (2014)

Screenwriting: Creative Labour and Professional Practice. London: Routledge; D. Ashton and C. Noonan (2013) *Cultural Work and Higher Education*. London: Palgrave Macmillan; P. A. Banks (2019) *Diversity and Philanthropy at African American Museums: Black Renaissance*. Abingdon: Routledge; M. Banks (2017) *Creative Justice: Cultural Industries, Work and Inequality*. London: Rowman & Littlefield; C. Childress (2017) *Under the Cover: The Creation, Production and Reception of a Novel*. Princeton: Princeton University Press; A. Gerber (2017) *The Work of Art: Value in Creative Careers*. Stanford: Stanford University Press; D. Hesmondhalgh and S. Baker (2011) *Creative Labour*. New York: Routledge; Lena, *Entitled*; S. Luckman (2015) *Craft and the Creative Economy*. London and New York: Palgrave Macmillan; A. McRobbie (2016) *Be Creative*. Cambridge: Polity Press; C. Nwonka and S. Malik (2018) 'Cultural discourses and practices of in-stitutionalised diversity in the UK film sector: "Just get something black made"', *Sociological Review*, 66 (6): 1111–27; A. Rogers (2016) *Performing Asian Transnationalisms: Theatre, Identity, and the Geographies of Performance*. London: Routledge; A. Saha (2018) *Race and the Cultural Industries*. Cambridge: Polity Press; N. Wreyford (2018) *Gender Inequality in Screenwriting Work*. London: Palgrave; N. Yuen (2016) *Reel Inequality: Hollywood Actors and Racism*. New Brunswick: Rutgers University Press.

18 https://createlondon.org/event/panic-what-happened-to-social-mobility-in-the-arts (accessed 30/01/2020).

19 https://createlondon.org/event/panic2018 (accessed 30/01/2020).

20 More detail about this, and many of the other data sources and analyt-ical techniques we use in the book are in Appendix 2, and are in some of the papers we reference throughout each chapter.

21 O. Brook, D. O'Brien, and M. Taylor (2018) *Panic: Social Class, Taste, and Inequality in the Creative Industries*, available from http://createlondon.org/event/panic-paper (accessed 20/01/2020).

22 We are delighted that published work with Peter Campbell, University of Liverpool, Sam Friedman, London School of Economics, Daniel Laurison, Swarthmore College, Siobhan McAndrew, University of Bristol, Andrew Miles, University of Manchester, Kate Oakley, University of Glasgow, and Laurie Hanquinet, Université libre de Bruxelles, has informed the analysis in this book.

23 P. Campbell, D. O'Brien, and M. Taylor (2019) 'Cultural engagement and the economic performance of the cultural and creative indus-tries: an occupational critique', *Sociology*, 53 (2): 347–67; L. Hanquinet, D. O'Brien, and M. Taylor (2019) 'The coming crisis of cultural

engagement? Measurement, methods, and the nuances of niche activities', *Cultural Trends*, 28 (2–3): 198–219; S. McAndrew, D. O'Brien, and M. Taylor (2020) 'The values of culture? Social closure in the political identities, policy preferences, and social attitudes of cultural and creative workers', *The Sociological Review*, 68 (1): 33–54; K. Oakley, D. Laurison, D. O'Brien, and S. Friedman (2017) 'Cultural capital: arts graduates, spatial inequality, and London's impact on cultural labor markets', *American Behavioral Scientist*, 61 (12): 1510–31; O'Brien *et al.*, 'Are the creative industries meritocratic?'; M. Taylor and D. O'Brien (2017) '"Culture is a meritocracy": why creative workers' attitudes may reinforce social inequality', *Sociological Research Online*, 22 (4): 27–47.

24 Brook *et al.*, *Panic*.

25 E.g. summarised in a recent debate in the *British Journal of Sociology*, L. Bear (2014) 'Capital and time: uncertainty and qualitative measures of inequality sociology', *The British Journal of Sociology*, 65 (4): 639–49; D. Perrons (2014) 'Gendering inequality: a note on Piketty's *Capital in the Twenty-First Century*', *The British Journal of Sociology*, 65 (4): 667–77; D. Piachaud (2014) 'Piketty's capital and social policy', *The British Journal of Sociology*, 65 (4): 696–707; T. Piketty (2014) '*Capital in the Twenty-First Century*: a multidimensional approach to the history of capital and social classes', *The British Journal of Sociology*, 65 (4): 736–47; M. Savage (2014) 'Piketty's challenge for sociology', *The British Journal of Sociology*, 65 (4): 591–605; H. Boushey, B. Delong, and M. Steinbaum (2017) *After Piketty: The Agenda for Economics and Inequality*. Cambridge, MA: Harvard University Press.

26 For example, reactions to R. Wilkinson and K. Pickett (2009) *The Spirit Level*. London: Penguin or D. Dorling (2014) *Inequality and the 1%*. London: Penguin.

27 T. Piketty (2014) *Capital in the Twenty-First Century*. Cambridge, MA: Harvard University Press; J. Stiglitz (2013) *The Price of Inequality*. London: Penguin; B. Milanovic (2018) *Global Inequality: A New Approach for the Age of Globalization*. London: Belknap Press.

28 Piketty, *Capital*.

29 M. Blyth (2013) *Austerity: The History of a Dangerous Idea*. Oxford: Oxford University Press; A. Tooze (2018) *Crashed: How a Decade of Financial Crises Changed the World*. London: Allen Lane.

30 W. Bottero (2020) *A Sense of Inequality*. London: Rowman & Littlefield.

31 J. Acker (2006) 'Inequality regimes: gender, race and class in organisations', *Gender and Society*, 20 (4): 441–64.

Notes

32 A. J. Fielding (1992) 'Migration and social mobility: south east England as an escalator region', *Regional Studies*, 26: 1–15; S. Friedman, D. Laurison, and L. Macmillan (2017) *Social Mobility, the Class Pay Gap and Intergenerational Worklessness: New Insights from the Labour Force Survey*. London: Social Mobility Commission.

33 M. Granovetter (1995) *Getting a Job*, 2nd edition. Chicago: University of Chicago Press.

34 B. Skeggs (2011) 'Imagining personhood differently: person value and autonomist working-class value practices', *The Sociological Review*, 59 (3): 496–513; G. Kuipers, T. Franssen, and S. Holla (2019) 'Clouded judgments? Aesthetics, morality and everyday life in early 21st century culture', *European Journal of Cultural Studies*, 22 (4): 383–98.

35 https://gender-pay-gap.service.gov.uk (accessed 30/01/2020).

36 F. Blau (2012) *Gender, Inequality, and Wages*. Oxford: Oxford University Press; S. Banet-Weiser (2018) *Empowered: Popular Feminism and Popular Misogyny*. Durham, NC: Duke University Press.

37 M. Lamont (2019) 'From "having" to "being": self-worth and the current crisis of American society', *British Journal of Sociology*, 70 (3): 660–707.

38 I. Tyler and T. Slater (2018) 'Rethinking the sociology of stigma', *The Sociological Review*, 66 (4): 721–43.

39 B. Skeggs (1997) *Formations of Class and Gender*. London: Sage; T. Jensen and I. Tyler (2015) 'Benefits broods: the cultural and political crafting of anti-welfare commonsense', *Critical Social Policy*, 35 (4): 470–91.

40 Kuipers *et al.*, 'Clouded judgments?'.

41 R. Hoggart (1957) *The Uses of Literacy*. Harmondsworth: Penguin; A. Miles and A. Sullivan (2012) 'Understanding participation in culture and sport: mixing methods, reordering knowledges', *Cultural Trends*, 21 (4): 311–24; Miles and Gibson, 'Everyday participation and cultural value: part 1'; Miles and Gibson, 'Everyday participation and cultural value: part 2'; R. Williams (1958) *Culture and Society*. London: Chatto & Windus; R. Williams (1961) *The Long Revolution*. London: Chatto & Windus; G. Yudice (2009) 'Cultural diversity and cultural rights', *Hispanic Issues Online*, 5 (1): 110–37.

42 S. Hall (1973) *Encoding and Decoding in the Television Discourse*. Birmingham: Centre for Contemporary Cultural Studies.

43 P. Du Gay, S. Hall, L. Janes, H. MacKay, and K. Negus (1997) *Doing Cultural Studies*. London: Sage.

44 N. Garnham (2005) 'From cultural to creative industries: an analysis of the implications of the "creative industries" approach to arts and media policy making in the United Kingdom', *International Journal*

of Cultural Policy, 11 (1): 15–29; D. Hesmondhalgh and A. Pratt (2005) 'Cultural industries and cultural policy', *International Journal of Cultural Policy*, 11 (1): 1–13; S. Lash and C. Lury (2007) *Global Culture Industry*. Cambridge: Polity; S. Lash and J. Urry (1994) *Economies of Signs and Space*. London: Sage; A. McRobbie (2002) 'Clubs to companies: notes on the decline of political culture in speeded up creative worlds', *Cultural Studies*, 16 (4): 516–31; J. O'Connor (2000) 'The definition of the "cultural industries"', *The European Journal of Arts Education*, 2 (3): 15–27; A. Pratt (1997) 'The cultural industries production system: a case study of employment change in Britain, 1984–91', *Environment and Planning A*, 29 (11): 1953–74.

45 F. Bianchini and M. Parkinson (eds) (1994) *Cultural Policy and Urban Regeneration: The West European Experience*. Manchester: Manchester University Press; G. Evans (2001) *Cultural Planning: An Urban Renaissance?* London: Routledge; G. Evans and P. Shaw (2004) *The Contribution of Culture to Regeneration in the UK*. London: London Met; C. Landry (2000) *The Creative City: A Toolkit for Urban Innovators*. London: Earthscan; C. Landry and F. Bianchini (1995) *The Creative City*. London: Demos; J. Myerscough (1988) *The Economic Importance of the Arts on Merseyside*. London: Policy Studies Institute.

46 H. Bakhshi, A. Freeman, and P. Higgs (2013) *A Dynamic Mapping of the UK's Creative Industries*. London: Nesta; DCMS (2018) *DCMS Sector Economic Estimates Methodology*, available from www.gov.uk/government/uploads/system/uploads/attachment_data/file/681217/DCMS_Sectors_Economic_Estimates_-_Methodology.pdf (accessed 19/02/2018); D. Hesmondhalgh (2019) *The Cultural Industries*, 4th edition. London: Sage.

47 Bakhshi *et al.*, *A Dynamic Mapping of the UK's Creative Industries*; BEIS, *Industrial Strategy*.

48 DCMS (2018) *DCMS Sector Economic Estimates 2017:GVA*, available from www.gov.uk/government/statistics/dcms-sectors-economic-estimates-2017-gva (accessed 30/01/2020).

49 Saha, *Race and the Cultural Industries*; Wreyford, *Gender Inequality in Screenwriting Work*.

50 K. Crenshaw (1991) 'Mapping the margins: intersectionality, identity politics, and violence against women of color', *Stanford Law Review*, 43 (6): 1241–99; H. Collins and S. Bilge (2016) *Intersectionality* Cambridge: Polity Press; N. Yuval-Davis (2006) 'Intersectionality and feminist politics', *European Journal of Women's Studies*, 13 (3): 193–209.

51 W. Bottero (2004) 'Class identities and the identity of class', *Sociology*, 38 (5): 985–1003; D. Cannadine (1998) *Class in Britain*. London: Penguin; S. Friedman and D. Laurison (2019) *The Class Ceiling: Why it Pays to*

be Privileged. Bristol: Policy Press; J. H. Goldthorpe, C. Llewellyn, and C. Payne (1987) *Social Mobility and Class Structure in Modern Britain*. Oxford: Clarendon; J. H. Goldthorpe and C. Mills (2008) 'Trends in intergenerational class mobility in modern Britain: evidence from national surveys, 1972–2005', *National Institute Economic Review*, 205: 83–100; R. Crompton (2008) *Class and Stratification*. Cambridge: Polity; J. H. Goldthorpe (2016) 'Social class mobility in modern Britain: changing structure, constant process', *Journal of the British Academy*, 4: 89–111; N. Rollock, D. Gilborn, C. Vincent, and D. Ball (2014) *The Colour of Class: The Educational Strategies of the Black Middle Classes*. London: Routledge; M. Savage (2000) *Class Analysis and Social Transformations*. London: Routledge; M. Savage (2010) *Identities and Social Change in Britain Since 1940: The Politics of Method*. Oxford: Oxford University Press; M. Savage (2015) *Social Class in the Twenty First Century*. London: Penguin; B. Skeggs (2004) *Class, Self and Culture*. London: Routledge.

52 M. Savage, F. Devine, N. Cunningham, M. Taylor, Y. Li, J. Hjellbrekke, B. Le Roux, S. Friedman, and A. Miles (2013) 'A new model of social class? Findings from the Great British Class Survey experiment', *Sociology*, 47: 219–50; Savage, *Social Class*.

53 The debates are captured across several special issues and special sections: *Sociology*, 48 (3) and *Sociological Review*, 63 (2), as well as M. Savage, F. Devine, N. Cunningham, S. Friedman, D. Laurison, A. Miles, and M. Taylor (2015) 'On social class, anno 2014', *Sociology*, 49 (6): 1011–30.

54 A. Guveli (2006) *New Social Classes within the Service Class in the Netherlands and Britain: Adjusting the EGP Class Schema for the Technocrats and the Social and Cultural Specialists*, available from https://repository.ubn.ru.nl/bitstream/handle/2066/56427/56427.pdf (accessed 04/09/2019); M. Flemmen (2014) 'The politics of the service class', *European Societies*, 16 (4): 543–69.

55 T. Piketty (2018) *Brahmin Left vs Merchant Right: Rising Inequality and the Changing Structure of Political Conflict (Evidence from France, Britain and the US, 1948–2017)*, WID.world Working paper series number 2018/7, available from http://piketty.pse.ens.fr/files/Piketty2018.pdf (accessed 20/01/2020).

56 McRobbie, *Be Creative*.

57 D. Grusky and K. Weeden (2001) 'Decomposition without death: a research agenda for a new class analysis', *Acta Sociologica*, 44 (3): 203–18;

K. Weeden and D. Grusky (2005) 'The case for a new class map', *American Journal of Sociology*, 111: 141–212; J. Jonsson, D. Grusky, M. Di Carlo, R. Pollak, and M. Brinton (2009) 'Microclass mobility: social reproduction in four countries', *American Journal of Sociology*, 114 (4): 977–1936; J. Jonsson *et al* (2011) 'It's a decent bet that our children will become professors too', in D. B. Grusky and S. Szelényi (eds), *The Inequality Reader: Contemporary and Foundational Readings in Race, Class, and Gender*. Boulder: Westview Press.

2 Is culture good for you?

1   The most comprehensive summary of these debates can be found in E. Belfiore and O. Bennett (2008) *The Social Impact of the Arts: An Intellectual History*. Basingstoke: Palgrave Macmillan.

2   T. Bennett (1995) *The Birth of the Museum*. London: Routledge.

3   Belfiore and Bennett, *Social Impact of the Arts*; Bennett, *Birth of the Museum*; T. Bennett (2015) *Making Culture, Changing Society*. London: Routledge.

4   L. Gibson (2008) 'In defence of instrumentality', *Cultural Trends*, 17 (4): 247–57.

5   D. Donoghue (1983) *The Arts without Mystery*. London: BBC; J. Luxford (2010) 'Art for art's sake: was it ever thus? A historical perspective', in N. Beech and B. Townley (eds), *Managing Creativity: Exploring the Paradox*. Cambridge: Cambridge University Press.

6   See Luxford, 'Art for art's sake' for a brief summary.

7   A critical summary can be found in E. Chiapello (2004) 'Evolution and co-optation: the artist critique of management and capitalism', *Third Text*, 18 (6): 585–94.

8   D. Hesmondhalgh (2013) *Why Music Matters*. London: Wiley.

9   There are numerous examples. Recent papers include ACE (2019) *The Durham Commission on Creativity and Education*, available from www.artscouncil.org.uk/publication/durham-commission-creativity-and-education (accessed 16/12/2019); ACE (2019) *Value of Arts and Culture in Place-Shaping*, available from www.artscouncil.org.uk/publication/value-arts-and-culture-place-shaping (accessed 16/12/2019); along with older interventions, e.g. DCMS (2010) *Understanding the Drivers, Impact and Value of Engagement in Culture and Sport*. London: DCMS; Myerscough, *The Economic Importance of the Arts on Merseyside*.

10   Crossick and Kaszynska, *Understanding the Value of Arts & Culture*.

Notes

11 House of Commons Digital, Culture, Media and Sport Select Committee, *Changing Lives*.

12 All-Party Parliamentary Group on Arts, Health and Wellbeing (2017) *Creative Health: The Arts for Health and Wellbeing*, available from www. artshealthandwellbeing.org.uk/appg-inquiry/Publications/Creative_ Health_Inquiry_Report_2017.pdf (accessed 20/05/2020).

13 Summarised in D. O'Brien (2014) *Cultural Policy*. London: Routledge; also see J. Holden (2004) *Capturing Cultural Value: How Culture has Become a Tool of Government Policy*. London: Demos.

14 Belfiore and Bennett, *Social Impact of the Arts*; also F. Matarasso (1997) *Use or Ornament?* London: Comedia; P. Merli (2002) 'Evaluating the social impact of participation in arts activities: a critical review of François Matarasso's "Use or ornament?"', *International Journal of Cultural Policy*, 8 (1): 107–18.

15 Summarised in O'Brien, *Cultural Policy*.

16 E.g. Myerscough, *The Economic Importance of the Arts on Merseyside*.

17 Bianchini and Parkinson, *Cultural Policy and Urban Regeneration*.

18 N. Garnham (1987) 'Concepts of culture: public policy and the cultural industries', in A. Gray and J. McGuigan (eds), *Studies in Culture: An Introductory Reader* (54–61). London: Arnold.

19 For one example, see C. Gibson and L. Kong (2005) 'Cultural economy: a critical review', *Progress in Human Geography*, 29 (5): 541–61.

20 P. Campbell (2014) 'Imaginary success? The contentious ascendance of creativity', *European Planning Studies*, 22 (5): 995–1009.

21 P. du Gay and M. Pryke (eds) (2002) *Cultural Economy: Cultural Analysis and Commercial Life*. London: Sage.

22 C. Bishop (2012) *Artificial Hells*. London: Verso, offers a critical summary.

23 Matarasso, *Use or Ornament?*.

24 B. Garcia, R. Melville, and T. Cox (2010) *Creating an Impact: Liverpool's Experience as European Capital of Culture*. Liverpool: Impacts08.

25 Garcia *et al.*, *Creating an Impact*.

26 S. Miles (2004) 'NewcastleGateshead Quayside: cultural investment and identities of resistance', *Capital and Class*, 84: 183–90; S. Miles (2010) *Spaces for Consumption*. London: Routledge; A. Minton (2003) *Northern Soul: Culture, Creativity and Quality of Place in Newcastle and Gateshead*. London: Demos.

27 P. Watt (2009) 'Housing stock transfers, regeneration and state-led gentrification in London', *Urban Policy and Research*, 27 (3): 229–42; O.

Mould (2018) *Against Creativity*. London: Verso; L. Lees, T. Slater, and E. Wyly (2008) *Gentrification*. New York: Routledge; H. Hawkins (2016) *Creativity*. London: Routledge.

28 S. Clift and P. Camic (2016) *Oxford Textbook of Creative Arts, Health, and Wellbeing*. Oxford: Oxford University Press; D. Fancourt (2017) *Arts in Health*. Oxford: Oxford University Press; T. Stickley and S. Clift (2017) *Arts, Health and Wellbeing: A Theoretical Inquiry for Practice*. Newcastle upon Tyne: Cambridge Scholars Publishing; N. Daykin (2019) *Arts, Health and Well-Being: A Critical Perspective on Research, Policy and Practice*. London: Routledge.

29 S. Oman (2015) '"Measuring national well-being: what matters to you?" What matters to whom?', in S. White (ed.), *Cultures of Wellbeing: Method, Place, Policy*. London: Palgrave.

30 R. Williams (1993) 'Culture is ordinary', in A. Gray and J. McGuigan (eds), *Studying Culture: An Introductory Reader* (5–14). London: Arnold.

31 P. Bourdieu (1984) *Distinction: A Social Critique of the Judgement of Taste*. London: Routledge.

32 D. O'Brien (2010) *Measuring the Value of Culture*. London: DCMS.

33 Bourdieu, *Distinction*.

34 K. Negus (2002) 'The work of cultural intermediaries and the enduring distance between production and consumption', *Cultural Studies*, 16 (4): 501–15; S. Nixon and P. Du Gay (2002) 'Who needs cultural intermediaries?', *Cultural Studies*, 16 (4): 495–500; J. Smith Maguire and J. Matthews (eds) (2014) *The Cultural Intermediaries Reader*. London: Sage.

35 S. Purhonen, R. Heikkilä, I. K. Hazir, T. Lauronen, C. J. F. Rodríguez, and J. Gronow (2018) *Enter Culture, Exit Arts? The Transformation of Cultural Hierarchies in European Newspaper Culture Sections, 1960–2010*. London: Routledge.

36 M. Choueiti, S. L. Smith, and K. Pieper, with A. Case (2018) *Critic's Choice 2: Gender and Race/Ethnicity of Film Reviewers across 300 Top Films from 2015–2017*. Pennsylvania: Annenberg Inclusion Initiative.

37 Gibson, 'In defence of instrumentality'.

38 M. Terras (2018) *Picture-Book Professors*. Cambridge: Cambridge University Press.

39 B. Skeggs and H. Wood (2012) *Performance, Audience and Value*. London: Routledge; S. De Benedictis, K. Allen, and T. Jensen (2017) 'Portraying poverty: the economics and ethics of factual welfare television', *Cultural Sociology*, 11 (3): 337–58.

40 Crossick and Kaszynska, *Understanding the Value of Arts & Culture*.

41 These themes are also present in policy-makers' understandings of culture, e.g. P. Bazalgette (2016) *The Empathy Instinct: How to Create a More Civil Society*. London: John Murray; D. Henley (2016) *The Arts Dividend: Why Investment in Culture Pays*. London: Elliott & Thompson; D. Henley (2019) *Creativity: Why It Matters*. London: Elliott & Thompson.

42 K. Rumbold, K. Simecek, V. Ellis, P. Riddell, J. Bessell, A. Williams, C. Rathbone, and E. Howell (2015) 'The uses of poetry: measuring the value of engaging with poetry in lifelong learning and development', *Cultural Value*, available from https://usesofpoetry.files.wordpress.com/2015/12/ahrc_cultural_value_rda-uses-of-poetry-rumbold.pdf (accessed 20/05/2020).

43 C. Chattoo (2018) 'Oscars so white: gender, racial, and ethnic diversity and social issues in U.S. documentary films (2008–2017)', *Mass Communication and Society*, 21 (3): 368–94; I. Molina-Guzmán (2016) '#OscarsSoWhite: how Stuart Hall explains why nothing changes in Hollywood and everything is changing', *Critical Studies in Media Communication*, 33 (5): 438–54; S. Smith, M. Choueiti, A. Choi, and K. Pieper (2019) *Inclusion in the Director's Chair*, available from http://assets.uscannenberg.org/docs/inclusion-in-the-directors-chair-2019.pdf (accessed 26/12/2019); S. Smith, M. Choueiti, A. Choi, K. Pieper, H. Clark, K. Hernandez, J. Martinez, B. Lopez, and M. Mota (2019) *Latinos in Film*, available from http://assets.uscannenberg.org/docs/aii-study-latinos-in-film-2019.pdf (accessed 26/12/2019); S. Smith, M. Choueiti, and S. Gall (n.d.) *Asymmetrical Academy Awards 2: Another Look at Gender in Best Picture Nominated films from 1977 to 2010*, available from https://annenberg.usc.edu/sites/default/files/MDSCI_Gender_Representation_1977_2010.pdf (accessed 26/12/2019); Chouieti *et al.*, *Critic's Choice 2*.

44 V. Bain (2019) *Counting the Music Industry: The Gender Gap*, available from https://img1.wsimg.com/blobby/go/c35ef375-9fb4-4753-8e7d-b9088ef68d25/downloads/Counting%20the%20Music%20Industry%20full%20report%202019.pdf?ver=1576691396956 (accessed 12/01/2019).

45 R. Hill (2016) *Gender, Metal and the Media: Women Fans and the Gendered Experience of Music*. London: Palgrave; M. Demoor, F. Saeys, and S. Lievens (2008) ' "And the winner is?" Researching the relationship between gender and literary awards in Flanders, 1981–2000', *Journal of Gender Studies*: 27–39; S. Smith, M. Choueitei, and K. Pieper (2019) *Inclusion in the Recording Studio?*, available from http://assets.uscannenberg.org/docs/aii-inclusion-recording-studio-2019.pdf

(accessed 26/12/2019); Y. Wang and E.-A. Horvat (2019) *Gender Differences in the Global Music Industry: Evidence from MusicBrainz and The Echo Nest*, available from www.aaai.org/ojs/index.php/ICWSM/article/view/3249/3117 (accessed 26/12/2019); C. Scharff (2017) *Gender, Subjectivity, and Cultural Work: The Classical Music Profession.* London: Routledge; A. Bull (2019) *Class, Control and Classical Music.* Oxford: Oxford University Press.

46 J. Kidd, S. Cairns, A. Drago, A. Ryall, and M. Stearn (2014) *Challenging History in the Museum: International Perspectives.* London: Routledge; C. Wintle (2017) 'Decolonising UK world art institutions, 1945–1980', *On Curating*, 35: 106–12; Banks, *Diversity and Philanthropy at African American Museums*; S. Wajid and R. Minott (2019) 'Detoxing and decolonising museums', in R. Janes and R. Sandell (eds), *Museum Activism.* London: Routledge.

3 Who works in culture?

1 E.g. S. Friedman and D. O'Brien (2017) 'Resistance and resignation: responses to typecasting in British acting', *Cultural Sociology*, 11 (3): 359–76; Friedman and Laurison, *The Class Ceiling*; D. Hesmondhalgh (2018) 'The media's failure to represent the working class: explanations from media production and beyond', in J. Deery and A. Press (eds), *Media and Class: TV, Film and Digital Culture.* London: Routledge; M. Banks and K. Oakley (2016) 'The dance goes on forever? Art schools, class and UK higher education', *International Journal of Cultural Policy*, 22 (1): 41–57; D. Eikhof and D. Warhust (2013) 'The promised land? Why social inequalities are systemic in the creative industries', *Employee Relations*, 35 (5): 495–508; N. Olah (2019) *Steal as Much as You Can.* London: Repeater Books.

2 The field is extensive, and we'll encounter key references throughout the substantive analysis in the book. Key examples include Bull, *Class, Control, and Classical Music*; Conor *et al.*, *Gender and Creative Labour*; R. Gill (2014) 'Unspeakable inequalities: post feminism, entrepreneurial subjectivity, and the repudiation of sexism among cultural workers', *Social Politics*, 21 (4): 509–28; S. Malik (2013) 'Creative diversity: UK public service broadcasting after multiculturalism', *Popular Communication*, 11 (3): 227–41; G. Mellinger (2003) 'Counting color: ambivalence and contradiction in the American Society of Newspaper Editors'

discourse of diversity', *Journal of Communication Inquiry*, 27 (2): 129–51; C. Nwonka (2015) 'Diversity pie: rethinking social exclusion and diversity policy in the British film industry', *Journal of Media Practice*, 16 (1): 73–90; Nwonka and Malik, 'Cultural discourses and practices of institutionalised diversity in the UK film sector'; Saha, *Race and the Cultural Industries*; Scharff, *Gender, Subjectivity, and Cultural Work*.

3   Much of the research at the start of this section is drawn from two papers: O'Brien *et al.*, 'Are the creative industries meritocratic?' and Oakley *et al.*, 'Cultural capital'.

4   DCMS, *DCMS Sector Economic Estimates Methodology*.

5   Office for National Statistics (2019) *Labour Force Survey: User Guidance*, available from www.ons.gov.uk/employmentandlabourmarket/peopleinwork/employmentandemployeetypes/methodologies/labourforcesurveyuserguidance; see also Office for National Statistics, Social Survey Division, Northern Ireland Statistics and Research Agency, Central Survey Unit (2020) *Quarterly Labour Force Survey, January - March, 2020*. [data collection]. UK Data Service. SN: 8639, http://doi.org/10.5255/UKDA-SN-8639-1, and related studies.

6   D. Rose and D. J. Pevalin (2003) *A Researcher's Guide to the National Statistics Socio-Economic Classification*. London: Sage.

7   See R. Connelly, V. Gayle, and P. Lambert (2016) 'A review of occupation-based social classifications for social survey research', *Methodological Innovations*, 9: 1–14 for an overview, along with N. Kreiger, D. Williams, and N. Moss (1997) 'Measuring social class in US public health research: concepts, methodologies, and guidelines', *Annual Review of Public Health*, 18: 341–78; K. Roberts (2011) *Class in Contemporary Britain*. London: Palgrave; Crompton, *Class and Stratification*.

8   Office for National Statistics (2019) *User Guide to the LFS Questionnaire*, available from www.ons.gov.uk/employmentandlabourmarket/peopleinwork/employmentandemployeetypes/methodologies/labourforcesurveyuserguidance (accessed 26/12/2019).

9   O'Brien *et al.*, 'Are the creative industries meritocratic?' and Oakley *et al.*, 'Cultural capital'.

10 Bain, *Counting the Music Industry*.

11 Again, given the relative size of the museums, galleries, and libraries occupations sector in the 2019 LFS we should be cautious with this figure.

12 Friedman and Laurison, *The Class Ceiling*.

13 This section draws on McAndrew *et al.*, 'The values of culture?' and Taylor and O'Brien, 'Culture is a meritocracy'.

14 J. Broadbent and L. Kirkham (2008) 'Glass ceilings, glass cliffs or new worlds? Revisiting gender and accounting', *Accounting, Auditing and Accountability Journal*, 21 (4): 465–73; J. D. Levinson and D. Young (2010) 'Implicit gender bias in the legal profession: an empirical study', *Duke Journal of Gender Law and Policy*, 18 (1); K. Miller and D. Clark (2008) '"Knife before wife": an exploratory study of gender and the UK medical profession', *Journal of Health Organization and Management*, 22 (3): 238–53; Friedman and Laurison, *The Class Ceiling*.

15 R. Florida (2002) *The Rise of the Creative Class*. New York: Basic Books.

16 J. Peck (2005) 'Struggling with the creative class', *International Journal of Urban and Regional Research*, 29 (4): 740–70.

17 J. Littler (2018) *Against Meritocracy: Culture, Power and Myths of Mobility*. London: Routledge.

18 McAndrew *et al.*, 'The values of culture?'.

19 www.britishelectionstudy.com.

20 People very strongly pro-Remain rate themselves as 10 and anti as 0.

21 It's difficult to make specific comments about the group of people working in cultural and creative jobs that are classified as 'intermediate'. This largely reflects the ways in which creative jobs are classified.

22 These points show the average scores for each of these groups, while the bars around them show a measure of uncertainty for each group: there is more uncertainty for each of these things for the people working in creative industries in intermediate and routine jobs, as there are not as many of them in the sample. These average scores are after we have adjusted for a wide range of relevant other dimensions, such as people's ages, their educational qualifications, their gender. This means these differences just reflect occupational differences as far as possible.

23 Brook *et al.*, *Panic*.

24 J. Mijs (2019) 'The paradox of inequality: income inequality and belief in meritocracy go hand in hand', *Socio-Economic Review*, doi: 10.1093/ser/mwy051.

25 In the top part of the chart are that that agreed that talent, hard work, and ambition are important. This is the majority of respondents, with very few people indicating that these things are not at all important, not very important, or fairly important. However, there is still variation – only those respondents who indicated that all three of these aspects are essential are the ones right at the top of the graph. The smaller number of people below the horizontal line have a wide range of scores. Some of these disagreed very strongly that talent and hard work were how we

can best account for people's success in creative work, while others are more neutral. The reverse is true for the horizontal axis of social reproduction – those that didn't agree with social reproduction as an explanation of success are clustered closer to the central, indicating that they thought that coming from a wealthy background, and so on, might be important, but that it is not essential. The right-hand side of the graph is more sparse – only a few of our respondents indicated that your gender, your ethnicity, your class, and knowing the right people were all essential – and the far left of the graph is similarly sparse, with only a few people indicating that none of these things was at all important.

26 Bennett *et al.*, *Culture, Class, Distinction*.

27 Bennett *et al.*, *Culture, Class, Distinction*.

28 Friedman and Laurison, *The Class Ceiling*.

29 Hesmondhalgh, 'The media's failure to represent the working class'; De Benedictis *et al.*, 'Portraying poverty'; Skeggs and Wood, *Performance, Audience and Value*. See also K. Beswick (2019) *Social Housing in Performance*. London: Bloombury for a discussion of these issues in on-stage representation.

30 L. Rivera (2012) 'Hiring as cultural matching: the case of elite professional service firms', *American Sociological Review*, 77 (6): 999–1022; L. Rivera (2015) *Pedigree: How Elite Students Get Elite Jobs*. Princeton: Princeton University Press.

31 S. Koppman (2015) 'Different like me – why cultural omnivores get creative jobs', *Administrative Science Quarterly*, 61 (2): 291–331.

4 Who consumes culture?

1 E.g. Bourdieu, *Distinction*; Bennett *et al.*, *Culture, Class, Distinction*; P. DiMaggio and M. Useem (1978) 'Social class and arts consumption: the origins and consequences of class differences in exposure to arts in America', *Theory and Society*, 5 (2): 141–61; R. Peterson and R. Kern (1996) 'Changing highbrow taste: from snob to omnivore', *American Sociological Review*, 61 (5): 900–7; Lena, *Entitled*; S. Friedman (2015) *Comedy and Distinction*. London: Routledge; A. Miles and A. Leguina (2017) 'Fields of participation and lifestyle in England: revealing the regional dimension from a reanalysis of the Taking Part survey using multiple factor analysis', *Cultural Trends*, 26 (1): 4–17. See also V. Alexander (2003) *Sociology of the Arts*. London: Wiley; and M. Savage and L. Hanquinet (2018)

Routledge International Handbook of the Sociology of Art and Culture. London: Routledge for overviews.

2 Bunting *et al.*, 'Calling participation to account'.

3 A. R. Upchurch (2016) *The Origins of the Arts Council Movement: Philanthropy and Policy.* London: Palgrave; V. Durrer, T. Miller, and D. O'Brien (2017) *The Routledge Handbook of Global Cultural Policy.* London: Routledge.

4 DCMS (2019) *Taking Part Survey,* available from https://assets. publishing.service.gov.uk/government/uploads/system/uploads/attachment_data/file/807859/Taking_Part_Survey_October_2017_ to_September_2018__Provisional_.pdf (accessed 20/05/2020).

5 Figures 4.1–4.8 are based on estimates from the 2017/2018 wave of the Taking Part survey, which is administered by the DCMS on an annual basis. The survey has National Statistic status, owing to its high-quality design and implementation; we can therefore be confident that these estimates are close to the true value within the population.

6 We are looking at over-sixteens here, but deal with young people's cultural consumption in Chapter 6.

7 In order to qualify, people need only to have gone once. Someone who had been to a film at a cinema just once counts just as much as someone who had been multiple times a week.

8 S. Cunningham and J. D. Potts (2015) 'Creative industries and the wider economy', in C. Jones, M. Lorenzen, and J. Sapsed (eds), *The Oxford Handbook of Creative Industries.* Oxford: Oxford University Press.

9 Here, by 'social class', we're classifying people into one of three groups. 'Managerial/professional' means that someone lives in a household where the main income earner works in a managerial or professional job: this includes jobs we might think of as being classically elite, like CEOs, doctors, lawyers, architects, and it also includes roles like nurses and teachers. For 'intermediate', we're looking at jobs like police officers (up to sergeant), driving instructors, and electricians, while for 'semi-routine and routine' we're looking at jobs like traffic wardens, receptionists, bus drivers, and cleaners. This group also includes people who are long-term unemployed, and who've never worked. Because we're looking at households, someone would be classified as 'managerial/ professional' if they don't engage in paid work, and undertake large amounts of domestic labour, but their spouse works in a managerial role.

10 As a result of the small numbers the ratios may range from 3:1 to a more extreme 6:1. We are, however, confident that there are class based differences in artforms with smaller numbers of participants

Notes

11 Office for National Statistics (2019) *UK Population by Ethnicity: Age Groups*, available from www.ethnicity-facts-figures.service.gov.uk/uk-population-by-ethnicity/demographics/age-groups/latest.

12 P. Stark, C. Gordon, and D. Powell (2013) *Rebalancing Our Cultural Capital*, available at gpsculture.co.uk (accessed 20/05/2020).

13 This analysis draws on Campbell *et al.*, 'Cultural engagement and the economic performance of the cultural and creative industries'.

14 M. Greenacre (1988) 'Correspondence analysis of multivariate categorical data by weighted least-squares', *Biometrika*, 75 (3): 457–67; M. Flemmen, V. Jarness, and L. Rosenlund (2018) 'Social space and cultural class divisions: the forms of capital and contemporary lifestyle differentiation', *British Journal of Sociology*, 69 (1): 124–53.

15 The categories of artform vary slightly from our earlier analysis because we're using several years' worth of data. We've omitted a few categories in the middle, to make the graph easier to read.

16 The categories aren't perfect for this sort of analysis, because there are small numbers of particular jobs, such as dancers. To help get meaningful results with decent sample sizes, we've grouped together occupations into the following categories: libraries or archives, artistic or literary occupations, architecture, media, design, ICT, textiles, and into other skilled roles. Those last two groups are both part of 'crafts'.

17 Campbell *et al.*, 'Cultural engagement and the economic performance of the cultural and creative industries'.

18 Bourdieu, *Distinction*.

19 This section draws on Hanquinet *et al.*, 'The coming crisis of cultural engagement?'.

20 M. Taylor (2016) 'Taking Part: the next five years (2016) by the Department for Culture, Media and Sport', *Cultural Trends*, 25 (4): 291–4.

21 We might also look at reviews, (e.g. A. Goldberg, M. T. Hannan, and B. Kovács (2016) 'What does it mean to span cultural boundaries? Variety and atypicality in cultural consumption', *American Sociological Review*, 81 (2): 215–41) or media coverage (e.g. Purhonen *et al.*, *Enter Culture, Exit Arts?*) to give two examples of other methods and datasets for thinking about patterns of taste.

22 R. Groves and L. Lyberg (2010) 'Total survey error: past, present, and future', *Public Opinion Quarterly*, 74 (5): 849–79.

23 You can read more about *Audience Finder* at audiencefinder.org.

24 See methods appendix and relevant Hanquinet *et al.* paper, 'The coming crisis of cultural engagement?'.

25 A. Rae (2019) 'I ranked every UK constituency by deprivation and then coloured them by party affiliation – for fun', *CityMetric*, available at www.citymetric.com/politics/i-ranked-every-uk-constituency-deprivation-and-then-coloured-them-party-affiliation-fun (accessed 20/05/2020).

26 T. W. Chan and J. H. Goldthorpe (2005) 'The social stratification of theatre, dance and cinema attendance', *Cultural Trends*, 14 (3): 193–212.

27 S. Scherger (2009) 'Cultural practices, age and the life course', *Cultural Trends*, 18 (1): 23–45; M. Savage, L. Hanquinet, N. Cunningham, and J. Hjellbrekke (2018) 'Emerging cultural capital in the city: profiling London and Brussels', *International Journal of Urban and Regional Research*, 42 (1): 138–49.

28 A. Reeves (2015) 'Neither class nor status: arts participation and the social strata', *Sociology*, 49 (4): 624–42.

29 S. Trienekens (2002) '"Colourful" distinction: the role of ethnicity and ethnic orientation in cultural consumption', *Poetics*, 30 (4): 281–98.

30 T. Katz-Gerro and O. Sullivan (2010) 'Voracious cultural consumption: the intertwining of gender and social status', *Time & Society*, 19 (2): 193–219.

5 When does inequality begin in cultural workers' lives?

1 E.g. P. A. Banks (2012) 'Cultural socialization in black middle-class families', *Cultural Sociology*, 6 (1): 61–73; J. M. Calarco (2018) *Negotiating Opportunities: How the Middle Class Secures Advantages in School*. Oxford: Oxford University Press; I. Nagel (2010) 'Cultural participation between the ages of 14 and 24: intergenerational transmission or cultural mobility?', *European Sociological Review*, 26 (5): 541–56; A. Reeves (2015) '"Music's a family thing": cultural socialisation and parental transference', *Cultural Sociology*, 9 (4): 493–514; S. Scherger and M. Savage (2010) 'Cultural transmission, educational attainment and social mobility', *The Sociological Review*, 58 (3): 406–28; A. Sullivan (2001) 'Cultural capital and educational attainment', *Sociology*, 35 (4): 893–912; A. Sullivan (2008) 'Cultural capital, cultural knowledge and ability', *Sociological Research Online*, 12 (6): 91–104; A. Zimdars, A. Sullivan, and A. Heath (2009) 'Elite higher education admissions in the arts and sciences: is cultural capital the key?', *Sociology*, 43 (4): 648–66; D. Wallace (2019) 'The racial politics of cultural capital: perspectives

from black middle-class pupils and parents in a London comprehensive', *Cultural Sociology*, 13 (2): 159–77.

2 Rivera, 'Hiring as cultural matching'; Rivera, *Pedigree*.

3 Koppman, 'Different like me'.

4 A. Lareau (2003) *Unequal Childhoods*. Oakland: University of California Press; A. Lareau (2015) 'Cultural knowledge and social inequality', *American Sociological Review*, 80 (1): 1–27; A. Lareau, S. A. Evans, and A. Yee (2016) 'The rules of the game and the uncertain transmission of advantage: middle-class parents' search for an urban kindergarten', *Sociology of Education*, 89 (4): 279–99.

5 Lareau, *Unequal Childhoods*.

6 S. Khan (2012) *Privilege: The Making of an Adolescent Elite at St. Paul's School*. Princeton: Princeton University Press.

7 Friedman and Laurison, *The Class Ceiling*.

8 S. Davies and J. Rizk (2018) 'The three generations of cultural capital research: a narrative review', *Review of Educational Research*, 88 (3): 331–65.

9 Bourdieu, *Distinction*; P. Bourdieu (2011 [1986]) 'The forms of capital', in M. Granovetter and R. Swedberg (eds), *The Sociology of Economic Life* (78–92). Boulder: Westview Press.

10 See the debates in J. H. Goldthorpe (2007) '"Cultural capital": some critical observations', *Sociologica*, 1 (2); P. DiMaggio (2007) 'Comment on John Goldthorpe 2', *Sociologica*, 1 (2); M. Savage, A. Warde, and F. Devine (2007) 'Comment on John Goldthorpe 3', *Sociologica*, 1 (2); O. Lizardo (2008) 'Comment on John Goldthorpe 5: three cheers for unoriginality', *Sociologica*, 2 (2).

11 K. Robson (2009) 'Teenage time use as investment in cultural capital', in Robson and Sanders (eds) *Quantifying Theory: Pierre Bourdieu* (105–16). Dordrecht: Springer.

12 Friedman and Laurison, *The Class Ceiling*.

13 Reeves and de Vries, 'Can cultural consumption increase future earnings?'.

14 Sullivan, 'Cultural capital and educational attainment'; Sullivan, 'Cultural capital, cultural knowledge and ability'.

15 Scherger and Savage, 'Cultural transmission'.

16 A. A. Jack (2019) *The Privileged Poor: How Elite Colleges are Failing Disadvantaged Students*. Cambridge, MA: Harvard University Press.

17 K. Sedgman (2018) *The Reasonable Audience*. Cham: Palgrave Pivot.

18 Lena, *Entitled*.

19 L. Hanquinet (2017) 'Exploring dissonance and omnivorousness: another look into the rise of eclecticism', *Cultural Sociology*, 11 (2): 165–87; L. Hanquinet, (2017) 'Inequalities: when culture becomes a capital', in V. Durrer, T. Miller, and D. O'Brien (eds), *The Routledge Companion to Global Cultural Policy*. London: Routledge.

20 Purhonen *et al. Enter Culture, Exit Arts?*

21 Social Mobility Commission (2019) *An Unequal Playing Field: Extra-Curricular Activities, Soft Skills and Social Mobility*, available from https://assets.publishing.service.gov.uk/government/uploads/system/uploads/attachment_data/file/818679/An_Unequal_Playing_Field_report.pdf (accessed 20/05/2020).

22 Cited in House of Commons Digital, Culture, Media and Sport Select Committee, *Changing Lives*.

23 All Party Parliamentary Group for Music Education (2019) *Music Education: State of the Nation*, available from www.ism.org/images/images/State-of-the-Nation-Music-Education-WEB.pdf (accessed 20/05/2020).

24 F. Howard (2017) 'The arts in youth work: a spectrum of instrumentality?', *Youth and Policy*, available at www.youthandpolicy.org/articles/the-arts-in-youth-work (accessed 27/12/2019); F. Howard (2019) *Pedagogies for the 'Dis-Engaged': Who Gets What from Arts Education?*, available from www.bera.ac.uk/blog/pedagogies-for-the-disengaged-who-gets-what-from-arts-education (accessed 27/12/2019).

25 It does not ask about early years. There is, obviously, much more uncertainty about recall of early years experiences.

26 Respondents are asked: 'When you were growing up, did you do any of the following? Go to museums or art galleries; Go to the theatre or to see a dance or classical music performance; Go to historic sites (this includes historic attractions such as old buildings, historic parks and gardens and archaeological sites); Go to the library; Read books for enjoyment (not required for school or religious studies); Draw or paint; Write stories, poems, plays or music; Play musical instrument(s), act, dance, or sing; Take part in sports activities.' They are also asked how much their parents or other adults in the household encouraged them to do each of the following when they were growing up: 'Read books that were not required for school or religious studies; Draw, paint, write stories, poems, plays, or music; Take part in sport; Play musical instrument(s), act, dance, or sing'.

27 H. Taylor (2019) *Why Women Read Fiction: The Stories of Our Lives*. Oxford: Oxford University Press.

28 V. Cann (2018) *Girls Like This, Boys Like That: The Reproduction of Gender in Contemporary Youth Cultures*. London: I. B. Tauris.
29 BEIS (2018) *Industrial Strategy: Creative Industries Sector Deal*. London: HMSO.
30 Reeves, ' "Music's a family thing" '; Sullivan, 'Cultural capital and educational attainment'; Sullivan, 'Cultural capital, cultural knowledge and ability'.
31 Koppman, 'Different like me'.
32 Rivera, 'Hiring as cultural matching'; Rivera, *Pedigree*.

6 Is it still good work if you're not getting paid?

1 DCMS, *DCMS Sector Economic Estimates 2017*.
2 IPPR (2017) *The Inbetweeners: The New Role of Internships in the Graduate Labour Market*. London: IPPR.
3 M. Campbell (2018) ' "Shit is hard, yo": young people making a living in the creative industries, *International Journal of Cultural Policy*, DOI: 10.1080/10286632.2018.1547380; M. Curtin and K. Sanson (2016) *Precarious Creativity*. Oakland: University of California Press; G. De Peuter (2014) 'Confronting precarity in the Warhol economy', *Journal of Cultural Economy*, 7 (1): 31–47; G. De Peuter, N. Cohen, and E. Brophy (2015) 'Interrogating internships: unpaid work, creative industries, and higher education', *Triple C*, 13 (2): 329–602; B. E. Duffy (2018) *(Not) Being Paid to Do What You Love: Gender, Social Media, and Aspirational Work*. New Haven: Yale University Press; D. Eikhof and C. Warhurst (2012) 'The promised land? Why social inequalities are systemic in the creative industries', *Employee Relations*, 35 (5): 495–508; K. Fast, H. Ornebring, and M. Karlsson (2016) 'Metaphors of free labor: a typology of unpaid work in the media sector', *Media, Culture and Society*, 38 (7): 963–78; R. Gill and A. Pratt (2008) 'In the social factory? Immaterial labour, precariousness and cultural work', *Theory, Culture & Society*, 25 (7–8): 1–30; Hesmondhalgh and Baker, *Creative Labour*; A. Mears (2015) 'Working for free in the VIP', *American Sociological Review*, 80 (6): 1099–122; G. Morgan and P. Nelligan, (2018) *The Creativity Hoax: Precarious Work and the Gig Economy*. London and New York: Anthem Press; N. Percival and D. Hesmondhalgh (2014) 'Unpaid work in the UK television and film industries: resistance and changing attitudes', *European Journal of Communication*, 29 (2): 188–203;

R. Perlin (2011) *Intern Nation*. London: Verso; A. Ross (2010) *Nice Work if You Can Get It*. New York: New York University Press; S. Siebert and F. Wilson (2013) 'All work and no pay: consequences of unpaid work in the creative industries', *Work, Employment and Society*, 27 (4): 711–21; C. Umney and L. Kretsos (2013) '"That's the experience": passion, work precarity and life transitions among London jazz musicians', *Work, Employment and Society*, 28 (4): 571–88; S. P. Vallas and A. Christin (2018) 'Work and identity in an era of precarious employment: how workers respond to "personal branding" discourse', *Work and Occupations*, 45 (1): 3–37; A. Frenette (2013) 'Making the intern economy: Role and career challenges of the music industry intern', *Work and Occupations*, 40(4): 364–97; A. Frenette and R. E. Ocejo (2018) 'Sustaining enchantment: How cultural workers manage precariousness and routine' *Race, Identity and Work (Research in the Sociology of Work)*, 32: 35–60.

4 C. Cullinane and R. Montacute (2018) *Pay as You Go? Internship Pay, Quality and Access in the Graduate Jobs Market*, available from www.suttontrust.com/wp-content/uploads/2018/11/Pay-As-You-Go-1.pdf (accessed 27/12/2019); Equity (2018) *Professionally Made Professionally Paid: A Guide to Combating Low-Pay and No-Pay Work in the Entertainment Industry*, available from www.equity.org.uk/media/2849/equity_pmpp-campaign.pdf (accessed 27/12/2019).

5 Arts Council England (2011) *Internships in the Arts: A Guide for Arts Organisations*, available from www.artscouncil.org.uk/sites/default/files/download-file/internships_in_the_arts_final.pdf (accessed 28/12/2019).

6 D. Hesmondhalgh (2010) 'Normativity and social justice in the analysis of creative labour', *Journal for Cultural Research*, 14 (3): 231–49; Hesmondhalgh and Baker, *Creative Labour*; A. Ross (2007) 'Nice work if you can get it: the mercurial career of creative industries policy', *Work Organisation, Labour and Globalisation*, 1 (1): 13–30; E. Wilf (2011) 'Sincerity versus self-expression: modern creative agency and the materiality of semiotic forms', *Cultural Anthropology*, 26 (3): 462–84.

7 M. Banks, R. Gil, and S. Taylor (eds) (2013) *Theorizing Cultural Work: Labour, Continuity, and Change in the Cultural and Creative Industries*. London: Routledge; A. McRobbie (2002) 'From Holloway to Hollywood: happiness at work in the new cultural economy', in P. du Gay and M. Pryke (eds), *Cultural Economy*. New York: Sage; McRobbie, *Be Creative*; A. McRobbie (2016) 'Towards a sociology of fashion micro-enterprises: methods for creative economy research',

Sociology, 50 (5): 934–48; V. Mayer (2011) *Below the Line: Producers and Production Studies in the New Television Economy*. Durham, NC: Duke University Press.

8 V. Dubois (2015) *Culture as a Vocation: Sociology of Career Choices in Cultural Management*. London: Routledge; McRobbie, *Be Creative*.

9 A. McRobbie (2011) 'Rethinking creative economy as radical social enterprise', *Variant*, 41: 32–3.

10 These sit alongside demographic categories such as disability and sexuality, which also have a major impact on getting in and getting on.

11 Gill and Pratt, 'In the social factory?'.

12 C. Murray and M. Gollmitzer (2012) 'Escaping the precarity trap: a call for creative labour policy', *International Journal of Cultural Policy*, 18 (4): 419–38.

13 G. Standing (2011) 'The precariat', *Contexts*, 13 (10): 10–12; G. Standing (2014) *The Precariat Charter*. London: Bloomsbury.

14 McRobbie, *Be Creative*.

15 D. Dean and A. Greene (2017) 'How do we understand worker silence despite poor conditions – as the actress said to the woman bishop', *Human Relations*, 70 (10): 1237–57.

16 De Peuter, 'Confronting precarity in the Warhol economy'.

17 Percival and Hesmondhalgh, 'Unpaid work in the UK television and film industries'.

18 Percival and Hesmondhalgh, 'Unpaid work in the UK television and film industries'.

7 Was there a golden age?

1 W. Manger (2014) 'Julie Walters: working class kids can't afford drama school – soon only posh kids will be actors', *Daily Mirror*, available from www.mirror.co.uk/tv/tv-news/julie-walters-working-class-kids-4750761 (accessed 27/12/2019); D. Hutchison (2016) 'Julie Hesmondhalgh condemns loss of support for working-class actors', *The Stage*, available from www.thestage.co.uk/news/2016/julie-hesmondhalgh-condemns-loss-of-support-for-working-class-actors (accessed 27/12/2019); V. Thorpe (2018) 'Why does British theatre leave working-class actors in the wings?', *Guardian*, available from www.theguardian.com/stage/2018/jul/08/british-theatre-working-class-actors-waiting-in-the-wings (accessed 27/12/2019).

2 Frieze (2018) '"Culture is a birthright": eight leading UK Artists on the perils of excluding arts in schools', available from https://frieze. com/article/culture-birthright-eight-leading-uk-artists-perils-excluding-arts-schools (accessed 27/12/2019); All Party Parliamentary Group for Music Education, *Music Education*; J. Savage and D. Barnard (2019) *The State of Play: A Review of Music Education in England 2019*, available from www.musiciansunion.org.uk/StateOfPlay (accessed 27/12/2019); Warwick Commission (2015) *Enriching Britain: Culture, Creativity and Growth*, available from https://warwick.ac.uk/research/warwickcommission/futureculture/finalreport/warwick_commission_final_report.pdf (accessed 27/12/2019); S. Bhardwa (2018) 'Grayson Perry criticises lack of diversity on art degrees', *Times Higher Education*, available from www.timeshighereducation.com/news/grayson-perry-criticises-lack-diversity-art-degrees#survey-answer (accessed 27/12/2019).

3 Recent overviews of the term, and introductions to the field and associated debates include E. Bukodi and J. H. Goldthorpe (2018) *Social Mobility and Education in Britain*. Oxford: Oxford University Press; L. Major and S. Machin (2018) *Social Mobility and Its Enemies*. London: Pelican; D. Exley (2019) *The End of Aspiration? Social Mobility and Our Children's Fading Prospects*. Bristol: Policy Press; Friedman and Laurison, *The Class Ceiling*.

4 Office for National Statistics, *User Guide to the LFS Questionnaire*; see Friedman and Laurison, *The Class Ceiling*, for an application of this data in the context of social mobility.

5 Connelly *et al.*, 'A review of occupation-based social classifications'; Roberts, *Class in Contemporary Britain*.

6 A summary of recent historical perspectives can be found in a special issue of *Cultural and Social History* and C. de Bellaigue, H. Mills, and E. Worth (2019) '"Rags to riches?" New histories of social mobility in modern Britain – introduction', *Cultural and Social History*, 16 (1): 1–11.

7 Studies using income include J. Blanden and S. Machin (2007) *Recent Changes in Intergenerational Mobility in Britain*. London: Sutton Trust; J. Blanden, P. Gregg, and L. Macmillan (2007) 'Accounting for intergenerational income persistence: non-cognitive skills, ability and education', *Economic Journal*, 117(519): C43–60; J. Blanden, P. Gregg, and L. Macmillan (2013) 'Intergenerational persistence in income and social class: the effect of within-group inequality', *Journal of the Royal Statistical Society Series A (Statistics in Society)*, 176 (2): 541–63; a (highly critical) overview of the debate between income and occupational

approaches can be found in J. H. Goldthorpe (2013) 'Understanding – and misunderstanding – social mobility in Britain: the entry of the economists, the confusion of politicians and the limits of educational policy', *Journal of Social Policy*, 42 (3): 431–50.

8   R. Breen and R. Breen Jr. (eds) (2004) *Social Mobility in Europe*. Oxford: Oxford University Press; J. H. Goldthorpe and R. Erikson (1992) *The Constant Flux: A Study of Class Mobility in Industrial Societies*. Oxford: Clarendon Press; Goldthorpe, 'Social class mobility in modern Britain'.

9   F. Buscha and P. Sturgis (2018) 'Declining social mobility? Evidence from five linked censuses in England and Wales 1971–2011', *The British Journal of Sociology*, 69 (1): 154–82; P. Sturgis and F. Buscha (2015) 'Increasing inter-generational social mobility: is educational expansion the answer?', *The British Journal of Sociology*, 66 (3): 512–33; P. Brown (2013) 'Education, opportunity and the prospects for social mobility', *British Journal of Sociology of Education*, 34 (5–6): 678–700; Littler, *Against Meritocracy*.

10 D. Reay (2013) 'Social mobility, a panacea for austere times: tales of emperors, frogs, and tadpoles', *British Journal of Sociology of Education*, 34 (5–6): 660–77.

11 R. Breen and J. H. Goldthorpe (1997) 'Explaining educational differentials: towards a formal rational action theory', *Rationality and Society*, 9 (3): 275–305; H. G. Van de Werfhorst and S. Hofstede (2007) 'Cultural capital or relative risk aversion? Two mechanisms for educational inequality compared', *The British Journal of Sociology*, 58 (3): 391–415.

12 Goldthorpe, 'Social class mobility in modern Britain'.

13 Goldthorpe and Mills, 'Trends in intergenerational class mobility'; Friedman *et al.*, *Social Mobility*.

14 It is also important to note the gendered aspect of our discussion here. We'll see more about women and social mobility in Chapter 8.

15 Bukodi and Goldthorpe, *Social Mobility and Education in Britain*.

16 Goldthorpe, 'Social class mobility in modern Britain'.

17 www.gov.uk/government/organisations/social-mobility-commission (accessed 20/05/2020).

18 Grusky and Weeden, 'Decomposition without death'.

19 T. Strømme and M. Hansen (2017) 'Closure in the elite professions: the field of law and medicine in an egalitarian context', *Journal of Education and Work*, 30 (2): 168–85.

20 Banks, *Creative Justice*.

21 N. Shelton, C. Marshall, R. Stuchbury, E. Grundy, A. Dennett, J. Tomlinson, W. Xun (2019) 'Cohort Profile: the Office for National Statistics Longitudinal Study (The LS)', *International Journal of Epidemiology*, 48 (2): 383–4.

22 The ONS-LS also links life event data including births, deaths and cancer registrations. New LS members are added every year through births and immigration; existing members leave through emigration (including to Scotland and Northern Ireland) or death, however their data is still available for analysis.

23 We couldn't include people if neither parent had an occupation that could be assigned to an NS-SEC code when they were teenagers (which is under 10% in each cohort).

24 J. H. Goldthorpe (1987) *Social Mobility and Class Structure in Modern Britain*, 2nd edition. Oxford: Clarendon Press.

25 First, because we are only including people who were living in England and Wales as teenagers, so migrants are only included if they arrived as young children (which of course also applies to White migrants). Second, because ethnic minority immigrants in the UK are better educated than the White population as a whole, but often don't get work appropriate to their education (Y. Li and A. Heath (2016) 'Class matters: a study of minority and majority social mobility in Britain, 1982–2011', *American Journal of Sociology*, 122 (1): 162–200). This means that measuring the social class origin of second-generation immigrants by parental occupation is more likely to tell a partial story.

26 O. Brook, D. O'Brien, and M. Taylor (2018) 'There was no golden age: social mobility into cultural and creative occupations', available from https://osf.io/preprints/socarxiv/7njy3 (accessed 20/05/2020).

8 How is inequality experienced?

1 N. Puwar (2001) 'The racialised somatic norm and the senior civil service', *Sociology*, 35 (3): 651–70; N. Puwar (2004) *Space Invaders: Race, Gender and Bodies out of Place*. London: Berg.

2 S. Friedman, D. O'Brien, and D. Laurison (2017) '"Like skydiving without a parachute": how class origin shapes occupational trajectories in British acting', *Sociology*, 51 (5): 992–1010. See also D. Vandebroek (2017) *Distinctions in the Flesh*. London: Routledge.

3 Bourdieu, 'The forms of capital'.

4   Collins and Bilge, *Intersectionality*; Crenshaw, 'Mapping the margins';
    Yuval-Davis, 'Intersectionality and feminist politics'.
5   E.g. R. Chakrabarti (2014) 'Social mobility: is there a downside?', *BBC
    News*, available from www.bbc.co.uk/news/uk-25815084 (accessed
    20/05/2020); S. Moore (2017) 'To most political leaders, social mobility
    is no more than a vague goal. Like world peace', *Guardian*, available from
    www.theguardian.com/commentisfree/2017/jun/28/to-most-political-
    leaders-social-mobility-is-no-more-than-a-vague-goal-like-world-peace
    (accessed 27/01/2020); D. Foster (2018) 'Helping gifted children is all
    very well – but what about the rest?', *Guardian*, available from www.
    theguardian.com/commentisfree/2018/feb/20/gifted-children-
    generation-gifted-bbc-talented-struggling (accessed 27/01/2020).
6   These critiques are summarised in recent work from D. Reay (2017)
    Miseducation: Inequality, Education and the Working Classes. Bristol: Policy
    Press; Littler, *Against Meritocracy*; S. Lawler and G. Payne (2017) *Social
    Mobility for the 21st Century: Everyone a Winner?* London: Routledge; G.
    Payne (2017) *The New Social Mobility: How the Politicians Got It Wrong.*
    Bristol: Bristol University Press; L. Hanley (2017) *Respectable: The
    Experience of Class.* London: Allen Lane.
7   Reay, *Miseducation*; Littler, *Against Meritocracy*; Lawler and Payne, *Social
    Mobility for the 21st Century*.
8   Reay, *Miseducation*; S. Lawler (1999) '"Getting out and getting
    away": women's narratives of class mobility', *Feminist Review*, 63 (1):
    3–24; Hanley, *Respectable*.
9   Littler, *Against Meritocracy*.
10 K. Roberts (2017) 'Social mobility: lift going up, doors closing. Going
    down, doors wide open; any volunteers?', *Discover Society*, available from
    https://discoversociety.org/2014/01/06/social-mobility-lift-going-up-
    doors-closing-going-down-doors-wide-open-any-volunteers (accessed
    27/01/2020); Lawler and Payne, *Social Mobility for the 21st Century*.
11 Littler, *Against Meritocracy*.
12 Tyler and Slater, 'Rethinking the sociology of stigma'; Skeggs,
    'Imagining personhood differently'; B. Skeggs and V. Loveday (2012)
    'Struggles for value: value practices, injustice, judgment, affect and the
    idea of class', *British Journal of Sociology*, 63 (3): 472–90.
13 T. W. Chan (2019) 'Social mobility and the wellbeing of individuals',
    British Journal of Sociology, 69 (1): 183–206.
14 S. Friedman (2016) 'Habitus clivé and the emotional imprint of social
    mobility', *Sociological Review*, 64 (1): 129–47.

15 Rollock *et al.*, *The Colour of Class*.
16 A. Meghji (2019) *Black Middle-Class Britannia: Identities, Repertoires, Cultural Consumption*. Manchester: Manchester University Press.
17 Lawler, ' "Getting out and getting away" '.
18 E. Worth (2019) 'Women, education and social mobility in Britain during the long 1970s', *Cultural and Social History*, 16 (1): 67–83.
19 Puwar, 'The racialised somatic norm'; Puwar, *Space Invaders*.
20 Friedman *et al.*, ' "Like skydiving without a parachute" '; Friedman and O'Brien, 'Resistance and resignation'. Also Yuen, *Reel Inequality*.
21 See E. Dawson (2019) *Equity, Exclusion and Everyday Science Learning: The Experiences of Minoritised Groups*. London: Routledge, on the consequences of these issues for museum audiences.
22 Mellinger, 'Counting color'; N. Adams (2017) *Cultural Diversity Communication Strategies in UK and US Advertising Agencies: A Bourdieusian Analysis*, available from https://bura.brunel.ac.uk/bitstream/2438/15825/1/FulltextThesis.pdf (accessed 28/12/2019); Friedman and Laurison, *The Class Ceiling*.
23 Florida, *The Rise of the Creative Class*; A. Prieur and M. Savage (2013) 'Emerging forms of cultural capital', *European Societies*, 15 (2): 246–67; Hanquinet, 'Inequalities'.
24 Friedman and Laurison, *The Class Ceiling*.
25 A. Saha (2017) 'The politics of race in cultural distribution: addressing inequalities in British Asian theatre', *Cultural Sociology*, 11 (3): 302–17; Saha, *Race and the Cultural Industries*.
26 E.g. www.artscouncil.org.uk/diversity/creative-case-diversity.
27 Rollock *et al.*, *The Colour of Class*; D. Snoussi and L. Mompelat (2019) *'We Are Ghosts': Race, Class and Institutional Prejudice*, available from www.runnymedetrust.org/uploads/publications/We%20Are%20Ghosts.pdf (accessed 27/12/2019).
28 Rollock *et al.*, *The Colour of Class*.
29 H. Gray (2016) 'Precarious diversity: representation and demography', in M. Curtin and K. Sanson (eds), *Precarious Creativity*. Oakland: University of California Press; Mellinger, 'Counting color'; indeed some critics have pointed to organisations 'woke-washing': F. Sobande (in press) 'Woke-washing: "intersectional" femvertising and branding "woke" bravery', *European Journal of Marketing*, available from https://doi.org/10.1108/EJM-02-2019-0134 (accessed 20/05/2020).
30 S. Ahmed (2007) 'The language of diversity', *Ethnic and Racial Studies*, 30 (2): 235–56; S. Ahmed (2012) *On Being Included*. Durham, NC: Duke University Press.

9 Why don't women run culture?

1 Conor, *Screenwriting*; Gill, 'Unspeakable inequalities'; Wreyford, *Gender Inequality in Screenwriting Work*.

2 Conor *et al.*, *Gender and Creative Labour*.

3 E.g. S. Smith (2010) *Gender Oppression in Cinematic Content? A Look at Females an Screen & Behind-The-Camera in Top-Grossing 2007 Films. Report.* Annenberg School for Communication and Journalism, University of Southern California. D. D. Bielby and W. T. Bielby (1996) 'Women and men in film: gender inequality among writers in a culture industry', *Gender & Society*, 10 (3): 248–70; Conor *et al.*, *Gender and Creative Labour*; Conor, *Screenwriting*; Wreyford, *Gender Inequality in Screenwriting Work*; O'Brien, *Women, Inequality, and Media Work*.

4 Banet-Weiser, *Empowered*.

5 M. M. Lauzen and D. M. Dozier (1999) 'The role of women on screen and behind the scenes in the television and film industries: review of a program of research', *Journal of Communication Inquiry*, 23 (4): 355–73; Conor, *Screenwriting*; Wreyford, *Gender Inequality in Screenwriting Work*; O'Brien, *Women, Inequality, and Media Work*.

6 F. Henderson (2011) 'The culture behind closed doors: issues of gender and race in the writers' room', *Cinema Journal*, 50 (2): 145–52.

7 D. Eikhof (2017) 'Analysing decisions on diversity and opportunity in the cultural and creative industries: a new framework', *Organization*, 24 (3): 289–307.

8 Banks *et al.*, *Theorizing Cultural Work*.

9 D. Bielby (2009) 'Gender inequality in culture industries: women and men writers in film and television', *Sociologie du Travail*, 51 (2): 237–52.

10 A. Dimitrakaki and K. Lloyd (2017) 'Social reproduction struggles and art history', *Third Text*, 31 (1): 1–14.

11 D. Reay (1998) 'Rethinking social class: qualitative perspectives on class and gender', *Sociology*, 32 (2): 259–75.

12 K. Mendes, J. Ringrose, and J. Keller (2018) '#MeToo and the promise and pitfalls of challenging rape culture through digital feminist activism', *European Journal of Women's Studies*, 25 (2): 236–46.

13 There is a fourth, younger cohort, but we only have data on their jobs at one Census, so we can't say who leaves or where they go.

14 It's also worth noting that the same differences are found if we analyse all creative jobs rather than just our core creatives – though the (by far) largest differences in the people included are those working

in IT/software/computing, and in advertising and marketing. These occupational groups may be different in many ways to core creative work, but women still experience substantial exclusions from the workplace, in practice.

15 E.g. T. Dent (in press) 'Devalued women, valued men: motherhood, class and neoliberal feminism in the creative media industries', *European Journal of Cultural Studies*; S. Berridge (2019) 'Mum's the word: public testimonials and gendered experiences of negotiating caring responsibilities with work in the film and television industries', *European Journal of Cultural Studies*, 22 (5–6): 646–64; Gill, 'Unspeakable inequalities'.

16 Interviews were analysed for key words and phrases: 'my child/ren', 'my kid/s', 'my son', 'my daughter', 'pregnant/cy', 'matern(ity)', and 'childcare'. The interviews were then read to identify whether the interviewee was in fact a parent, and whether and how they discussed the relationship between parenting and their creative career.

17 Dent, 'Devalued women, valued men'; Berridge, 'Mum's the word'.

18 Banet-Weiser, *Empowered*.

19 PIPA (2017) *PIPA Best Practice Research Project Final Report*, available from www.pipacampaign.com/wp-content/uploads/2016/10/PIPA-Best-Practice-Research-Project-Final-Report-03–11–17-online-2.pdf (accessed 20/05/2020).

20 Wreyford, *Gender Inequality in Screenwriting Work*.

21 O'Brien, *Women, Inequality, and Media Work*.

22 Berridge, 'Mum's the word'.

23 Dent, 'Devalued women, valued men'.

24 B. Conor, R. Gill, and S. Taylor (2015) *Gender and Creative Labour*. London: Wiley-Blackwell.

25 M. Hicks (2018) *Programmed Inequality: How Britain Discarded Women Technologists and Lost Its Edge in Computing*. Boston: MIT Press.

10 What about the men?

1 This chapter draws on O. Brook, D. O'Brien, and M. Taylor (2019) 'Inequality talk: how discourses by senior men reinforce exclusions from creative occupations', *European Journal of Cultural Studies*.

2 Friedman and Laurison, *The Class Ceiling*.

3 Puwar, 'The racialised somatic norm'; Puwar, *Space Invaders*; Saha, *Race and the Cultural Industries*; Bull, *Class, Control, and Classical Music*; Scharff,

Gender, Subjectivity, and Cultural Work; Hesmondhalgh, 'The media's failure to represent the working class'; De Benedictis *et al.*, 'Portraying poverty'; K. Randle, C. Forson, and M. Calveley (2015) 'Towards a Bourdieusian analysis of the social composition of the UK film and television workforce', *Work, Employment and Society*, 29 (4): 590–606; Childress, *Under the Cover*; Gerber, *The Work of Art*.

4 Nwonka and Malik, 'Cultural discourses and practices of institutionalised diversity in the UK film sector'; Sobande, 'Woke-washing'.

5 Conor *et al.*, *Gender and Creative Labour*; Nwonka, 'Diversity pie'; Nwonka and Malik, 'Cultural discourses and practices of institutionalised diversity in the UK film sector'.

6 A. McRobbie (2007) 'Top girls? Young women and the post-feminist sexual contract', *Cultural Studies*, 21 (4–5): 718–37.

7 R. Gill (2011) 'Sexism reloaded, or, it's time to get angry again!', *Feminist Media Studies*, 11 (1): 61–71; Gill, 'Unspeakable inequalities'.

8 Malik, 'Creative diversity'.

9 Malik, 'Creative diversity'.

10 S. Sandberg (2013) *Lean In: Women, Work, and the Will to Lead*. London: WH Allen.

11 Gill, 'Unspeakable inequalities'.

12 M. Savage, G. Bagnall, and B. Longhurst (2001) 'Ordinary, ambivalent and defensive: class identities in the northwest of England', *Sociology*, 35 (4): 875–92; Bottero, 'Class identities and the identity of class'; S. Irwin (2015) 'Class and comparison: subjective social location and lay experiences of constraint and mobility', *British Journal of Sociology*, 66 (2): 259–81; S. Irwin (2018) 'Lay perceptions of inequality and social structure', *Sociology*, 52 (2): 211–27; G. Payne and C. Grew (2005) 'Unpacking "class ambivalence": some conceptual and methodological issues in accessing class cultures', *Sociology*, 39: 893–910; F. Sutcliffe-Braithwaite (2017) 'Discourses of "class" in Britain in "new times"', *Contemporary British History*, 31 (2): 294–317; R. Sherman (2018) '"A very expensive ordinary life": consumption, symbolic boundaries and moral legitimacy among New York elites', *Socio-Economic Review*, 16 (2): 411–33.

13 A. Miles, M. Savage, and F. Bühlmann (2011) 'Telling a modest story: accounts of men's upward mobility from the National Child Development Study', *British Journal of Sociology*, 62 (3): 418–41; A. Miles and M. Savage (2012) 'The strange survival story of the English gentleman, 1945–2010', *Cultural and Social History*, 9 (4): 595–612.

14 Friedman, 'Habitus clivé'.

15 Miles and Savage, 'The strange survival story of the English gentleman'.
16 Scharff, *Gender, Subjectivity, and Cultural Work*.

11 Conclusion

1 BBC (1967, 10 May). *Man Alive: Top Class People* [BBC iPlayer]. Available from www.bbc.co.uk/programmes/p0141jdn (accessed 20/05/2020).
2 BBC (1966, 23 February) *Man Alive: Not In Our Class Dear* [BBC iPlayer]. Available from www.bbc.co.uk/programmes/p0141n80 (accessed 20/05/2020).
3 We write this even as contemporary sociology is considering the limits of the project of making inequality visible as a basis for social change, as demonstrated by Bottero, *A Sense of Inequality*.
4 O'Brien, *Women, Inequality, and Media Work*.
5 M. Banks (2018) 'Creative economies of tomorrow? Limits to growth and the uncertain future', *Cultural Trends*, 27 (5): 367–80; T. Campbell and S. Selwood (2018) 'Culture and the environment', *Cultural Trends*, 27 (1): 1–3; R. Maxwell and T. Miller (2012) *Greening the Media*. Oxford: Oxford University Press; K. Oakley and J. Ward (2018) 'The art of the good life: culture and sustainable prosperity', *Cultural Trends*, 27 (1): 4–17.
6 Hesmondhalgh, 'The media's failure to represent the working class'.
7 Cann, *Girls Like This, Boys Like That*.

Bibliography

ACE (2019) *The Durham Commission on Creativity and Education*. Available from www.artscouncil.org.uk/publication/durham-commission-creativity-and-education (accessed 16/12/2019).

ACE (2019) *Value of Arts and Culture in Place-Shaping*. Available from www.artscouncil.org.uk/publication/value-arts-and-culture-place-shaping (accessed 16/12/2019).

Acker, J. (2006) 'Inequality regimes: gender, race and class in organisations', *Gender and Society*, 20 (4): 441–64.

Adams, N. (2017) *Cultural Diversity Communication Strategies in UK and US Advertising Agencies: A Bourdieusian Analysis*. Available from https://bura.brunel.ac.uk/bitstream/2438/15825/1/FulltextThesis.pdf (accessed 28/12/2019).

Ahmed, S. (2007) 'The language of diversity', *Ethnic and Racial Studies*, 30 (2): 235–56.

Ahmed, S. (2012) *On Being Included*. Durham, NC: Duke University Press.

Alacovska, A. (2017) 'The gendering power of genres: how female Scandinavian crime fiction writers experience professional authorship', *Organization*, 24 (3): 377–96.

Alexander, V. (2003) *Sociology of the Arts*. London: Wiley.

All Party Parliamentary Group for Music Education (2019) *Music Education: State of the Nation*. Available from www.ism.org/images/images/State-of-the-Nation-Music-Education-WEB.pdf (accessed 20/05/2020).

All-Party Parliamentary Group on Arts, Health and Wellbeing (2017) *Creative Health: The Arts for Health and Wellbeing*. Available from www.artshealthandwellbeing.org.uk/appg-inquiry/Publications/Creative_Health_Inquiry_Report_2017.pdf (accessed 20/05/2020).

Allen, K. (2014) 'What do you need to make it as a woman in this industry? Balls! Work placements, gender and the cultural industries'.

In D. Ashton and C. Noonan (eds), *Cultural Work and Higher Education* (232–53). Basingstoke: Palgrave Macmillan.

A-N (2016) *Paying Artists: A Manifesto for Artist-led Work*. Available from www.payingartists.org.uk/wp-content/uploads/2016/10/Paying-Artists-Artist-Led-Manifesto.pdf (accessed 21/02/2017).

Anderson, B. (1983) *Imagined Communities: Reflections on the Origin and Spread of Nationalism*. New York and London: Verso.

Arts Council England (2011) *Internships in the Arts: A Guide for Arts Organisations*. Available from www.artscouncil.org.uk/sites/default/files/download-file/internships_in_the_arts_final.pdf (accessed 28/12/2019).

Ashton, D. and Noonan, C. (2013) *Cultural Work and Higher Education*. London: Palgrave Macmillan.

Atkinson, A. (2015) *Inequality: What Can be Done?* Cambridge, MA: Harvard University Press.

Bain, V. (2019) *Counting the Music Industry: The Gender Gap*. Available from https://countingmusic.co.uk/ (accessed 20/05/2020).

Bakhshi, H., Freeman, A., and Higgs, P. (2013) *A Dynamic Mapping of the UK's Creative Industries*. London: Nesta.

Banet-Weiser, S. (2018) *Empowered: Popular Feminism and Popular Misogyny*. Durham, NC: Duke University Press.

Banks, M. (2017) *Creative Justice: Cultural Industries, Work and Inequality*. London: Rowman & Littlefield.

Banks, M. (2018) 'Creative economies of tomorrow? Limits to growth and the uncertain future', *Cultural Trends*, 27 (5): 367–80.

Banks, M. and Oakley, K. (2015) 'Class, UK art workers and the myth of mobility'. In R. Maxwell (ed.), *The Routledge Companion to Labor and Media* (170–9). New York: Routledge.

Banks, M. and Oakley, K. (2016) 'The dance goes on forever? Art schools, class and UK higher education', *International Journal of Cultural Policy*, 22 (1): 41–57.

Banks, M., Gill, R., and Taylor, S. (eds) (2013) *Theorizing Cultural Work: Labour, Continuity and Change in the Cultural and Creative Industries*. London: Routledge.

Banks, M., Lovatt, A., O'Connor, J., and Raffo, C. (2000) 'Risk and trust in the cultural industries', *Geoforum*, 31: 453–64.

Banks, P. A. (2012) 'Cultural socialization in black middle-class families', *Cultural Sociology*, 6 (1): 61–73.

Banks, P. A. (2019) *Diversity and Philanthropy at African American Museums: Black Renaissance*. Abingdon: Routledge.

Bibliography

Bazalgette, P. (2016) *The Empathy Instinct: How to Create a More Civil Society*. London: John Murray.

BBC (1966, 23 February) *Man Alive: Not In Our Class Dear* [BBC iPlayer]. Available from www.bbc.co.uk/programmes/p0141n80 (accessed 20/05/2020).

BBC (1967, 10 May) *Man Alive: Top Class People* [BBC iPlayer]. Available from www.bbc.co.uk/programmes/p0141jdn (accessed 20/05/2020).

Bear, L. (2014) 'Capital and time: uncertainty and qualitative measures of inequality sociology', *British Journal of Sociology*, 65 (4): 639–49.

Beck, U. (1992) *Risk Society*. London: Sage.

BEIS (2018) *Industrial Strategy: Creative Industries Sector Deal*. London: HMSO.

Belfiore, E. and Bennett, O. (2008) *The Social Impact of the Arts: An Intellectual History*. Basingstoke: Palgrave Macmillan.

Belfiore, E. and Gibson, L. (eds) (2020) *Histories of Cultural Participation, Values and Governance*. London: Palgrave.

Bennett, T. (1995) *The Birth of the Museum*. London: Routledge.

Bennett, T. (2013) *Making Culture, Changing Society*. London: Routledge.

Bennett, T., Savage, M., Silva, E. B., Warde, A., Gayo-Cal, M., and Wright, D. (2009) *Culture, Class, Distinction*. London: Routledge.

Berridge, S. (2019) 'Mum's the word: public testimonials and gendered experiences of negotiating caring responsibilities with work in the film and television industries', *European Journal of Cultural Studies*, 22 (5–6): 646–64.

Beswick, K. (2019) *Social Housing in Performance*. London: Bloomsbury.

Bhardwa, S. (2018) 'Grayson Perry criticises lack of diversity on art degrees'. *Times Higher Education*. Available from www.timeshighereducation.com/news/grayson-perry-criticises-lack-diversity-art-degrees#survey-answer (accessed 27/12/2019).

Bianchini, F. and Parkinson, M. (eds) (1994) *Cultural Policy and Urban Regeneration: The West European Experience*. Manchester: Manchester University Press.

Bielby, D. D. (2009) 'Gender inequality in culture industries: women and men writers in film and television', *Sociologie du travail*, 51 (2): 237–52.

Bielby, D. D. and Bielby, W. T. (1996) 'Women and men in film: gender inequality among writers in a culture industry', *Gender & Society*, 10 (3): 248–70.

Bilton, C. (1999) 'Risky business', *International Journal of Cultural Policy*, 6 (1): 17–39.

Bishop, C. (2012) *Artificial Hells*. London: Verso.

Blanden, J. and Machin, S. (2007) *Recent Changes in Intergenerational Mobility in Britain*. London: Sutton Trust.

Blanden, J., Gregg, P., and Macmillan, L. (2007) 'Accounting for intergenerational income persistence: non-cognitive skills, ability and education', *Economic Journal*, 117 (519): C43–60.

Blanden, J., Gregg, P., and Macmillan, L. (2013) 'Intergenerational persistence in income and social class: the effect of within-group inequality', *Journal of the Royal Statistical Society Series A (Statistics in Society)*, 176 (2): 541–63.

Blau, F. (2012) *Gender, Inequality, and Wages*. Oxford: Oxford University Press.

Blyth, M. (2013) *Austerity: The History of a Dangerous Idea*. Oxford: Oxford University Press.

Bottero, W. (2004) 'Class identities and the identity of class', *Sociology*, 38 (5): 985–1003.

Bottero, W. (2020) *A Sense of Inequality*. London: Rowman & Littlefield.

Bourdieu, P. (1984) *Distinction: A Social Critique of the Judgment of Taste*. London: Routledge.

Bourdieu, P. (2011 [1986]) 'The forms of capital'. In M. Granovetter and R. Swedberg (eds), *The Sociology of Economic Life* (78–92). Boulder: Westview Press.

Boushey, H., Delong, B., and Steinbaum, M. (2017) *After Piketty: The Agenda for Economics and Inequality*. Cambridge, MA: Harvard University Press.

Breen, R. and Breen Jr, R. (eds) (2004) *Social Mobility in Europe*. Oxford: Oxford University Press.

Breen, R. and Goldthorpe, J. H. (1997) 'Explaining educational differentials: towards a formal rational action theory', *Rationality and Society*, 9 (3): 275–305.

Broadbent, J. and Kirkham, L. (2008) 'Glass ceilings, glass cliffs or new worlds? Revisiting gender and accounting', *Accounting, Auditing & Accountability Journal*, 21 (4): 465–73.

Broockman, D., Ferenstein, G., and Malhotra, M. (2017) *Wealthy Elites' Policy Preferences and Economic Inequality: The Case of Technology Entrepreneurs*. Stanford Graduate School of Business Working Paper No. 3581.

Brook, O., O'Brien, D., and Taylor, M. (2018) *Panic: Social Class, Taste, and Inequality in the Creative Industries*. Available from http://createlondon. org/event/panic-paper/ (accessed 20/05/2020).

Brook, O., O'Brien, D., and Taylor, M. (2018) 'There was no golden age: social mobility into cultural and creative occupations'. Available from https://osf.io/preprints/socarxiv/7njy3/ (accessed 20/05/2020).

Brown, P. (2013) 'Education, opportunity and the prospects for social mobility', *British Journal of Sociology of Education*, 34 (5–6): 678–700.

Bukodi, E. and Goldthorpe, J. (2018) *Social Mobility and Education in Britain*. Oxford: Oxford University Press.

Bull, A. (2019) *Class, Control, and Classical Music*. Oxford: Oxford University Press.

Bunting, C., Gilmore, A., and Miles, A. (2020) 'Calling participation to account: Taking Part in the politics of method'. In E. Belfiore and L. Gibson (eds), *Histories of Cultural Participation, Values and Governance* (183–210). London: Palgrave.

Buscha, F. and Sturgis, P. (2018) 'Declining social mobility? Evidence from five linked censuses in England and Wales 1971–2011', *British Journal of Sociology*, 69 (1): 154–82.

Cabinet Office (2018) *Measuring Socio-Economic Background in Your Workforce: Recommended Measures for Use by Employers*. Available from https://assets.publishing.service.gov.uk/government/uploads/system/uploads/attachment_data/file/768371/Measuring_Socio-economic_Background_in_your_Workforce__recommended_measures_for_use_by_employers.pdf (accessed 20/05/2020).

Calarco, J. M. (2018) *Negotiating Opportunities: How the Middle Class Secures Advantages in School*. Oxford: Oxford University Press.

Campbell, M. (2018) ' "Shit is hard, yo": young people making a living in the creative industries', *International Journal of Cultural Policy*. DOI: 10.1080/10286632.2018.1547380.

Campbell, P. (2014) 'Imaginary success? The contentious ascendance of creativity', *European Planning Studies*, 22 (5): 995–1009.

Campbell, P., O'Brien, D., and Taylor, M. (2019) 'Cultural engagement and the economic performance of the cultural and creative industries: an occupational critique', *Sociology*, 53 (2): 347–67.

Campbell, T. and Selwood, S. (2018) 'Culture and the environment', *Cultural Trends*, 27 (1): 1–3.

Cann, V. (2018) *Girls Like This, Boys Like That: The Reproduction of Gender in Contemporary Youth Cultures*. London: I. B. Tauris.

Cannadine, D. (1998) *Class in Britain*. London: Penguin.

Chakrabarti, R. (2014) 'Social mobility: is there a downside?' *BBC News*. Available from www.bbc.co.uk/news/uk-25815084 (accessed 27/01/2020).

Chan, T. W. (2019) 'Social mobility and the wellbeing of individuals', *British Journal of Sociology*, 69 (1): 183–206.

Bibliography

Chan, T. W. and Goldthorpe, J. H. (2005) 'The social stratification of the-atre, dance and cinema attendance', *Cultural Trends*, 14 (3): 193–212.

Chattoo, C. (2018) 'Oscars so white: gender, racial, and ethnic diver-sity and social issues in U.S. documentary films (2008–2017)', *Mass Communication and Society*, 21 (3): 368–94.

Chiapello, E. (2004) 'Evolution and co-optation: the artist critique of management and capitalism', *Third Text*, 18 (6): 585–94.

Childress, C. (2017) *Under the Cover: The Creation, Production and Reception of a Novel*. Princeton: Princeton University Press.

Choueiti, M., Smith, S. L., and Pieper, K., with Case, A. (2018) *Critic's Choice 2: Gender and Race/Ethnicity of Film Reviewers across 300 Top Films from 2015–201*. Pennsylvania: Annenberg Inclusion Initiative.

Clift, S. and Camic, P. (2016) *Oxford Textbook of Creative Arts, Health, and Wellbeing*. Oxford: Oxford University Press.

Collins, H. and Bilge, S. (2016) *Intersectionality*. Cambridge: Polity Press.

Connelly, R., Gayle, V., and Lambert, P. (2016) 'A review of occupation-based social classifications for social survey research', *Methodological Innovations*, 9: 1–14.

Conor, B. (2014) *Screenwriting: Creative Labour and Professional Practice*. London: Routledge.

Conor, B., Gill, R., and Taylor, S. (2015) *Gender and Creative Labour*. London: Wiley-Blackwell.

Creative Industries Council (2019) *Arts and Culture: Why the UK?* Available from www.thecreativeindustries.co.uk/industries/arts-culture/arts-culture-why-the-uk (accessed 13/12/2019).

Crenshaw, K. (1991) 'Mapping the margins: intersectionality, identity politics, and violence against women of color', *Stanford Law Review*, 43 (6): 1241–99.

Crompton, R. (2008) *Class and Stratification*. Cambridge: Polity.

Crossick, G. and Kaszynska, P. (2016) *Understanding the Value of Arts & Culture: The AHRC Cultural Value Project*. Available from www.ahrc.ac.uk/documents/publications/cultural-value-project-final-report/ (accessed 20/05/2020).

Cullinane, C. and Montacute, R. (2018) *Pay as You Go? Internship Pay, Quality and Access in the Graduate Jobs Market*. Available from www.suttontrust.com/wp-content/uploads/2018/11/Pay-As-You-Go-1.pdf (accessed 27/12/2019).

Cunningham, S. and Potts, J. D. (2015) 'Creative industries and the wider economy'. In C. Jones, M. Lorenzen, and J. Sapsed (eds), *The Oxford Handbook of Creative Industries*. Oxford: Oxford University Press.

Curtin, M. and Sanson, K. (2016) *Precarious Creativity*. Oakland: University of California Press.

Davies, S. and Rizk, J. (2018) 'The three generations of cultural capital research: a narrative review', *Review of Educational Research*, 88 (3): 331–65.

Dawson, E. (2019) *Equity, Exclusion and Everyday Science Learning: The Experiences of Minoritised Groups*. London: Routledge.

Daykin, N. (2019) *Arts, Health and Well-Being: A Critical Perspective on Research, Policy and Practice*. London: Routledge.

DCMS (2010) *Taking Part: the National Survey of Culture, Leisure and Sport, 2005-2006; Adult and Child Data*. [data collection]. *2nd Edition*. UK Data Service. SN: 5717, http://doi.org/10.5255/UKDA-SN-5717-1.

DCMS (2010) *Taking Part: the National Survey of Culture, Leisure and Sport, 2008-2009; Adult and Child Data*. [data collection]. UK Data Service. SN: 6530, http://doi.org/10.5255/UKDA-SN-6530-1.

DCMS (2010) *Understanding the Drivers, Impact and Value of Engagement in Culture and Sport*. London: DCMS.

DCMS (2011) *Taking Part: the National Survey of Culture, Leisure and Sport, 2010-2011; Adult and Child Data*. [data collection]. UK Data Service. SN: 6855, http://doi.org/10.5255/UKDA-SN-6855-1.

DCMS (2013) *Taking Part: the National Survey of Culture, Leisure and Sport, 2012-2013; Adult and Child Data*. [data collection]. UK Data Service. SN: 7371, http://doi.org/10.5255/UKDA-SN-7371-1.

DCMS (2016) *The Culture White Paper*. Available from https://assets. publishing.service.gov.uk/government/uploads/system/uploads/attachment_data/file/510798/DCMS_The_Culture_White_Paper__3_.pdf (accessed 20/05/2020).

DCMS (2018) *DCMS Sector Economic Estimates 2017: GVA*. Available from www.gov.uk/government/statistics/dcms-sectors-economic-estimates-2017-gva (accessed 20/05/2020).

DCMS (2018) *DCMS Sector Economic Estimates Methodology*. Available from www.gov.uk/government/uploads/system/uploads/attachment_data/file/681217/DCMS_Sectors_Economic_Estimates_-_Methodology.pdf (accessed 19/02/2018).

DCMS (2019) *Taking Part Survey*. Available from https://assets.publishing. service.gov.uk/government/uploads/system/uploads/attachment_data/file/807859/Taking_Part_Survey_October_2017_to_September_2018__Provisional_.pdf (accessed 20/05/2020).

Bibliography

DCMS (2019) *Taking Part: the National Survey of Culture, Leisure and Sport, 2017-2018: Adult and Child Data.* [data collection]. UK Data Service. SN: 8442, http://doi.org/10.5255/UKDA-SN-8442-1.

Dean, D., and Greene, A. (2017) 'How do we understand worker silence despite poor conditions – as the actress said to the woman bishop', *Human Relations*, 70 (10): 1237–57.

de Bellaigue, C., Mills, H., and Worth, E. (2019) '"Rags to riches?" New histories of social mobility in modern Britain – introduction', *Cultural and Social History*, 16 (1): 1–11.

De Benedictis, S., Allen, K., and Jensen, T. (2017) 'Portraying poverty: the economics and ethics of factual welfare television', *Cultural Sociology*, 11 (3): 337–58.

Demoor, M., Saeys, F., and Lievens, S. (2008) '"And the winner is?" Researching the relationship between gender and literary awards in Flanders, 1981–2000', *Journal of Gender Studies*: 27–39.

Dent, T. (2019) 'Devalued women, valued men: motherhood, class and neoliberal feminism in the creative media industries', *Media, Culture and Society*. DOI: 10.1177/0163443719876537.

De Peuter, G. (2014) 'Confronting precarity in the Warhol economy', *Journal of Cultural Economy*, 7 (1): 31–47.

De Peuter, G., Cohen, N., and Brophy, E. (2015) 'Interrogating internships: unpaid work, creative industries, and higher education', *Triple C*, 13 (2): 329–602.

De Vries, R. (2014) *Internship or Indenture?* The Sutton Trust. Available from www.suttontrust.com/wp-content/uploads/2020/01/Unpaid-Internships.pdf (accessed 20/05/2020).

DiMaggio, P. (2007) 'Comment on John Goldthorpe 2', *Sociologica*, 1 (2).

DiMaggio, P. and Useem, M. (1978) 'Social class and arts consumption: the origins and consequences of class differences in exposure to arts in America', *Theory and Society*, 5 (2): 141–61.

Dimitrakaki, A. and Lloyd, K. (2017) 'Social reproduction struggles and art history', *Third Text*, 31 (1): 1–14.

Donoghue, D. (1983) *The Arts without Mystery*. London: BBC.

Dorling, D. (2014) *Inequality and the 1%*. London: Penguin.

Dubois, V. (2015) *Culture as a Vocation: Sociology of Career Choices in Cultural Management*. London: Routledge.

Duffy, B. E. (2018) *(Not) Being Paid to Do what you Love: Gender, Social Media, and Aspirational Work*. New Haven: Yale University Press.

Du Gay, P. and Pryke, M. (eds) (2002) *Cultural Economy: Cultural Analysis and Commercial Life*. London: Sage.

Du Gay, P., Hall, S., Janes, L., MacKay, H., and Negus, K. (1997) *Doing Cultural Studies: The Story of the Sony Walkman*. London: Sage.

Durrer, V., Miller, T., and O'Brien, D. (2017) *The Routledge Handbook of Global Cultural Policy*. London: Routledge.

Eikhof, D. (2017) 'Analysing decisions on diversity and opportunity in the cultural and creative industries: a new framework', *Organization*, 24 (3): 289–307.

Eikhof, D. and Warhurst, C. (2013) 'The promised land? Why social inequalities are systemic in the creative industries', *Employee Relations*, 35 (5): 495–508.

Elgenius, G. (2011) *Symbols of Nations and Nationalism: Celebrating Nationhood*. Basingstoke: Palgrave Macmillan.

Equity (2018) *Professionally Made Professionally Paid: A Guide to Combating Low-Pay and No-Pay Work in the Entertainment Industry*. Available from www.equity.org.uk/media/2849/equity_pmpp-campaign.pdf (accessed 27/12/2019).

Evans, G. (2001) *Cultural Planning: An Urban Renaissance?* London: Routledge.

Evans, G. and Shaw, P. (2004) *The Contribution of Culture to Regeneration in the UK*. London: London Met.

Evans, G. and Tilley, J. (2017) *The New Politics of Class: The Political Exclusion of the British Working Class*. Oxford: Oxford University Press.

Exley, D. (2019) *The End of Aspiration? Social Mobility and Our Children's Fading Prospects*. Bristol: Policy Press.

Fancourt, D. (2017) *Arts in Health*. Oxford: Oxford University Press.

Fast, K., Ornebring, H., and Karlsson, M. (2016) 'Metaphors of free labor: a typology of unpaid work in the media sector', *Media, Culture and Society*, 38 (7): 963–78.

Fieldhouse, E., Green, J., Evans, G., Schmitt, H., van der Eijk, C., Mellon, J. and Prosser, C. (2017) British Election Study Internet Panel Wave 13. DOI: 10.15127/1.293723.

Fielding, A. J. (1992) 'Migration and social mobility: south east England as an escalator region', *Regional Studies*, 26: 1–15.

Flemmen, M. (2014) 'The politics of the service class', *European Societies*, 16 (4): 543–69.

Flemmen, M., Jarness, V., and Rosenlund, L. (2018) 'Social space and cultural class divisions: the forms of capital and contemporary lifestyle differentiation', *British Journal of Sociology*, 69 (1): 124–53.

Florida, R. (2002) *The Rise of the Creative Class*. New York: Basic Books.

Bibliography

Foster, D. (2018) 'Helping gifted children is all very well – but what about the rest?' *Guardian*. Available from www.theguardian.com/ commentisfree/2018/feb/20/gifted-children-generation-gifted-bbc-talented-struggling (accessed 27/01/2020).

Frenette, A. (2013) 'Making the intern economy: Role and career challenges of the music industry intern', *Work and Occupations*, 40(4): 364–97.

Frenette, A. and Ocejo, R. E. (2018) 'Sustaining enchantment: How cultural workers manage precariousness and routine' *Race, Identity and Work (Research in the Sociology of Work)*, 32: 35–60.

Friedman, S. (2015) *Comedy and Distinction*. London: Routledge.

Friedman, S. (2016) 'Habitus clivé and the emotional imprint of social mobility', *Sociological Review*, 64 (1): 129–47.

Friedman, S. and Laurison, D. (2019) *The Class Ceiling: Why it Pays to be Privileged*. Bristol: Policy Press.

Friedman, S. and O'Brien, D. (2017) 'Resistance and resignation: responses to typecasting in British acting', *Cultural Sociology*, 11 (3): 359–76.

Friedman, S., Laurison, D., and Macmillan, L. (2017) *Social Mobility, the Class Pay Gap and Intergenerational Worklessness: New Insights from the Labour Force Survey*. London: Social Mobility Commission.

Friedman, S., O'Brien, D., and Laurison, D. (2017) '"Like skydiving without a parachute": how class origin shapes occupational trajectories in British acting', *Sociology*, 51 (5): 992–1010.

Frieze (2018) '"Culture is a birthright": eight leading UK artists on the perils of excluding arts in schools'. Available from https://frieze.com/ article/culture-birthright-eight-leading-uk-artists-perils-excluding-arts-schools (accessed 27/12/2019).

Garcia, B. and Cox, T. (2013) *European Capitals of Culture: Success Strategies and Long-Term Effects*. Available from www.europarl.europa.eu/RegData/ etudes/etudes/join/2013/513985/IPOL-CULT_ET(2013)513985_ EN.pdf (accessed 13/12/2019).

Garcia, B., Melville, R., and Cox, T. (2010) *Creating an Impact: Liverpool's Experience as European Capital of Culture*. Liverpool: Impacts08.

Garnham, N. (1987) 'Concepts of culture: public policy and the cultural industries'. In Ann Gray and Jim McGuigan (eds), *Studies in Culture: An Introductory Reader* (54–61). London: Arnold.

Garnham, N. (2005) 'From cultural to creative industries: an analysis of the implications of the "creative industries" approach to arts and media policy making in the United Kingdom', *International Journal of Cultural Policy*, 11 (1): 15–29.

Bibliography

Gerber, A. (2017) *The Work of Art: Value in Creative Careers*. Stanford: Stanford University Press.

Gibson, C. and Kong, L. (2005) 'Cultural economy: a critical review', *Progress in Human Geography*, 29 (5): 541–61.

Gibson, L. (2008) 'In defence of instrumentality', *Cultural Trends*, 17 (4): 247–57.

Gill, R. (2002) 'Cool, creative and egalitarian? Exploring gender in project-based new media work in Europe', *Information, Communication and Society*, 5 (1): 70–89.

Gill, R. (2011) '"Life is a pitch": managing the self in new media work'. In M. Deuze (ed.), *Managing Media Work* (249–62). London: Sage.

Gill, R. (2011) 'Sexism reloaded, or, it's time to get angry again!' *Feminist Media Studies*, 11 (1): 61–71.

Gill, R. (2014) 'Unspeakable inequalities: post feminism, entrepreneurial subjectivity, and the repudiation of sexism among cultural workers', *Social Politics*, 21 (4): 509–28.

Gill, R. and Pratt, A. (2008) 'In the social factory? Immaterial labour, precariousness and cultural work', *Theory, Culture & Society*, 25 (7–8): 1–30.

Gilroy, P. (2012) ' "My Britain is fuck all": zombie multiculturalism and the race politics of citizenship', *Identities*, 19 (4): 380–97.

Goldberg, A., Hannan, M. T., and Kovács, B. (2016) 'What does it mean to span cultural boundaries? Variety and atypicality in cultural consumption', *American Sociological Review*, 81 (2): 215–41.

Goldthorpe, J. H. (1987) *Social Mobility and Class Structure in Modern Britain*, 2nd edition. Oxford: Clarendon Press.

Goldthorpe, J. H. (2007) '"Cultural capital": some critical observations', *Sociologica*, 1 (2).

Goldthorpe, J. H. (2013) 'Understanding – and misunderstanding – social mobility in Britain: the entry of the economists, the confusion of politicians and the limits of educational policy', *Journal of Social Policy*, 42 (3): 431–50.

Goldthorpe, J. H. (2016) 'Social class mobility in modern Britain: changing structure, constant process', *Journal of the British Academy*, 4: 89–111.

Goldthorpe, J. H. and Erikson, R. (1992) *The Constant Flux: A Study of Class Mobility in Industrial Societies*. Oxford: Clarendon Press.

Goldthorpe, J. H. and Mills, C. (2008) 'Trends in intergenerational class mobility in modern Britain: evidence from national surveys, 1972–2005', *National Institute Economic Review*, 205: 83–100.

Goldthorpe, J. H., Llewellyn, C., and Erikson, R. (1987) *Social Mobility and Class Structure in Modern Britain*. Oxford: Clarendon Press.

Granovetter, M. (1995) *Getting a Job*, 2nd ediion. Chicago: University of Chicago Press.

Gray, H. (2016) 'Precarious diversity: representation and demography'. In M. Curtin and K. Sanson (eds), *Precarious Creativity* (241–53). Oakland: University of California Press.

Greenacre, M. J. (1988) 'Correspondence analysis of multivariate categorical data by weighted least-squares', *Biometrika*, 75 (3): 457–67.

Groves, R. and Lyberg, L. (2010) 'Total survey error: past, present, and future', *Public Opinion Quarterly*, 74 (5): 849–79.

Grusky, D. and Weeden, K. (2001) 'Decomposition without death: a research agenda for a new class analysis', *Acta Sociologica*, 44 (3): 203–18.

Guveli, A. (2006) *New Social Classes within the Service Class in the Netherlands and Britain: Adjusting the EGP Class Schema for the Technocrats and the Social and Cultural Specialists*. Available from https://repository.ubn.ru.nl/bitstream/handle/2066/56427/56427.pdf (accessed 04/09/2019).

Hall, S. (1973) *Encoding and Decoding in the Television Discourse*. Birmingham: Centre for Contemporary Cultural Studies.

Hanley, L. (2017) *Respectable: The Experience of Class*. London: Allen Lane.

Hanquinet, L. (2017) 'Exploring dissonance and omnivorousness: another look into the rise of eclecticism', *Cultural Sociology*, 11 (2): 165–87.

Hanquinet, L. (2017) 'Inequalities: when culture becomes a capital'. In V. Durrer, T. Miller, and D. O'Brien (eds), *The Routledge Companion to Global Cultural Policy* (327–41). London: Routledge.

Hanquinet, L., O'Brien, D. and Taylor, M. (2019) 'The coming crisis of cultural engagement? Measurement, methods, and the nuances of niche activities', *Cultural Trends*, 28 (2–3): 198–219.

Hawkins, H. (2016) *Creativity*. London: Routledge.

Henderson, F. (2011) 'The culture behind closed doors: issues of gender and race in the writers' room', *Cinema Journal*, 50 (2): 145–52.

Henley, D. (2016) *The Arts Dividend: Why Investment in Culture Pays*. London: Elliott & Thompson.

Henley, D. (2019) *Creativity: Why It Matters*. London: Elliott & Thompson.

Hesmondhalgh, D. (2010) 'Normativity and social justice in the analysis of creative labour', *Journal for Cultural Research*, 14 (3): 231–49.

Hesmondhalgh, D. (2013) *Why Music Matters*. London: Wiley.

Hesmondhalgh, D. (2018) 'The media's failure to represent the working class: explanations from media production and beyond'. In J. Deery

Bibliography

and A. Press (eds), *Media and Class: TV, Film and Digital Culture* (21–37). London: Routledge.

Hesmondhalgh, D. (2019) *The Cultural Industries*, 4th edition. London: Sage.

Hesmondhalgh, D. and Baker, S. (2011) *Creative Labour*. New York: Routledge.

Hesmondhalgh, D. and Pratt, A. (2005) 'Cultural industries and cultural policy', *International Journal of Cultural Policy*, 11 (1): 1–14.

Hicks, M. (2018) *Programmed Inequality: How Britain Discarded Women Technologists and Lost Its Edge in Computing*. Boston: MIT Press.

Hill, R. (2016) *Gender, Metal and the Media: Women Fans and the Gendered Experience of Music*. London: Palgrave.

Hobsbawm, E. and Ranger, T. (eds) (1983) *The Invention of Tradition*. Cambridge: Cambridge University Press.

Hoggart, R. (1957) *The Uses of Literacy*. Harmondsworth: Penguin.

Holden, J. (2004) *Capturing Cultural Value: How Culture has Become a Tool of Government Policy*. London: Demos.

House of Commons Digital, Culture, Media and Sport Select Committee (2019) *Changing Lives: The Social Impact of Participation in Culture and Sport*, Eleventh Report of Session 2017–19, 14 May 2019 HC 734.

Howard, F. (2017) 'The arts in youth work: a spectrum of instrumentality?', *Youth and Policy*. Available from www.youthandpolicy.org/articles/the-arts-in-youth-work (accessed 27/12/2019).

Howard, F. (2019) *Pedagogies for the 'Dis-Engaged': Who Gets What from Arts Education?* Available from www.bera.ac.uk/blog/pedagogies-for-the-disengaged-who-gets-what-from-arts-education (accessed 27/12/2019).

Hutchison, D. (2016) 'Julie Hesmondhalgh condemns loss of support for working-class actors'. *The Stage*. Available from www.thestage.co.uk/news/2016/julie-hesmondhalgh-condemns-loss-of-support-for-working-class-actors/ (accessed 27/12/2019).

IPPR (2017) *The Inbetweeners: The New Role of Internships in the Graduate Labour Market*. London: IPPR.

Irwin, S. (2015) 'Class and comparison: subjective social location and lay experiences of constraint and mobility'. *British Journal of Sociology*, 66 (2): 259–81.

Irwin, S. (2018) 'Lay perceptions of inequality and social structure', *Sociology*, 52 (2): 211–27.

Jack, A. (2019) *The Privileged Poor: How Elite Colleges are Failing Disadvantaged Students*. Cambridge, MA: Harvard University Press.

Jennings, W. and Stoker, G. (2016) 'The bifurcation of politics: two Englands', *Political Quarterly*, 87 (3): 372–82.

Jennings, W. and Stoker, G. (2017) 'Tilting towards the cosmopolitan axis? Political change in England and the 2017 general election', *Political Quarterly*, 88 (3): 359–69.

Jensen, T. and Tyler, I. (2015) 'Benefits broods: the cultural and political crafting of anti-welfare commonsense', *Critical Social Policy*, 35 (4): 470–91.

Jonsson, J., Grusky, D., Di Carlo, M., and Pollak, R. (2011) 'It's a decent bet that our children will become professors too'. In D. B. Grusky and S. Szelényi (eds), *The Inequality Reader: Contemporary and Foundational Readings in Race, Class, and Gender* (499–516). Boulder: Westview Press.

Jonsson, J. O., Grusky, D. B., Di Carlo, M., Pollak, R., and Brinton, M. C. (2009) 'Microclass mobility: social reproduction in four countries', *American Journal of Sociology*, 114 (4): 977–1936.

Katz-Gerro, T. and Sullivan, O. (2010) 'Voracious cultural consumption: the intertwining of gender and social status', *Time & Society*, 19 (2): 193–219.

Kelan, E. (2018) 'Men doing and undoing gender at work: a review and research agenda', *International Journal of Management Reviews*, 20 (2): 544–58.

Kemeny, T., Nathan, M., and O'Brien, D. (2019) 'Creative differences? Measuring creative economy employment in the United States and the UK', *Regional Studies*, 54 (3): 377–87.

Khan, S. (2012) *Privilege: The Making of an Adolescent Elite at St. Paul's School*. Princeton: Princeton University Press.

Kidd, J., Cairns, S., Drago, A., Ryall, A., and Stearn, M. (2014) *Challenging History in the Museum: International Perspectives*. London: Routledge.

Koppman, S. (2016) 'Different like me: why cultural omnivores get creative jobs', *Administrative Science Quarterly*, 61 (2): 291–331.

Kreiger, N., Williams, D., and Moss, N. (1997) 'Measuring social class in US public health research: concepts, methodologies, and guidelines', *Annual Review of Public Health*, 18: 341–78.

Kuipers, G., Franssen, T., and Holla, S. (2019) 'Clouded judgments? Aesthetics, morality and everyday life in early 21st century culture', *European Journal of Cultural Studies*, 22 (4): 383–98.

Lamont, M. (2019) 'From "having" to "being": self-worth and the current crisis of American society', *British Journal of Sociology*, 70 (3): 660–707.

Landry, C. (2000) *The Creative City: A Toolkit for Urban Innovators*. London: Earthscan.

Landry, C. and Bianchini, F. (1995) *The Creative City*. London: Demos.

Lareau, A. (2003) *Unequal Childhoods*. Oakland: University of California Press.

Bibliography

Lareau, A. (2015) 'Cultural knowledge and social inequality', *American Sociological Review*, 80 (1): 1–27.

Lareau, A., Evans, S. A., and Yee, A. (2016) 'The rules of the game and the uncertain transmission of advantage: middle-class parents' search for an urban kindergarten', *Sociology of Education*, 89 (4): 279–99.

Lash, S. and Lury, C. (2007) *Global Culture Industry*. Cambridge: Polity.

Lash, S. and Urry, J. (1994) *Economies of Signs and Space*. London: Sage.

Lauzen, M. M. and Dozier, D. M. (1999) 'The role of women on screen and behind the scenes in the television and film industries: review of a program of research', *Journal of Communication Inquiry*, 23 (4): 355–73.

Lawler, S. (1999) '"Getting out and getting away": women's narratives of class mobility', *Feminist Review*, 63 (1): 3–24.

Lawler, S. and Payne, G. (2017) *Social Mobility for the 21st Century: Everyone a Winner?* London: Routledge.

Lees, L., Slater, T., and Wyly, E. (2008) *Gentrification*. New York: Routledge.

Lena, J. (2019) *Entitled: Discriminating Tastes and the Expansion of the Arts*. Princeton: Princeton University Press.

Levinson, J. D. and Young, D. (2010) 'Implicit gender bias in the legal profession: an empirical study', *Duke Journal of Gender Law & Policy*, 18 (1): 1–33.

Li, Y. and Heath, A. (2016) 'Class matters: a study of minority and majority social mobility in Britain, 1982–2011', *American Journal of Sociology*, 122 (1): 162–200.

Littler, J. (2018) *Against Meritocracy: Culture, Power and Myths of Mobility*. London: Routledge.

Lizardo, O. (2008) 'Comment on John Goldthorpe 5: three cheers for unoriginality', *Sociologica*, 2 (2).

Luckman, S. (2015) *Craft and the Creative Economy*. London and New York: Palgrave Macmillan.

Luxford, J. (2010) 'Art for art's sake: was it ever thus? A historical perspective'. In N. Beech and B. Townley (eds), *Managing Creativity: Exploring the Paradox* (87–105). Cambridge: Cambridge University Press.

McAndrew, S., O'Brien, D., and Taylor, M. (2020) 'The values of culture? Social closure in the political identities, policy preferences, and social attitudes of cultural and creative workers', *The Sociological Review*, 68 (1): 33–54.

McRobbie, A. (2002) 'Clubs to companies: notes on the decline of political culture in speeded up creative worlds', *Cultural Studies*, 16 (4): 516–31.

McRobbie, A. (2002) 'From Holloway to Hollywood: happiness at work in the new cultural economy'. In P. du Gay and M. Pryke (eds), *Cultural Economy*. New York: Sage.

McRobbie, A. (2007) 'Top girls? Young women and the post-feminist sexual contract', *Cultural Studies*, 21 (4–5): 718–37.

McRobbie, A. (2011) 'Rethinking creative economy as radical social enterprise', *Variant*, 41: 32–3.

McRobbie, A. (2016) *Be Creative*. Cambridge: Polity Press.

McRobbie, A. (2016) 'Towards a sociology of fashion micro-enterprises: methods for creative economy research', *Sociology*, 50 (5): 934–48.

Major, L. and Machin, S. (2018) *Social Mobility and Its Enemies*. London: Pelican.

Malik, S. (2013) 'Creative diversity: UK public service broadcasting after multiculturalism', *Popular Communication*, 11 (3): 227–41.

Manger, W. (2014) 'Julie Walters: working class kids can't afford drama school – soon only posh kids will be actors'. *Daily Mirror*. Available from www.mirror.co.uk/tv/tv-news/julie-walters-working-class-kids-4750761 (accessed 27/12/2019).

Matarasso, F. (1997) *Use or Ornament? The Social Impact of Participation in the Arts*. Stroud: Comedia.

Mayer, V. (2011) *Below the Line: Producers and Production Studies in the New Television Economy*. Durham, NC: Duke University Press.

Maxwell, R. and Miller, T. (2012) *Greening the Media*. Oxford: Oxford University Press.

Mears, A. (2015) 'Working for free in the VIP', *American Sociological Review*, 80 (6): 1099–122.

Meghji, A. (2019) *Black Middle-Class Britannia: Identities, Repertoires, Cultural Consumption*. Manchester: Manchester University Press,

Mellinger, G. (2003) 'Counting color: ambivalence and contradiction in the American Society of Newspaper Editors' discourse of diversity', *Journal of Communication Inquiry*, 27 (2): 129–51.

Mendes, K., Ringrose, J., and Keller, J. (2018) '#MeToo and the promise and pitfalls of challenging rape culture through digital feminist activism', *European Journal of Women's Studies*, 25 (2): 236–46.

Menger, P.-M. (2014) *The Economics of Creativity: Art and Achievement under Uncertainty*. Cambridge, MA: Harvard University Press.

Merli, P. (2002) 'Evaluating the social impact of participation in arts activities: a critical review of François Matarasso's "use or ornament?"', *International Journal of Cultural Policy*, 8 (1): 107–18.

Mijs, J. (2019) 'The paradox of inequality: income inequality and belief in meritocracy go hand in hand', *Socio-Economic Review*. doi: 10.1093/ser/mwy051.

Bibliography

Milanovic, B. (2018) *Global Inequality: A New Approach for the Age of Globalization*. London: Belknap Press.

Miles, A. and Gibson, L. (eds) (2016) 'Everyday participation and cultural value: part 1', *Cultural Trends*, 25 (3) (Special Issue).

Miles, A. and Gibson, L. (eds) (2017) 'Everyday participation and cultural value: part 2', *Cultural Trends*, 26 (1) (Special Issue).

Miles, A. and Leguina, A. (2017) 'Fields of participation and lifestyle in England: revealing the regional dimension from a reanalysis of the Taking Part survey using multiple factor analysis', *Cultural Trends*, 26 (1): 4–17.

Miles, A. and Savage, M. (2012) 'The strange survival story of the English gentleman, 1945–2010', *Cultural and Social History*, 9 (4): 595–612.

Miles, A. and Sullivan, A. (2012) 'Understanding participation in culture and sport: mixing methods, reordering knowledges', *Cultural Trends*, 21 (4): 311–24.

Miles, A., Savage, M., and Bühlmann, F. (2011) 'Telling a modest story: accounts of men's upward mobility from the National Child Development Study', *British Journal of Sociology*, 62 (3): 418–41.

Miles, S. (2004) 'NewcastleGateshead Quayside: cultural investment and identities of resistance', *Capital and Class*, 84: 183–90.

Miles, S. (2010) *Spaces for Consumption*. London: Routledge.

Miller, K. and Clark, D. (2008) '"Knife before wife": an exploratory study of gender and the UK medical profession', *Journal of Health Organization and Management*, 22 (3): 238–53.

Minton, A. (2003) *Northern Soul: Culture, Creativity and Quality of Place in Newcastle and Gateshead*. London: Demos.

Molina-Guzmán, I. (2016) '#OscarsSoWhite: how Stuart Hall explains why nothing changes in Hollywood and everything is changing', *Critical Studies in Media Communication*, 33 (5): 438–54.

Moore, S. (2017) 'To most political leaders, social mobility is no more than a vague goal. Like world peace'. *Guardian*. Available from www.theguardian.com/commentisfree/2017/jun/28/to-most-political-leaders-social-mobility-is-no-more-than-a-vague-goal-like-world-peace (accessed 27/01/2020).

Morgan, G. and Nelligan, P. (2018) *The Creativity Hoax: Precarious Work and the Gig Economy*. London and New York: Anthem Press.

Mould, O. (2018) *Against Creativity*. London: Verso.

Murray, C. and Gollmitzer, M. (2012) 'Escaping the precarity trap: a call for creative labour policy', *International Journal of Cultural Policy*, 18 (4): 419–38.

Bibliography

Myerscough, J. (1988) *The Economic Importance of the Arts on Merseyside*. London: Policy Studies.

Nagel, I. (2010) 'Cultural participation between the ages of 14 and 24: intergenerational transmission or cultural mobility?' *European Sociological Review*, 26 (5): 541–56.

Negus, K. (2002) 'The work of cultural intermediaries and the enduring distance between production and consumption', *Cultural Studies*, 16 (4): 501–15.

Nelligan, P. (2015) *Walking the Vocational Tightrope: Narratives of Aspiration, Creativity and Precarious Labour* (Unpublished PhD). University of Western Sydney.

Nixon, S. and Du Gay, P. (2002) 'Who needs cultural intermediaries?', *Cultural Studies*, 16 (4): 495–500.

Nwonka, C. (2015) 'Diversity pie: rethinking social exclusion and diversity policy in the British film industry', *Journal of Media Practice*, 16 (1): 73–90.

Nwonka, C. and Malik, S. (2018) 'Cultural discourses and practices of institutionalised diversity in the UK film sector: "just get something black made"', *Sociological Review*, 66 (6): 1111–27.

Oakley, K. (2013) 'Good work? Rethinking cultural entrepreneurship'. In C. Bilton and S. Cummings (eds), *Handbook of Management and Creativity* (145–59). London: Edward Elgar.

Oakley, K., Laurison, D., O'Brien, D., and Friedman, S. (2017) 'Cultural capital: arts graduates, spatial inequality, and London's impact on cultural labor markets', *American Behavioral Scientist*, 61 (12): 1510–31.

Oakley, K. and Ward, J. (2018) 'The art of the good life: culture and sustainable prosperity', *Cultural Trends*, 27 (1): 4–17.

O'Brien, A. (2019) *Women, Inequality, and Media Work*. London: Palgrave.

O'Brien, D. (2010) *Measuring the Value of Culture*. London: DCMS.

O'Brien, D. (2014) *Cultural Policy*. London: Routledge.

O'Brien, D., Laurison, D., Miles, A., and Friedman, S. (2016) 'Are the creative industries meritocratic? An analysis of the 2014 British Labour Force Survey', *Cultural Trends*, 25 (2): 116–31.

O'Connor, J. (2000) 'The definition of the "cultural industries"', *The European Journal of Arts Education*, 2 (3): 15–27.

Office for National Statistics (2019) *Labour Force Survey: User Guidance*. Available from www.ons.gov.uk/employmentandlabourmarket/ peopleinwork/employmentandemployeetypes/methodologies/ labourforcesurveyuserguidance (accessed 26/12/2019).

Office for National Statistics (2019) *User Guide to the LFS Questionnaire*. Available from www.ons.gov.uk/employmentandlabourmarket/peopleinwork/employmentandemployeetypes/methodologies/labourforcesurveyuserguidance (accessed 26/12/2019).

Office for National Statistics (2019) *UK Population by Ethnicity: Age Groups*. Available from www.ethnicity-facts-figures.service.gov.uk/uk-population-by-ethnicity/demographics/age-groups/latest (accessed 20/05/2020).

Office for National Statistics, Social Survey Division, Northern Ireland Statistics and Research Agency, Central Survey Unit. (2020) *Quarterly Labour Force Survey, January - March, 2020*. [data collection]. UK Data Service. SN: 8639, http://doi.org/10.5255/UKDA-SN-8639-1.

Olah, N. (2019) *Steal as Much as You Can*. London: Repeater Books.

Oman, S. (2015) '"Measuring national well-being: what matters to you?" What matters to whom?' In S. White (ed.), *Cultures of Wellbeing: Method, Place, Policy* (66–94). London: Palgrave.

Osborne, T. (2003) 'Against "creativity": a philistine rant', *Economy and Society*, 32 (4): 507–25.

Paret, M. (2016) 'Towards a precarity agenda', *Global Labour Journal*, 7 (2): 111–22.

Payne, G. (2017) *Social Mobility for the 21st Century: Everyone a Winner?* London: Routledge.

Payne, G. (2017) *The New Social Mobilty: How the Politicians Got it Wrong*. Bristol: Policy Press.

Payne, G. and Grew, C. (2005) 'Unpacking "class ambivalence": some conceptual and methodological issues in accessing class cultures', *Sociology*, 39: 893–910.

Peck, J. (2005) 'Struggling with the creative class', *International Journal of Urban and Regional Research*, 29 (4): 740–70.

Percival, N. and Hesmondhalgh, D. (2014) 'Unpaid work in the UK television and film industries: resistance and changing attitudes', *European Journal of Communication*, 29 (2): 188–203.

Perlin, R. (2011) *Intern Nation*. London: Verso.

Perrons, D. (2014) 'Gendering inequality: a note on Piketty's *Capital in the Twenty-First Century*', *The British Journal of Sociology*, 65 (4): 667–77.

Peterson, R. and Kern, R. (1996) 'Changing highbrow taste: from snob to omnivore', *American Sociological Review*, 61 (5): 900–7.

Piachaud, D. (2014) 'Piketty's capital and social policy', *The British Journal of Sociology*, 65 (4): 696–707.

Pikettty, T. (2014) *Capital in the Twenty-First Century*. Cambridge, MA: Harvard University Press.

Piketty, T. (2014) '*Capital in the Twenty-First Century*: a multidimensional approach to the history of capital and social classes', *The British Journal of Sociology*, 65 (4): 736–47.

Piketty, T. (2018) *Brahmin Left vs Merchant Right: Rising Inequality and the Changing Structure of Political Conflict (Evidence from France, Britain and the US, 1948–2017)*. WID.world working paper series number 2018/7. Available from http://piketty.pse.ens.fr/files/Piketty2018.pdf.

PIPA (2017) *PIPA Best Practice Research Project Final Report*. Available from www.pipacampaign.com/wp-content/uploads/2016/10/PIPA-Best-Practice-Research-Project-Final-Report-03–11–17-online-2.pdf (accessed 20/05/2020).

Platt, L. (2019) *Understanding Inequalities*. Cambridge: Polity Press.

Pratt, A. (1997) 'The cultural industries production system: a case study of employment change in Britain, 1984–91', *Environment and Planning A*, 29 (11): 1953–74.

Prieur, A. and Savage, M. (2013) 'Emerging forms of cultural capital', *European Societies*, 15 (2): 246–67.

Prince, R. (2010) 'Fleshing out expertise: the making of creative industries experts in the United Kingdom', *Geoforum*, 41 875–84.

Purhonen, S., Heikkilä, R., Hazir, I. K., Lauronen, T., Rodríguez, C. J. F., and Gronow, J. (2018) *Enter Culture, Exit Arts? The Transformation of Cultural Hierarchies in European Newspaper Culture Sections, 1960–2010*. London: Routledge.

Puwar, N. (2001) 'The racialised somatic norm and the senior civil service', *Sociology*, 35 (3): 651–70.

Puwar, N. (2004) *Space Invaders: Race, Gender and Bodies out of Place*. London: Berg.

Rae, A. (2019) 'I ranked every UK constituency by deprivation and then coloured them by party affiliation – for fun'. *CityMetric*. Available from www.citymetric.com/politics/i-ranked-every-uk-constituency-deprivation-and-then-coloured-them-party-affiliation-fun (accessed 27/01/2020).

Rae, D. (2004) 'Entrepreneurial learning: a practical model from the creative industries', *Education + training*, 46 (8/9): 492–500.

Ramdarshan Bold, M. (2019) *Inclusive Young Adult Fiction: Authors of Colour in the United Kingdom*. Basingstoke: Palgrave Macmillan.

Bibliography

Randle, K., Forson, C., and Calveley, M. (2015) 'Towards a Bourdieusian analysis of the social composition of the UK film and television workforce', *Work, Employment and Society*, 29 (4): 590–606.

Reay, D. (1998) 'Rethinking social class: qualitative perspectives on class and gender', *Sociology*, 32 (2): 259–75.

Reay, D. (2013) 'Social mobility, a panacea for austere times: tales of emperors, frogs, and tadpoles', *British Journal of Sociology of Education*, 34 (5–6): 660–77.

Reay, D. (2017) *Miseducation: Inequality, Education and the Working Classes*. Bristol: Policy Press.

Reeves, A. (2015) '"Music's a family thing": cultural socialisation and parental transference', *Cultural Sociology*, 9 (4): 493–514.

Reeves, A. (2015) 'Neither class nor status: arts participation and the social strata', *Sociology*, 49 (4): 624–42.

Reeves, A. and de Vries, R. (2016) 'Does media coverage influence public attitudes towards welfare recipients? The impact of the 2011 English riots', *British Journal of Sociology*, 67 (2): 281–306.

Reeves, A. and de Vries, R. (2019) 'Can cultural consumption increase future earnings? Exploring the economic returns to cultural capital', *British Journal of Sociology*, 70 (1): 214–40.

Rivera, L. (2012) 'Hiring as cultural matching: the case of elite professional service firms', *American Sociological Review*, 77 (6): 999–1022.

Rivera, L. (2015) *Pedigree: How Elite Students Get Elite Jobs*. Princeton: Princeton University Press.

Roberts, K. (2011) *Class in Contemporary Britain*. London: Palgrave.

Roberts, K. (2017) 'Social mobility: lift going up, doors closing. Going down, doors wide open; any volunteers?' *Discover Society*. Available from https://discoversociety.org/2014/01/06/social-mobility-lift-going-up-doors-closing-going-down-doors-wide-open-any-volunteers/ (accessed 27/01/2020).

Robson, K. (2009) 'Teenage time use as investment in cultural capital'. In Robson and Sanders (eds) *Quantifying Theory: Pierre Bourdieu* (105–16). Dordrecht: Springer.

Rogers, A. (2016) *Performing Asian Transnationalisms: Theatre, Identity, and the Geographies of Performance*. London: Routledge.

Rogers, A. and Thorpe, A. (2014) 'A controversial company: debating the casting of the RSC's The Orphan of Zhao', *Contemporary Theatre Review*, 24 (4): 428–35.

Rollock, N., Gilborn, D., Vincent, C. and Ball, D. (2014) *The Colour of Class: The Educational Strategies of the Black Middle Classes*. London: Routledge.

Rose, D. and Pevalin, D. J. (2003) *A Researcher's Guide to the National Statistics Socio-Economic Classification*. London: Sage.

Ross, A. (2007) 'Nice work if you can get it: the mercurial career of creative industries policy', *Work Organisation, Labour and Globalisation*, 1 (1): 13–30.

Ross, A. (2010) *Nice Work If You Can Get It*. New York: New York University Press.

Rumbold, K., Simecek, K., Ellis, V., Riddell, P., Bessell, J., Williams, A., Rathbone, C., and Howell, E. (2015) 'The uses of poetry: measuring the value of engaging with poetry in lifelong learning and development', *Cultural Value*. Available from https://usesofpoetry.files.wordpress.com/2015/12/ahrc_cultural_value_rda-uses-of-poetry-rumbold.pdf (accessed 20/05/2020).

Saha, A. (2016) 'The rationalizing/racializing logic of capital in cultural production', *Media Industries*, 3 (1): 1–16.

Saha, A. (2017) 'The politics of race in cultural distribution: addressing inequalities in British Asian theatre', *Cultural Sociology*, 11 (3): 302–17.

Saha, A. (2018) *Race and the Cultural Industries*. Cambridge: Polity Press.

Sandberg, S. (2013) *Lean In: Women, Work, and the Will to Lead*. London: WH Allen.

Savage, J. and Barnard, D. (2019) *The State of Play: A Review of Music Education in England 2019*. Available from www.musiciansunion.org.uk/StateOfPlay (accessed 27/12/2019).

Savage, M. (2000) *Class Analysis and Social Transformations*. London: Routledge.

Savage, M. (2010) *Identities and Social Change in Britain Since 1940: The Politics of Method*. Oxford: Oxford University Press.

Savage, M. (2014) 'Piketty's challenge for sociology', *The British Journal of Sociology*, 65 (4): 591–605.

Savage, M. (2015) *Social Class in the Twenty First Century*. London: Penguin.

Savage, M. and Hanquinet, L. (2018) *Routledge International Handbook of the Sociology of Art and Culture*. London: Routledge.

Savage, M., Bagnall, G. and Longhurst, B. (2001) 'Ordinary, ambivalent and defensive: class identities in the northwest of England', *Sociology*, 35 (4): 875–92.

Savage, M., Warde, A., and Devine, F. (2007) 'Comment on John Goldthorpe 3' *Sociologica* 1 (2).

Savage, M., Devine, F., Cunningham, N., Friedman, S., Laurison, D., Miles, A., and Taylor, M. (2015) 'On social class, anno 2014', *Sociology*, 49 (6): 1011–30.

Savage, M., Devine, F., Cunningham, N., Taylor, M., Li, Y., Hjellbrekke, J., Le Roux, B., Friedman, S., and Miles, A. (2013) 'A new model of social class? Findings from the Great British Class Survey Experiment', *Sociology*, 47 (2): 19–50.

Scharff, C. (2015) *Equality and Diversity in the Classical Music Profession*. London: Kings College London.

Scharff, C. (2017) *Gender, Subjectivity, and Cultural Work: The Classical Music Profession*. London: Routledge.

Scherger, S. (2009) 'Cultural practices, age and the life course', *Cultural Trends*, 18 (1): 23–45.

Scherger, S. and Savage, M. (2010) 'Cultural transmission, educational attainment and social mobility', *The Sociological Review*, 58 (3): 406–28.

Schwartz, S. (1999) 'A theory of cultural values and some implications for work', *Applied Psychology*, 48: 23–47.

Scully, B. (2016) 'Precarity north and south: a southern critique of Guy Standing', *Global Labour Journal*, 7 (2): 160–73.

Sedgman, K. (2018) *The Reasonable Audience*. Cham: Palgrave Pivot.

Shelton, N., Marshall, C. E., Stuchbury, R., Grundy, E., Dennett, A., Tomlinson, J. and Xun, W. (2019) 'Cohort Profile: the Office for National Statistics Longitudinal Study (The LS)', *International Journal of Epidemiology* 48 (2): 383–384.

Sherman, R. (2018) '"A very expensive ordinary life": consumption, symbolic boundaries and moral legitimacy among New York elites', *Socio-Economic Review*, 16 (2): 411–33.

Siebert, S. and Wilson, F. (2013) 'All work and no pay: consequences of unpaid work in the creative industries', *Work, Employment and Society*, 27 (4): 711–21.

Skeggs, B. (1997) *Formations of Class and Gender*. London: Sage.

Skeggs, B. (2004) *Class, Self and Culture*. London: Routledge.

Skeggs, B. (2011) 'Imagining personhood differently: person value and autonomist working-class value practices', *The Sociological Review*, 59 (3): 496–513.

Skeggs, B. and Loveday, V. (2012) 'Struggles for value: value practices, injustice, judgment, affect and the idea of class', *British Journal of Sociology*, 63 (3): 472–90.

Bibliography

Skeggs, B. and Wood, H. (2012) *Performance, Audience and Value.* London: Routledge.

Smith, S. (2010) *Gender Oppression in Cinematic Content? A Look at Females an Screen & Behind-The-Camera in Top-Grossing 2007 Films.* Report. Annenberg School for Communication and Journalism, University of Southern California. Retrieved 30 November, p. 2017.

Smith, S., Choueiti, M., and Gall, S. (n.d.) *Asymmetrical Academy Awards 2: Another Look at Gender in Best Picture Nominated Films from 1977 to 2010.* Available from https://annenberg.usc.edu/sites/default/files/MDSCI_Gender_Representation_1977_2010.pdf (accessed 26/12/2019).

Smith, S., Choueiti, M., and Pieper, K. (2019) *Inclusion in the Recording Studio?* Available from http://assets.uscannenberg.org/docs/aii-inclusion-recording-studio-2019.pdf (accessed 26/12/2019).

Smith, S., Choueiti, M., Choi, A., and Pieper, K. (2019) *Inclusion in the Director's Chair.* Available from http://assets.uscannenberg.org/docs/inclusion-in-the-directors-chair-2019.pdf (accessed 26/12/2019).

Smith, S., Choueiti, M., Choi, A., Pieper, K., Clark, H., Hernandez, K., Martinez, J., Lopez, B., and Mota, M. (2019) *Latinos in Film.* Available from http://assets.uscannenberg.org/docs/aii-study-latinos-in-film-2019.pdf (accessed 26/12/2019).

Smith Maguire, J. and Matthews, J. (eds) (2014) *The Cultural Intermediaries Reader.* London: Sage.

Snoussi, D. and Mompelat, L. (2019) *'We Are Ghosts': Race, Class and Institutional Prejudice.* Available from www.runnymedetrust.org/uploads/publications/We%20Are%20Ghosts.pdf (accessed 27/12/2019).

Sobande, F. (2019) 'Woke-washing: "intersectional" femvertising and branding "woke" bravery', *European Journal of Marketing.* DOI: 10.1108/EJM-02-2019-0134.

Social Mobility Commission (2019) *An Unequal Playing Field: Extra-Curricular Activities, Soft Skills and Social Mobility.* Available from https://assets.publishing.service.gov.uk/government/uploads/system/uploads/attachment_data/file/818679/An_Unequal_Playing_Field_report.pdf (accessed 20/05/2020).

Standing, G. (2011) 'The precariat', *Contexts*, 13 (10): 10–12.

Standing, G. (2014) *The Precariat Charter.* London: Bloomsbury.

Stark, P., Gordon, C., and Powell, D. (2013) *Rebalancing Our Cultural Capital.* Available from www.gpsculture.co.uk (accessed 20/05/2020).

Stickley, T. and Clift, S. (2017) *Arts, Health and Wellbeing: A Theoretical Inquiry for Practice.* Newcastle upon Tyne: Cambridge Scholars Publishing.

Bibliography

Stiglitz, J. (2013) *The Price of Inequality*. London: Penguin.

Strømme, T. and Hansen, M. (2017) 'Closure in the elite professions: the field of law and medicine in an egalitarian context', *Journal of Education and Work*, 30 (2): 168–85.

Sturgis, P. and Buscha, F. (2015) 'Increasing inter-generational social mobility: is educational expansion the answer?' *The British Journal of Sociology*, 66 (3): 512–33.

Sullivan, A. (2001) 'Cultural capital and educational attainment', *Sociology*, 35 (4): 893–912.

Sullivan, A. (2008) 'Cultural capital, cultural knowledge and ability', *Sociological Research Online*, 12 (6): 91–104.

Surridge, P. (2016) 'Education and liberalism: pursuing the link', *Oxford Review of Education*, 42: 146–64.

Sutcliffe-Braithwaite, F. (2017) 'Discourses of "class" in Britain in "new times"', *Contemporary British History*, 31 (2): 294–317.

Taylor, H. (2019) *Why Women Read Fiction: The Stories of Our Lives*. Oxford: Oxford University Press.

Taylor, M. (2016) 'Nonparticipation or different styles of participation? Alternative interpretations from Taking Part', *Cultural Trends*, 25 (3): 169–81.

Taylor, M. (2016) 'Taking Part: the next five years (2016) by the Department for Culture, Media and Sport', *Cultural Trends*, 25 (4): 291–4.

Taylor, M. and O'Brien, D. (2017) '"Culture is a meritocracy": why creative workers' attitudes may reinforce social inequality', *Sociological Research Online*, 22 (4): 27–47.

Terras, M. (2018) *Picture-Book Professors*. Cambridge: Cambridge University Press.

Thorpe, V. (2018) 'Why does British theatre leave working-class actors in the wings?' *Guardian*. Available from www.theguardian.com/stage/2018/jul/08/british-theatre-working-class-actors-waiting-in-the-wings (accessed 27/12/2019).

Tooze, A. (2018) *Crashed: How a Decade of Financial Crises Changed the World*. London: Allen Lane.

Trienekens, S. (2002) '"Colourful" distinction: the role of ethnicity and ethnic orientation in cultural consumption', *Poetics*, 30 (4): 281–98.

Tyler, I. and Slater, T. (2018) 'Rethinking the sociology of stigma', *The Sociological Review*, 66 (4): 721–43.

Umney, C. and Kretsos, L. (2013) '"That's the experience": passion, work precarity and life transitions among London jazz musicians', *Work, Employment and Society*, 28 (4): 571–88.

Upchurch, A. R. (2016) *The Origins of the Arts Council Movement: Philanthropy and Policy*. London: Palgrave.

Vallas, S. P. and Christin, A. (2018) 'Work and identity in an era of precarious employment: how workers respond to "personal branding" discourse', *Work and Occupations*, 45 (1): 3–37.

Vandebroek, D. (2017) *Distinctions in the Flesh*. London: Routledge.

Van de Werfhorst, H. G. and Hofstede, S. (2007) 'Cultural capital or relative risk aversion? Two mechanisms for educational inequality compared', *The British Journal of Sociology*, 58 (3): 391–415.

Wajid, S. and Minott, R. (2019) 'Detoxing and decolonising museums'. In R. Janes and R. Sandell (eds), *Museum Activism* (34–45). London: Routledge.

Wallace, D. (2019) 'The racial politics of cultural capital: perspectives from black middle-class pupils and parents in a London comprehensive', *Cultural Sociology*, 13 (2): 159–77.

Wang, Y. and Horvat, E.-A. (2019) *Gender Differences in the Global Music Industry: Evidence from MusicBrainz and The Echo Nest*. Available from www.aaai.org/ojs/index.php/ICWSM/article/view/3249/3117 (accessed 26/12/2019).

Warwick Commission (2015) *Enriching Britain: Culture, Creativity and Growth*. Available from https://warwick.ac.uk/research/warwickcommission/futureculture/finalreport/warwick_commission_final_report.pdf (accessed 27/12/2019).

Watt, P. (2009) 'Housing stock transfers, regeneration and state-led gentrification in London', *Urban Policy and Research*, 27 (3): 229–42.

Weeden, K. A. and Grusky, D. B. (2005) 'The case for a new class map', *American Journal of Sociology*, 111 (1): 141–212.

Wetherell, M., Stiven, H. and Potter, J. (1987) 'Unequal egalitariansim: a preliminary study of discourses concerning gender and employment opportunities', *British Journal of Social Psychology*, 26 (2): 59–71.

What Next? (2019) *What Next? Briefing Pack*. Available from www.whatnextculture.co.uk/wp-content/uploads/2019/11/What-Next-General-Election-Briefing-2019-4.pdf (accessed 13/12/2019).

Wilf, E. (2011) 'Sincerity versus self-expression: modern creative agency and the materiality of semiotic forms', *Cultural Anthropology*, 26 (3): 462–84.

Wilkinson, R. and Pickett, K. (2009) *The Spirit Level*. London: Penguin.

Williams, R. (1958) *Culture and Society*. London: Chatto & Windus.

Williams, R. (1961) *The Long Revolution*. London: Chatto & Windus.

Bibliography

Williams, R. (1993) 'Culture is ordinary'. In A. Gray and J. McGuigan (eds), *Studying Culture: An Introductory Reader* (5–14). London: Arnold.

Wintle, C. (2017) 'Decolonising UK world art institutions, 1945–1980', *On Curating*, 35: 106–12.

Worth, E. (2019) 'Women, education and social mobility in Britain during the long 1970s', *Cultural and Social History*, 16 (1): 67–83.

Wreyford, N. (2018) *Gender Inequality in Screenwriting Work*. London: Palgrave.

Yudice, G. (2009) 'Cultural diversity and cultural rights', *Hispanic Issues Online*, 5 (1): 110–37.

Yuen, N. (2016) *Reel Inequality: Hollywood Actors and Racism*. New Brunswick: Rutgers University Press.

Yuval-Davis, N. (2006) 'Intersectionality and feminist politics', *European Journal of Women's Studies*, 13 (3): 193–209.

Zimdars, A., Sullivan, A., and Heath, A. (2009) 'Elite higher education admissions in the arts and sciences: is cultural capital the key?', *Sociology*, 43 (4): 648–66.

Index

Page numbers in **bold** refer to figures, page numbers in *italic* refer to tables.

#MeToo movement 223

accents 209–10
access 20–1, 115, 130–3, 134–5
Adam 257–8, 261–2
age and age group 21
    cultural consumption and
        consumers by 89, **90**, 91, 108
    and social mobility 165–8, *178*,
        180, 188
    and unpaid work 138, **147**, 148,
        149, **150**, 151–2, 152–5,
        158–60, 163
AHRC Cultural Value Project 38–43
Aldridge, Alan 274
Alex 144
alienation 55, 196
All Party Parliamentary Group for
    Music Education 116
Anna 154–5, 155–6
Arts Council 106
Arts Emergency 6, 282
attendance
    by age group **90**, 91, 108
    by class 84, **85**, 86, 108

by disabled people 92
by ethnic group 86, **88**, 89,
    91, 108
by gender 86, **87**, 108
multiple correspondence
    analysis 93–9, **94**, **95**
ticketing data 99–107, **103**,
    105, 108
attitudes and values, occupational
    65–72, **69**, **71**
Audience Finder 100, 101–2, 104,
    106–7, 108

Banet-Weiser, Sarah 238
Banks, Mark 173–4
Belfiore, Eleonora 32
Ben 265
Berridge, Susan 240
Bourdieu, Pierre 37, 112
Bradford *see* Feversham Primary
    Academy, Bradford
Brexit referendum 67–8, **69**
British Election Study 67–8, **69**
British Social Attitudes survey
    (BSA) 67

Index

Brook, Orian 6, 7
BSA *see* British Social Attitudes
    survey
business models 278

Camille 125–6
Cann, Victoria 129, 283
career development
    schemes 215–16
caregiving 23, 168, 226, 229
Carys 123–4, 129, 134–5, 205
Catherine 52–3, 66, 200, 204–5
change 23, 46–51, 217–18, 253,
    267–70, 281
Changing Lives 31, 33–6, 36, 37, 48
Charlotte 234–5
childhood engagement 20,
    109–35
    and access 115, 130–3, 134–5
    and class 120, 128, 134
    creative workers 116–17,
        118, 119–20
    and gender 129
    importance of 111–16, 121
    level 126–9
    parental support 122,
        123–4, 124–6
    remembering 120–2
    in school and the home 122–4
Chloe 127–8, 130, 131
Chris 201–2, 207–8, 220
Christine 157
Claire 205–6, 215
class 4, 15–16, 96–7, 259, 260
    and childhood engagement 120,
        128, 134
    cultural consumption and
        consumers by 84, **85**, 86, 94,
        95, **95**, 96–8, 108

and cultural occupations 15–18,
    18–19, 21, 23, 51, 52–3, 55
and unpaid work 138–9, **147**,
    148, **149**, **150**, 152, 154,
    155–61, 163
    see also social mobility
class problem 63–5
community activity 33
community regeneration 34–5
computing 248
Create London 6, 282
creative diversity 254
creative freedom 212–13
*Creative Health: The Arts for Health
    and Wellbeing* 31, 36–8
creative industries 11, 12–13, 136
Crossick, Geoffrey 31, 37, 38–43
cultural capital 111–16, 117, 121,
    134–5, 184, 192, 208–11,
    274, 279
cultural consumption and
    consumers 2, 10, 14, 19–20,
    46, 77–108
    by age group 89, **90**, 91, 108
    attendance 79–80, **80**, 82–3, **82**
    by class 84, **85**, 86, 94, 95, **95**,
        96–8, 108
    creative workers' childhood
        116–17, **118**, 119–20
    by cultural occupations and
        workers 97–8, 99
    demographics 27, 83–92, **85**,
        87, **88**, **90**
    by disabled people 92
    by ethnic group 86, **88**, 89,
        91, 108
    by gender 86, **87**, 108
    multiple correspondence
        analysis 93–9, **94**, **95**

Index

participation 80–2, **81**, 82–3, **82**
patterns 78–82, **80**, **81**
social impact 32–5
ticketing data 99–107, **103**, **105**, 108
cultural engagement 20, 78, 114
childhood 20, 109–35
multiple correspondence analysis 93–9, **94**, **95**
cultural experiences 41–2
cultural forms 2
cultural hierarchies 11, 12
cultural knowledge 112
Cultural Learning Alliance 116
cultural matching 75–6, 111, 112, 134
cultural occupations and workers 2, 10–15, 54–76, 78
attitudes and values 65–72, **69**, **71**
benefits of 141–3
childhood engagement 20, 109–35
and class 15–18, 18–19, 21, 23, 51, 54, 56, 58–9, **59**, 62–5, **64**
commitment 44, 47, 50, 140–4
core occupations 175, 177, *178*
cultural consumption 97–8, 99
demographics 57–65, **59**, **60**, **61**, **64**, 280
ethnic backgrounds 59–60, **59**, **61**
experiences of mothers in 233–48
gender profile **59**, **60**, 61–2
as good work 140–4
ideal type version 247

importance of 25
inequality in 3–5, 65–6, 190–220
lack of diversity 65–6
motivation 45–6
non-creative and support jobs 13
pay 5, 21
social closure 75
social networks 73–4, **74**
structural inequalities 19
worker caricatures 14–15
workforce composition 57–61, **59**
cultural participation 82–3, **82**
cultural production 2, 10, 11, 12, 14
cultural sector, economic value 136
cultural studies 11
cultural value 38–43
culture 10, 11, 12, 29–43
benefits of 29–31, 140
childhood engagement 5, 20, 109–35
commitment to 44
definition 2, 133
in education 34
health impacts 36–8
importance of 1, 44, 121, 133
and inequality 2, 3–5, 25, 26–9, 53, 279–83
influence 46–51
positive contribution 26–53
power of 43–51
right to 45–6
social impact 32–5
transformational role 29–30
transformative power of 26–53
value 27–9, 38–43

Index

culture and inequality
   strong theory of 282–3
   weak theory of 281–2

David 257
DCMS *see* Department for
   Culture, Media and Sport
Deb 142, 245–6, 246
Department for Culture, Media
   and Sport (DCMS) 136
deprivation 101, 104, 107, 169
digital transformations 163
disabled people 92, **149**, **150**
discrimination 55, 254
diversity, lack of 41
diversity policies 215–16

economic capital 112, 169–70,
   201–3, 279
economic impact research 32–3
economic inequality 8, 9
economic resources, and unpaid
   work 144–6
education 34, 71, 116, 122–4, 129,
   208, 270–1
   art and culture debate 115–16
   and ethnic backgrounds 185–6
   inequality 110–11, 184–7, **186**
   and social mobility 167,
     184–7, **186**
Ellie 156–7
Emily 136–9
Emma 143
engaged citizen, the 41–3
ethnic group
   cultural consumption and
     consumers by 86, **88**, 89,
     91, 108
   and education **186**

and social mobility 196–7
   and unpaid work **149**, **150**
everyday cultural activities 2, 96
exclusion 62, 63, 255

Farida 124–5, 126, 134–5
Felicity 159
Feversham Primary Academy,
   Bradford 34
film industry 4, 39–40, 45, 49–51,
   56, 83–4, 86, 91, 95, 151, 277
Finn 142
Florida, Richard 66, 68
France 8, 17
free time 96
Friedman, Sam 65, 196, 211
frustration 257–8
fulfilment 141, 143
funding 30–1, 40, 83–4, 92,
   121, 277–8

gaps in the market 212, 216
Gavin 128–9, 130
GBCS *see* Great British Class
   Survey, The
gender and gender inequality 4, 8,
   23, 176, 221–48, 255, 258–9
   and childhood engagement 129
   cultural consumption and
     consumers by 86, **87**, 108
   film industry 39–40
   music industry 45
   ONS-LS data 226–9, **227**, **228**
   parenting 229–48
   and social mobility 197
   structural problems 224, 225
   and unpaid work **147**, 148, **150**
Gerald 45–6, 47, 153–4
Gill, Rosalind 254, 255, 256, 260

good work 140–4
government policy 5, 11, 12, 32, 213
Graham 159, 263–4, 264
Great British Class Survey, The (GBCS) 16
Guardian 6

Hanquinet, Laurie 114
happiness 141
Hazel 159, 233
health impacts 36–8
Henna 3–5, 47, 49–51, 273
Hesmondhalgh, David 151, 154, 283
Hesmondhalgh, Julie 167
Hicks, Mar 248
high culture 2, 96
higher education 185–7, **186**
hiring practices 269–70, 270–1
Holly 141
Howard 46–7, 249–51, 254, 256
Hull 34–5

identity 146, 243–6
immigration 9–10
impact frameworks 32–3
inclusivity, myth of 255–6
Index of Multiple Deprivation 101, 102
industry lore 211–12
inequality 8–10
  and class 96–7, 190–220, 259
  in cultural occupations and workers 65–6, 190–220
  and culture 2, 3–5, 25, 26–9, 53, 279–83
  education 110–11, 184–7, **186**
  language 78
  maintenance of 216
  making visible 275–9, 280–1
  recognition of 249–52, 257, 259–66, 269, 270, 271–2
  inequality talk 251–2, 257–9, 261–2, 264, 271
information, shared 42
Institute for Public Policy Research 138
instrumental benefits 30
internships 137–8, 146, 148
intersectional approach 27
interviewee profiles 284–91
interviews 6, 120–1
Isabel 131–2, 134–5, 187

Jack 265, 266, 269, 270
Jane 244–6, 247–8
Jenny 160, 161
Jessica 236–9, 241, 246
Jo 153
John 158, 209–10, 210–11

Kaszynska, Patrycja 31, 37, 38–43
Katie 221–2, 246
Kerry 160–1, 161
Khan, Shamus 111, 114–15, 116, 133
Kirsty 202–3, 204
Koppman, Sharon 111, 134

Labour Force Survey, ONS (LFS) 19, 57, 64–5, 175–6, 186, 248
language, inequality 78
Lareau, Annette 111, 113
Lauren 141, 158
Laurison, Daniel 65, 211
Lawrence 258

Index

leadership 250
LFS *see* Labour Force Survey, ONS
Lisa 165–8, 189
London, dominance of 168
Louisa 152–3
low culture 96
luck 263–4, 272
Lydia 132–3, 133, 134–5, 203–4

McRobbie, Angela 145, 162, 254, 255, 256
Malik, Sarita 216, 254, 256
Man Alive (TV documentary) 273–5, 276
marginalisation 46, 201, 217–18, 260, 278
Matt 47–9, 143, 144
Maura 141
Meena 43–4, 48
Meg 54–7, 135, 206–7, 217–18, 218–19, 219–20
Mel 242, 243, 246
men 47
  recognition of inequality 249–52, 257, 259–66, 269, 270, 271–2
  senior 249–72
  sense of success 260–6
meritocracy 19, 67, 71, 72, **72**, 250, 256, 271
methodology 6–7
Michaela 26–9, 44, 48, 51
Michelle 46, 47, 50
micro classes 134, 173
Miles, Andrew 260–1
Molly 152, 153
moral judgements 195
motherhood 221–2, 224–5, 229–48, 252–3

motivation, cultural workers 45–6
music industry 45, 244–6, 247–8

Nicole 236, 246
non-creative and support jobs 13
Nwonka, Clive 216

O'Brien, Anne 240, 277
O'Brien, Dave 6, 7
Office for National Statistics Longitudinal Study (ONS-LS) 175–6, 177, *178*, 179–80, **179**, 226–9, **227**, **228**, 246
ONS-LS *see* Office for National Statistics Longitudinal Study
opera 77–8, 83
outsider capital 213–14

Panic! Social Class, Taste and Inequalities in the Creative Industries 6–7, 7, 68, 70, 73–4
parental support 109–10, 122, 123–4, 124–6
parenting 221–2, 224–5, 229–48, 252–3
pay gap 9
people of colour
  barriers to success 201, 206–8, 211–15
  burden of representation 199–200
  misrepresentative depictions 57
  social mobility 193, 216–17
  under-representation 59–60, **59**
Percival, Neil 151, 154
Peuter, Greig de 146
Philpott, Trevor 275
policy interventions 217
political behaviour 17

Index

poshness 5
post-feminist discourses 255
precariousness 145–6, 162
privilege 131, 264, 265
publishing 40, 50, 62, 159, 257–8
Puwar, Nirmal 191, 197, 210

queer representation 50

race and racism 4, 8,
    214, 249–51
Rachel 211–15, 216, 216–17, 220
reflective individual, the 41–3
resources 192, 201–11, 279
Richard 141, 258–9, 259–60
risk and risk-aversion 4, 24, 144
Rivera, Lauren 111, 134
Rollock, Nicola 196
Ruth 233–4, 242–3

Saha, Anamik 212
Sam 190
Sandberg, Sheryl 255
Sasha 143
Savage, Mike 260–1
Sean 122–3, 133, 157
sexism and sexual harassment 222,
    223, 255, 276–7
shared experience 20, 21, 278–9
Shaw, Sandie 273–4
snobbery 275
SOC 2010 coding 174
social capital 112, 203–8, 274, 279
social change 49–51
social context 277–8
social hierarchies 78
social inequality 2, 8–9, 37, 39–40,
    53, 278, 280
social justice 169

social mobility 6, 15, 22, 165–89,
    191, 192, 209–10, 218–19
    absolute 170, 171–2, 180
    and age group 165–8, *178*,
        180, 188
    barriers to 200–11, 219
    and class 168–70, 179, **179**,
        181, 183–4, 196
    critiques of 194–5, 215–16
    definition 168–9
    downward 169, 171, 195
    and education 167, 184–7, **186**
    and ethnic backgrounds
        196–7
    exclusion from 187–8
    and gender 197
    microclass 173
    odds ratios 181–4, **182**, 187
    ONS-LS data 175–6, *178*,
        179–80, **179**
    people of colour 193, 216–17
    problem of 173–6
    qualitative analysis 189,
        190–220
    relative 170, 172, 181–3
    and the somatic norm
        193–200
    in the UK 170–2
    upward 168–9, 171, 195
    women 181
Social Mobility Commission 115
social networks 73–4, **74**,
    204–5, 241–2
social reproduction explanations
    71, 72, **72**
social status 16, 30
social transformation 29–30
social types 199
socio-cultural occupations 17

Index

somatic norm, the 191–2,
   193–200, 201, 210–11, 212,
   215–18, 219, 247, 251,
   252, 270
Speight, Johnny 273–4
Standing, Guy 145
Stefano 141–2
Stephanie 142, 231–2
strong theory, of culture and
   inequality 282–3
structural inequalities 19, 252,
   255–6, 269–70, 278–9
success, barriers to 200–11,
   211–15, 221–48
Sunderland 35
surveys 2, 6, 6–7

Taking Part survey 6–7, 79, 82,
   93, 100, 101, 102, 104,
   106–7, 108, 117, 120, 120–1,
   130, 133
talent 4, 19, 70–2, 111, 112, 131,
   188, 192, 201, 214, 217,
   219, 241, 245, 250, 255–6,
   257–9, 259–60, 262, 270–1,
   274, 279
Tasha 109–10, 125–6
taste 4, 39–40, 78, 283
Taylor, Mark 6, 7
television 40–1, 75, 83, 83–4, 151,
   210–11, 249–51
Terras, Melissa 40
theatre 237–9
Thomas 267–70, 270–1
ticketing data 5, 99–107, **103**,
   105, 108
trade-offs 216

UK City of Culture 35

*Understanding the Value of Arts
   & Culture* (Crossick and
   Kaszynska) 31, 37, 38–43
United States of America 8, 17,
   75–6, 114–15, 133, 134
Universal Declaration of Human
   Rights 25
unpaid work 21, 136–64, 184,
   188, 230
   and age group 138, **147**, 148,
      149, **150**, 151–2, 152–5,
      158–60, 163
   benefits of 153–4
   and class 138–9, **147**, 148, **149**,
      150, 152, 154, 155–61, 163
   and disability **149**, **150**
   and economic resources
      144–6, 169–70
   and ethnic backgrounds
      149, **150**
   and gender **147**, 148, **150**
   and good work 140–4
   levels 146, **147**, 148, **149**, **150**,
      151–2, 162, 164
   resistance to 154–5
   sense of inevitability of 157–8
   shared experience 139–40
   social support 160–1
   varieties 146
unspeakable inequalities 252–9,
   265, 268–9
USC Annenberg School for
   Communication and
   Journalism 39–40

value 27–9, 38–43, 282–3
values 9–10, 39, 66
Veronica 156

wages 5, 21, 136–7, 146
Walters, Julie 167
weak theory, of culture and
    inequality 281–2
Williams, Raymond 37
Wokingham 101
women 23
    barriers to success 201,
        211–15, 221–48
    burden of representation
        199–200
    career advice 244
    compromises 234–5
    dilemma 232
    hostility towards 240–1
    life choices 225–6
    loss of networks 241–2
    misrepresentative depictions 57
    motherhood 221–2, 224–5,
        229–48, 252–3
    ONS-LS data 226–9, **227**,
        228, 246
    social mobility 181, 197
    status 223
    structural problems facing
        224, 225
    support 236, 237–9, 246
women of colour 22
worth and value 9–10
Wreyford, Natalie 240

York Outer 101